H.T.Bradley

and SHIPWRECKS

TRUE TALES OF THE SEVEN SEAS

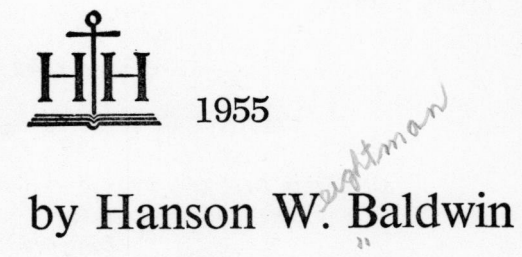 1955

by Hanson W. Baldwin

HANOVER HOUSE, GARDEN CITY, NEW YORK

ACKNOWLEDGMENTS   Grateful acknowledgment is made to Mrs. George Bambridge for the use of selections from the poem "The Sea and the Hills," taken from the book *The Five Nations,* and "Soldier an' Sailor Too," from *The Seven Seas,* by Rudyard Kipling. Acknowledgment is also made to Messrs. Methuen & Co. covering use of these selections in the Dominion of Canada.

MAPS BY RAFAEL PALACIOS

Library of Congress Catalog Card Number 55-7669

To My Wife . . .
and to all . . .

Who hath desired the Sea?—
the immense and contemptuous surges?
The shudder, the stumble, the swerve,
as the star-stabbing bowsprit emerges?

Kipling

And to our age's drowsy blood
Still shouts the inspiring sea.

J. R. Lowell

FOREWORD

These tales of men and ships in stress upon the oceans cover almost a century and a half of nautical history, and span the period—immense in its implications—from the days of sail to the age of the atom.

The common denominator is the "sea around us," probably the greatest environmental influence in the development of man. Man against the sea, or man against man upon the sea, or ships against the sea—this has long been the substance of poetry and romance as well as of history and progress. It is of this conflict—a fundamental one in all the centuries of recorded history—that this book treats. Shipwreck and disaster, endurance and battle, mystery and mutiny, heroism and cowardice all have their places in these pages.

All of the stories retold here actually happened; none are imaginary; none of the events are embellished. I have tried to present the full drama of shipwreck and battle without deviation from the factual record. To the best of my knowledge, all major sources have been studied, quoted, consulted, or checked in reconstructing these episodes. Interested readers will find sources listed under the Acknowledgments, and additional discussion under the Notes.

No single volume, of course, can claim to be a complete encyclo-

pedia of shipwreck, battle, and disaster; this one has no such preten-
sions. The separate chapters are representative episodes, each complete
in itself. Some of them are among the most famous incidents of modern
maritime history; others, even more fantastic than fiction, are but little
known. The actors vary; the scenes shift, but the stage is constant—
the everlasting sea.

Hanson W. Baldwin
December, 1954

Contents

Foreword   7

Herndon of the *Central America*—1857   13

Typhoon—1944   19

"The *Birken'ead* Drill"—Women and Children, First!—1852   35

R.M.S. *Titanic*—1912   46

"Sauve Qui Peut"—The Horrible Wreck of the Frigate *Medusa*—1816   63

Saga of a Stout Ship—The U.S.S. *Houston*—1942   76

Number 6—1910   92

The Cruise of the *Saginaw* Gig—1870   102

"Remember Always to Dare"—1918   121

The *Shō* Plan—The Battle for Leyte Gulf—1944   134

Mutiny on the Brig *Somers*—1842   183

Sea Raider—The Life and Death of the *Admiral Graf Spee*—1939   207

Contents

The Torpedoing of the *Lusitania*—1915   222

The Strange Case of the *Mary Celeste*—1872   239

Admiral Death—The Battle of Jutland—1916   267

Death of an Admiral—1893   287

The Greatest Sea-Air Battle in History—1945   297

Square-Rigger—1929   311

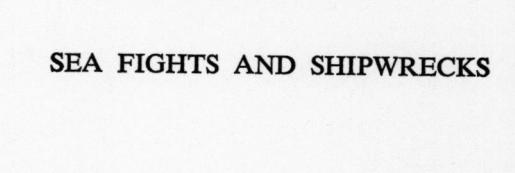

SEA FIGHTS AND SHIPWRECKS

1857

Herndon
of the *Central America*

All hope had gone. The *Central America* was dying—
dying in the darkness of a wild September night, her seams
opened to the sea, her top hamper wrecked and broken, her sails
shredded bits of canvas ripped from the bolt ropes.

Herndon, her captain, clung to a bridge stanchion as the hulk
rolled heavily in the trough of the giant seas. He had seen the sun
set—a pale and lusterless glow toward Hatteras—the last sunset he
would ever see. He had watched the quick twilight fade as the last
boat got away, laboring frightfully in the roar of waters. He had seen
the darkness shut down, the smashing rollers fade into the gloom. The
night wore on with dragging weariness, the ship settled deeper, and
Herndon knew it was the end. Slowly he turned toward his cabin. . . .

He had commanded her for almost two years—this ship that now
was sinking beneath his feet. She was skippered, like all Pacific Mail
ships, by a naval officer; Herndon had gone to her, with the rank of
commander, from the old *Potomac* of the Home Squadron. For almost
two years he had taken her back and forth on the run from New York
via Havana to the fever-ridden hole at Aspinwall. He had brought
many of the forty-niners home with their bulging sacks of gold; he
had taken giddy trollops and scores of adventurous young blades,
eager for fame and fortune, down the long seaway to the Isthmus—
gateway to California's gold. Two years, and the *Central America*
had helped to make history. Now it was all over, and the stout side-

wheeler with her lofty masts and reaching yards was to sink into the limbo of the past.

She had stood out of Havana past the old Morro on September 8, 1857, with her crew of 101, a full passenger list of 474—most of them from California—and about two million dollars in gold. Out of Havana in fair weather and high spirits, with Cuba behind them like a cloud on the horizon and ahead of them the well-traveled sea lane to Sandy Hook. Out of Havana she sailed with the northeast trades tautening her canvas and her paddle wheels chunk-chunking on the sea lane to New York.

Midnight of the ninth the wind had freshened; in the midwatch the barometer dropped rapidly, and by dawn a gale was roaring out of the nor'nor'east.

Two days of wind and weather—great seas rolling southward from the pole, spindrift pattering like hail on the storm sails, the paddles churning slowly as the ship labored. The sea made up; the *Central America* strained and groaned. On the forenoon of the eleventh her seams opened; the sea had won. But Herndon did not admit defeat. Red-eyed and tired, he ordered his men to the pumps. The wind shrieked at whole-gale force; the sea lipped eagerly about the opened seams and gurgled into the hold, giving her a starboard list. Huge seas broke aboard; green water fumed about the decks. By two bells of the afternoon watch the strakes had worked so far apart with the straining of the vessel that the inrushing water had extinguished some of the boiler fires, and the engine had soughed to a stop for lack of steam.

Herndon routed out the passengers—all hands to save ship. He organized bailing gangs; buckets, barrels, scoops, pots, and wheezing pumps sucked and dipped at the ocean in the hold. The passengers tailed on to whips, hoisted high the barrels, dumped them overside, dropped them again into the gaining water below decks. Herndon put some of them to shifting freight—from starboard to larboard—while he tried to keep his ship headed up with some wisps of canvas. All passengers not working on the whips were ordered to the windward side; the ship was trimmed; once more, briefly, she rode the combers on an even keel.

But the *Central America's* seams were wide to the eager sea. Pas-

sengers, men and women and even the older children, worked side
by side with the exhausted crew at the buckets and the barrels and
the pumps. It was no good. The water gained; tired muscles wearied
in the endless struggle. Slowly the ship settled. The water crept up into
the ashpits, above the grate bars, toward the boiler drums. The storm
spencer blew out of its boltropes; the ship's head fell off; she wallowed
in the troughs. The night came down as the storm shrieked on and
the ship settled. The pumps wheezed; the barrels came up out of the
flooded hold at a run—men and women on the whips, urged on to
new exertions by Herndon's encouragement. A sailor started an old
chantey:

> *"Whisky is the life of man.*
> *O Whisky Johnny!*
> *I'll drink whisky while I can.*
> *O Whisky Johnny!"*

During the night Herndon had the foreyard sent down; he tried
time and again to get the *Central America* before the wind, but there
was no canvas strong enough to hold in the gale. The head sails were
blown to tatters. Herndon ordered the clews of the foresail lashed to
the deck, hoping to hoist the yard, if only a few feet, show canvas, and
get her off; but the yard was scarcely clear of the bulwarks when the
wild wind took it entirely out of the boltropes.

Toward dawn axes bit into the foremast. It fell crashing to leeward,
and out of the foreyard and bits of timber and canvas were fashioned
a rough sea anchor. Aft tattered scraps of canvas were spread in the
rigging; but the *Central America,* the water rising toward her main
deck, would not answer; she rolled heavily in the troughs. Dawn of
the twelfth revealed a drifting hulk, battered and sinking. But the captain still refused to despair. They were in the shipping lanes, help
might come. "Rally all," he said. He kept them at the pumps, hoisted
the ensign upside down, had minute guns fired.

About noon the wind commenced to abate, but the gale had done
its work; the *Central America* was doomed. In early afternoon a ship
was sighted; hope rose—but the ship held her course. Later, more
yards against the clouded sky: a few wisps of canvas on another vessel,
scudding fast.

"A sail! A sail!"

The gun boomed; and the passing ship, the brig *Marine* out of Boston, Captain Burt, hove to—though she herself had been damaged by the storm. Herndon had the boats manned and lowered; the women and children climbed in; the boats commenced their perilous pull to leeward. Flung skyward, then dropped between the waves, they rode the combers, reached the brig, pulled back a long pull to the foundering vessel. A second time they made the dangerous passage with their gunwales awash—one hundred saved. As the last boat was ready to pull away, the sky darkening in the east, Herndon halted a passenger about to embark, and handed him his watch. The captain choked up—he who had stuck to his bridge, encouraged his crew, bravely fought the old fight against great waters. There was everything to live for (he was only forty-four): his wife; his sister, the wife of Commander Matthew Fontaine Maury; his daughter Ellen who later, after he was dead, was to marry Chester A. Arthur, twenty-first President of the United States; his service, and his friends. He thrust the watch at the passenger, spoke of his wife.

"Give it to her, and tell her—tell her—tell her from me . . ."

He could not go on; he shook his head and turned away. The boat pulled off; in a moment Herndon was back on the bridge, composed and awaiting the end.

It was not to be long in coming. The brig *Marine* had drifted several miles to leeward; the *Central America's* boats were battered, leaking, and half-filled with water—useless; the steamer was settling lower, listing to starboard, her main deck almost awash. But there was no panic; those hundreds left aboard saw their commander on the bridge, cool and quiet, looking out at the faint glow in the west.

The *Central America* foundered that night, carrying down with her the bags of California gold, her commander, and 423 of her passengers and crew. In addition to the hundred taken to the *Marine,* forty-nine passengers were picked out of the water next morning by the Norwegian bark *Ellen,* after clinging for hours to bits of wreckage. Three others were saved, days later, by the English brig *Mary,* after having drifted with the Gulf Stream more than 450 miles from the scene of the sinking. Herndon's last hours had been spent in vain attempts to save more lives. Rockets were sent up every fifteen minutes; life preservers were distributed as the ship settled to her doom, and the commander set the passengers and crew to work chopping away part of the hurricane deck to make an impromptu raft.

Toward the last, through the night, above the waves and wind, a boat's oars had been heard. But it was too late; the ship was going; Herndon had warned the boat off to keep her from being sucked down with the sinking ship.

"Keep off! Keep off!"

Everything had been done that could be done; it was only a question of moments. Herndon called his first officer, Van Rennselaer, and told him he was going below for his uniform. The commander went to his stateroom, and in a few minutes returned to the bridge. He had put on his full-dress uniform and removed the oilskin cover that concealed his naval-cap insignia. He took his stand on the wheelhouse, bracing himself against the ship's list.

A rocket went up—a fiery meteor illuminating briefly the dismasted foundering ship, the wrecked hopes of those who had gone west for gold. The waves seethed against the opened strakes; scud and spume and salt rind whitened the top hamper; green water lapped the decks. The *Central America* gave a final lurch. Herndon, clinging to the wheelhouse rail, uncovered, waved his hand. The side-wheel steamer, out of Aspinwall for New York, turned on her side and sank.

NOTES   I am indebted to Mrs. E. S. Lewars of Seminary Ridge, Gettysburg, Pa., for the information that one of those lost with the *Central America* was William Ulrich, a mulatto waiter. Ulrich had a distinguished patron, Thaddeus Stevens, who had procured for him the job which led to Ulrich's death. Ulrich was the son of a former slave—Ephraim Ulrich—who was bought and freed by Thaddeus Stevens of Gettysburg, the fiery figure whose name is forever associated with the stormy period of American history which culminated in the War Between the States.

ACKNOWLEDGMENTS   Republished from the *United States Naval Institute Proceedings* with permission of the editor.

This chapter is based primarily upon documents in the Navy Department library, particularly upon an account of the *Central America's* loss by Commander Matthew Fontaine Maury, "the pathfinder of the seas," who was Herndon's brother-in-law. I have quoted from these documents and have also drawn upon articles in the *United States Naval Institute Proceedings*.

1944

Typhoon

It was the greatest fleet that had ever sailed the seas, and it was fresh from its greatest triumph. But the hand of God was laid upon it and a great wind blew, and it was scattered and broken upon the ocean. The inexorable law of storms—the Bible of all seamen since the days of astrolabe and sail—was neglected, and the Third Fleet, proud in its might, paid the penalty—more men lost, more ships sunk and damaged than in many of the engagements of the Pacific War.

Storms have intervened before in history, and Nature has adjudicated the small affairs of Man. A great wind, as well as Drake of Devon, saved England from the Spanish Armada. Dampier the Navigator noted in his log book in 1687—the first Westerner to record the phenomenon—the violent ravages of a typhoon, which he called a "tuffoon." And at Apia harbor, Samoa, in 1889, wind and sea with catholic impartiality wrecked the men-of-war of two nations. But in five hundred years of naval history there had been no wind the like of that which struck the Third Fleet, Admiral William F. Halsey, commanding, and humbled it in its hour of victory, on December 17 and 18, 1944.

In mid-December the Battle for Leyte Gulf was history; the Japanese Empire only a few weeks before had been dealt a fatal blow. The invasion of Mindoro started on December 15, and the Third Fleet was weary from three days of wide-ranging strikes against the island of

Luzon in the Philippines. As the fleet retired to the east to refuel, the beginning of the end was in sight; enemy land-based air power in the Philippines had been neutralized or destroyed, and MacArthur's "I have returned" was already loud upon the lips of the world.

Admiral Halsey, flying his flag in the battleship *New Jersey*, was tired after 36,000 miles of steaming and ninety-five days of action (eighty-five of them at sea), and was trying to relax from the "constant threat of air attack" and the "burden of responsibility."

". . . it took me a long time to unwind," he records in his book, *Admiral Halsey's Story*. "Other men may have done it with the help of noble literature; I used to read *The Police Gazette*."

New Jersey dispatched the refueling rendezvous—14 degrees, 50 minutes north, 129 degrees, 57 minutes east, about five hundred miles east of Luzon—to the oilers and to Task Force 38—the carriers— Vice Admiral John S. ("Slew") McCain, commanding. Halsey started his *Police Gazette*, his deck tennis, and his movies—trying to relax. But it was not to be. On the night of December 16–17 the sea made up, and there was the queasiness of impending storm. Rear Admiral ("Mick") Carney, Chief of Staff to Halsey, noted a "tropical disturbance of some sort to the east of us," but nobody thought the storm would curve across the fleet's course. The enemy was the Japanese— not the cruel sea; this great fleet, unmatched in history, could disdain the elements.

Sunday, December 17   This day dawns dark and brooding, the sea choppy, the wind brisk but fickle, the ships fretful. Across hundreds of miles of ocean, the Third Fleet steams—the masts, the flight decks bowing and dipping, swinging in wide arcs across the horizon. Here, in all its panoply and power, is the fleet that has humbled Japan—a score of carriers, big and little; eight "battlewagons"; numerous cruisers; dozens of destroyers—spread wide in three great task groups across the ocean. The refueling rendezvous is changed three times in search of calmer seas; Third Fleet makes contact with the twenty-four big fleet oilers and their escort of Task Group 30.8, and despite the querulous swells refueling starts. The rigorous demands of combat, the support needed by those "G.I.'s" back on Mindoro permit no concession to Nature.

The destroyers—the little ships that dance in any sea, the ships with empty maws from their days of high-speed steaming—come alongside the tankers and the battleships in the morning. But the ocean will have none of it; this is a job for super-seamen. There's nothing but a mad swatch of white water between oilers and "tin cans" as the hungry little ships try to gulp their food through hoses leading from the oilers' tanks. Some get aboard hundreds of gallons before the lines break and the ships swing wildly apart, but most part line after line as boat-swains curse and the water boils aboard the well decks and the steel plates run with oil. Destroyer *Hull,* a name soon to be on the lips of all the fleet, from the ASW (anti-submarine warfare) group of a fuel-ing unit, puts forty bags of mail aboard battleship *South Dakota* with "much difficulty," but mail for thirty other ships of the fleet is undeliv-ered; the sea is wild.

"1107. Spence alongside New Jersey, starboard side, to fuel.

1128. Both for'd and after hoses to Spence parted."

U.S.S. *Buchanan* tries to transfer pilots by a swaying boatswain's chair to CVE-18—escort carrier *Altamaha*—but the sea's too rough. *San Jacinto,* light carrier, gets aboard 172,000 gallons from tanker *Monongahela* before the log noted at 1331 "discontinued fueling be-cause of adverse weather."

Wind—Force 26 knots. Barometer, 29.74. Temperature, 82. Visi-bility—5 miles. Sea—Force 4.

In early afternoon Com. Third Fleet orders fueling suspended, sets course to northwest, then later to southwest to escape storm center not clearly located. The barometer drops, the winds moan; there's the uneasy leaden feeling of a hand across the heavens, but the Third Fleet steams on in cruising formation—the destroyers screening the "big boys," the AA guns alert, the sonars "pinging," the radars . . . searching, searching. . . .

Monday, December 18 Third Fleet moves through trou-bled waters, the compulsion of combat dictating its movements. But the storm, with the catholic impartiality of Nature, sweeps across the war, puts in puny framework the efforts of Man. The night is haggard;

aboard the destroyers the sideboards are around the wardroom tables, the sleepers are braced in their bunks, but the sharp motion of the aroused ocean shakes and pounds the ships, makes sleep fitful and despairing. Barometers drop steadily, rain squalls and flung spray and spume reduce visibility; station-keeping is difficult—at times almost impossible. The seas make up; the winds beat and buffet; the fleet is battened down.

"But no estimates of the storm center were in agreement"; and not until dawn did Third Fleet realize it lay in the path of the grand-daddy of all typhoons. And units of Task Group 30.8—the fleet oilers, and their escorting destroyers and escort carriers—somewhat to the north and east of the main body, are directly athwart the "eye" of the approaching typhoon. Fleet course is ordered changed to 180 degrees —due south—but it is too late; the fury is upon them.

0400 to 0800 The Morning Watch

Nantahala (Oiler)—". . . this ship pitching deeply and heavily."
Altamaha (Escort Carrier)—". . . heavy weather making station-keeping only approximate."

Aboard *Dewey*, DD (destroyer) 349, the officer-of-the-deck reports to the captain that the barometer has dropped seven points between 7 and 8 A.M. Seas are so violent, winds so strong, *Dewey* finds it "impossible," when fleet course is changed, to countermarch to new station.

Morning fuel reports from many of the destroyers are ominous. All were low the day before; some had de-ballasted (pumped salt water out of their tanks) to prepare to refuel. They are riding light and high; stability is reduced. And their crews know that topside weight has been greatly increased since commissioning by more AA guns, fire control gear, and radar. *Yarnall* reports 20 per cent of fuel remaining; *Wedderburn,* 15 per cent; *Maddox, Hickox* and *Spence* 10 to 15 per cent.

0800 to 1200 The Forenoon Watch

The forenoon watch opens, in the words of an old seagoing term, "with hell to pay and no pitch hot."

The moaning violence of the wind is terrible; it shrieks and whinnies, roars and shudders, beats and clutches. The sea is convulsed, diabolic; the ships are laboring deeply—laid over by the wind, rolling rigidly through tremendous arcs with sharp violent jerks, pounding and pitching, buried deep beneath tons of water, rising heavily streaming foam and salt from gunnels and hawse pipes. Violent rain gusts, spindrift blown with the sting of hail, a rack of scud blot out visibility. Third Fleet is scattered; few ships see others; only on the radar scopes do the pips of light loom up to show in wild confusion Man's panoply of power.

The deeply-laden oilers, the heavy battleships, the larger carriers, roll and plunge deeply and work violently but not dangerously through the towering seas, but for the escort carriers, the light carriers and the destroyers, the struggle is to live; the war now is against Nature, not the Japanese; no man in all the fleet had ever felt before the full fury of such a howling, demonic wind. Some of the fleet is in the "dangerous semicircle" of the typhoon where no seaman ought to be; a few ships —though rocked and tossed like chips—are on the fringes of the terrible vortex, but at least one task unit is directly in the center, where the funnel of wind and the boiling ocean leap to climax.

Ship after ship falls away into the terrible troughs and will not answer her helm.

At 0820 the destroyer *Dewey*—DD 349—loses bridge steering control; at 0825 the SG radar, short-circuited by the flying scud, is out of operation.

At 0845 escort carrier *Altamaha* records in her deck log: "Mobile crane on hangar deck tore loose from moorings and damaged three aircraft," and, a few minutes later: "Wind and sea approaching hurricane violence. Ship laboring heavily and rolling violently as much as twenty-five to thirty degrees on either side."

The barometer drops as no seaman there had ever seen it fall before; the wind is up.

Aboard U.S.S. *Cowpens*, an F6F5 airplane, triple-lashed on the flight deck, breaks loose on a 45-degree roll, and smashes into the catwalk, starting a fire. Men fight it, as the wind howls and the roll indicator registers 45 degrees with the small bubble of the ship's inclinometer (roll indicator) "two-blocked and off the scale." Men fight it, as a bomb-handling truck breaks free on the hangar deck and smashes the belly tank of a fighter. Men fight it as a wall of solid green water rips open—like a can opener—the steel roller curtains on the port side of the hangar deck. Men fight it as the anenometer, with one of its cups gone, registers a wind velocity of more than one hundred knots. Men fight it as the wind and sea pull out of its steel roots the forward port 20 mm. gun sponsor and leave it hanging, and tear loose the radar antenna screen from the foremast and fling it into the boiling sea. And men fight it as the motor whaleboat is carried away by a wall of water, as bombs break their battens in the magazine and skitter about the deck, as jeeps and tractors, a kerry crane, and seven planes are flung and blown off the flight deck into the writhing sea. But in the end it is the sea which extinguishes the fire as it was the sea which started it; the F6F5 breaks clear of the catwalk and falls into the tumult of water.

As the day wears on the log books run out of the language of nautical superlatives. Several ships record the barometer at a flat 28 inches, an awesome low; *Dewey* reads hers at 27.30—possibly the world's lowest recorded reading. Oiler *Nantahala,* with other ships of a fueling unit to the northeast of the main body near the storm center, records a wind velocity of 124 knots. The wind shifts rapidly in direction as the typhoon circles, blowing from north and south and east and west—backing and filling as do all circular storms—and increasing in intensity to Force 17, far beyond that ancient nautical measuring-stick of mariners—the Beaufort scale—which defines Force 12, its maximum—"that which no canvas could withstand"—as a "hurricane above 65 knots."

Third Fleet is scattered now, station-keeping impossible, visibility five hundred yards to zero, only the radars—when operative—preventing collisions. Com. Third Fleet in *New Jersey,* his plan to refuel this day long since abandoned, his immediate commitment to MacArthur regretfully canceled, records in his war diary the reports of disaster:

0841. The Wasp *reported a life raft to her port, which appeared to have three persons on it.*

0907. The Independence *reported man overboard.*

0911. The Monterey *reported that, due to excessive roll, planes on her hangar deck had broken loose and caught fire.*

0942. The Kwajalein *reported she had lost steering control.*

1012. The Wisconsin *reported 1 Kingfisher* [plane] *overboard.*

1017. The Rudyerd Bay *reported she was dead in the water.*

1128 The Cape Esperance *reported fire on her flight deck.* . . .

The ships—the big and little—are racked and strained, punished and pommeled. The men are dazed; all hands are in lifejackets; none stand topside in exposed positions; muscles are sore and bodies bruised from clinging to stanchions, pounding against bulkheads; a miserable many retch from seasickness, but for hundreds terror calms the queasiness of the stomach. The violent rolls and the terrible mountains of water—seventy feet from trough to crest—are frightening, even to the experienced; some are plain scared, but most have confidence in the stoutness of their vessels.

But this is "one-hand-for-your-ship-and-one-for-yourself" weather; the business is to survive.

The voice of the storm drowns all other voices; the wind has a thousand notes—the bass of growling menace, the soprano of stays so tautly strained they hum like bowstrings. The tops of the wave crests are flattened off by the wind and hurled straight before its violence; rain and spindrift mix in a horizontal sheet of water; one cannot tell where ocean stops and sky begins. . . .

. . . And over all is the cacophony of the ships—the racked and groaning ships, the creaking of the bulkheads, the working of the stanchions, the play of rivets, the hum of blowers, the slide and tear and roar of chairs and books adrift, of wreckage slipping from bulkhead to bulkhead. . . .

Low fuel, attempts to keep station, or to change course to ease pounding spell havoc for some. The seas are so great, the wind so strong, that some of the lighter destroyers are derelicts; all possible combinations of rudders and screws fail to take them out of the troughs; they are sloughed and rolled and roughed far on their sides by wind and water—and drift, out of control, downwind.

The light and escort carriers fare little better; aboard *San Jacinto,* *Monterey, Altamaha* and others, planes slide and slip; wreckage crashes groaning from bulkhead to bulkhead; the hangar decks are infernos of flame and crashing metal, of fire and wind and sea.

Early in the morning watch *San Jacinto,* Captain Michael H. Kernodle, commanding, tries to "swing to new course to ease her." The skipper backs the starboard engines, goes ahead twenty knots on the port, but the howling wind will have none of it; *San Jacinto* falls off into the trough, rolls 42 degrees. A plane breaks loose on the hangar deck, skids into other planes—each lashed to steel deck pad eyes with fourteen turns of wire and rope—tears them loose, and the whole deckload crash from side to side with each roll, "rupturing and tearing away all air intakes and vent ducks passing through the hangar decks." Engine spares and other heavy material stowed on the hangar deck break loose and smash and tear into the bulkheads; oily water greases the deck; steam hisses from the ruptured exhausts; the fire sprinkling system, damaged by the wreckage, sprays water indiscriminately over the deck spaces; general flooding results through the broken ventilation vents in fire rooms and engine rooms; the evaporators are out of commission; the galley ovens out; the after gyro compass inoperative; electrical leads severed.

It is Man against the sea, but Man wins; personnel of the damage control and fire-fighting parties lash themselves to lines suspended from the overhead of the hangar deck, and swinging and slithering like pendulums across the slippery deck, risk their lives to secure the mass of sliding, groaning wreckage.

Aboard *Altamaha*—all 14,000 tons of her, planing like a surfboard on the tremendous rollers—the planes she mothers turn against her; fire mains burst; wreckage litters the elevator pit; heavy seas break over the fantail; damage repair parties shore the bulkheads.

In *Monterey,* Nos. 1 and 2 firerooms are abandoned at 0914 because of heavy smoke from a hangar deck fire; ready ammunition is jettisoned; the boilers are manned by skeleton crews using rescue breathing masks; a gasoline vapor explosion kills one seaman; another, trapped by the flames, is burned to death, a third asphyxiated; many injured.

Destroyer *Dewey* labors almost to the death. Throughout the morning watch, with the storm howling like a banshee, the quartermaster on watch scribbles painfully in the deck log, as casualty reports funnel to the bridge:

0950. . . . Dewey reported to CTG 30.8 she was out of control and passed through formation from starboard to port. Heavy rolling caused loss of lube oil suction repeatedly. . . .

1006. Captain ordered all port fuel tanks filled to capacity. 30,000 gallons of oil pumped to port side. Rolling through 40 to 50 degrees.

1020. Lost bridge steering control; steering aft. Telephone circuits began to go. Lost radar and TBS [radio—"Talk Between Ships"] contact with rest of formation. . . . Wind and sea rising, barometer falling.

1102. Doctor reported many men had been injured by falling.

1130. Main engines stopped—main switchboard shorted from salt water. Secured main generator. Electrical power and lights all gone. 500 to 1,000 gallons of water entering ⚓2 main forced draft intake on every big roll. Bucket brigade in mess hall and one aft kept water down.

1130. All control and communication lost from bridge. Dead in the water. The air . . . continually filled with salt spray 200 feet in the air or higher. Visibility zero. This blast of salt spray penetrated everything and grounded all electrical connections. . . . 8 inches of water in all living spaces produced undesirable "free surface effect." All hands told to remain on port side. Rolling and pounding worse. Inclinometer to 73 degrees to starboard and stopped for a few seconds. Engine room [indicated] 75 degrees. The masts and stacks . . . swinging and expected to carry away at any time. Tops of 3 ready ammo lockers torn off and 80 rounds of 5 inch spilled over the side. . . . All thin shielding of ship stove in—by water on starboard side— by wind on port.

1145. The wind . . . estimated to be more than 110 knots. All hands performed in a commendable manner, especially the engineers . . . no panic.

But *Dewey,* as the morning dies, still lives.

Not so destroyers *Monaghan* and *Spence.*

Monaghan, DD 354, with twelve battle stars on her bridge and a veteran of combat from Pearl Harbor to Leyte, lunges to her doom—the fleet unknowing—late in that wild windswept morning.

She's last heard and dimly seen when the morning is but half spent:

0936. Monaghan *to Com. T.G. 30.8*—"I am unable to come to the base course. Have tried full speed, but it will not work."

1006. Monaghan *to unknown ship*—"You are 1,200 yards off my port quarter. Am dead in water. Sheer off if possible."

1007. Monaghan *to* Hobby—"Bearing is 225, 1,400 yards . . ."

Then . . . silence . . .

Monaghan's 1,500 tons of steel are racked and strained; her starboard whaleboat drinks the sea as the davits dip into green water. But there's little intimation of disaster. About eight bells—as the Wagnerian dirge of the typhoon drowns the lesser noises of the laboring ship—the wind pushes *Monaghan* far on her starboard side. She struggles to rise again—and makes it, but sluggishly. In the after deck house forty or fifty men cling to stanchions and pray—silently, or aloud:

"Don't let us down now, Dear Lord. Bring it back, Oh God! bring it back!"

Slowly the ship recovers:

"Thanks, Dear Lord."

But the lights go out; again the deep roll to starboard, again and again she struggles back, shudderingly, from disaster.

Then, about noon, the wind brutalizes her; heavily *Monaghan* rolls to starboard—30, 40, 60, 70 degrees—tiredly she settles down flat on her side to die amid a welter of white waters and the screaming Valkyries of the storm. And there go with her eighteen officers and 238 men. . . .

Spence, DD 512, goes about the same time, but again the fleet unknowing. *Spence* is deballasted, light in fuel; she rides like a cork in the terrible canyon-like troughs. Power fails; the electrical board is shorted from the driven spray; the ship goes over 72 degrees to port—and stays there. The lights are out; the pumps are stopped—the ship's

heart dead before the body dies; she drifts derelict. Sometime before
noon, the Supply Officer—Lt. Alphonso Stephen Krauchunas, United
States Naval Reserve, one-time of Kalamazoo, destined to be *Spence's*
only officer survivor—sits on the edge of the bunk in the captain's
cabin talking tensely with the ship's doctor. An awful roll throws
Krauchunas on his back against the bulkhead "in a shower of books
and whatnot." Crawling on hands and knees on the bulkheads (walls)
of the passageway, Krauchunas gets topside just before the entering
ocean seeks him out. He fights clear along with seventy others—but
Spence, 2,000 tons of steel with the power of 60,000 horse, is done.

1200 to 1600 The Afternoon Watch

The afternoon watch brings some slight surcease to some ships,
climax and desperation to others. The fleet is widely dispersed across
a raging ocean; some ships have felt the full fury of the storm; others
are still to feel it. Between 1100 and 1400 of that day the peak is
reached; "mountainous seas . . . confused by backing winds made
the vessels roll to unprecedented angles."

For *Hull,* Destroyer ⚓350, with much of the mail of the fleet still
aboard, the afternoon watch of December 18, 1944, is to be her last.
The quartermaster has hardly turned the log page before it happens.

Small and old as destroyers go, *Hull* had made heavy weather of it
in the morning; the driven spray had shorted everything; in the CIC
(Combat Information Center) leaky seams admitted the sea and
"sparks were jumping back and forth among the electrical cables."

Hull's tanks are 70 per cent full of fuel oil; she's better off than her
lighter sisters, though she has no water ballast. But the storm brooks
no objections; gradually *Hull* loses the fight. Her radar is out; her
TBS inoperative; the whaleboat smashed and torn loose; depth charges
wrenched from the K-guns, and to "every possible combination of
rudder and engines" the ship will not respond, and is blown "bodily
before wind and sea, yawing between headings of 100 and 080 true."

Shortly after noon, as the seas tower into toppling mountains, the
ship lies over on her side in terrible sickening rolls, and the junior
officer of the watch is "catapulted completely through the air from
the port side of the pilot house to the upper portion of the starboard
side."

But still Lieutenant-Commander James Alexander Marks, the young skipper, has hope. . . .

". . . the ship had withstood the worst punishment any storm could offer."

("I had served in destroyers," he later noted, "in some of the worst storms of the North Atlantic and believed that no wind could be worse than that I had just witnessed.")

But the wind increases to an estimated 110 knots; "the force of the wind . . . [lays] the ship steadily over on her starboard side and holds her down in the water until the seas come flowing into the pilot house itself."

Early in the afternoon—probably before 1300—the leaping sea hurtled up into the port wing of the bridge and young Lieutenant Commander James Alexander Marks steps off his capsized ship—his first command—into a sea "whipped to a froth," a sea so wildly angry, so ravening for life that lifejackets are torn from the backs of the few survivors. . . .

Destroyer *Dewey,* battered and racked in the morning watch, makes it—though hurt almost mortally.

At 1230 No. 1 stack carries away and falls over the side in a clutter of wreckage, leaving a gaping wound in the main deck and four hundred pounds of steam escaping from the ruptured whistle line in a shuddering roar that mingles with the berserk voice of the typhoon. The falling funnel carries away the whaleboat davits; this easing of the topside weight—and the skipper's prescience in the morning watch in counter-ballasting the high side—the port side—with most of his fuel, probably save the ship. Nevertheless, green water slops over the starboard wing of the bridge as the ship lies over an estimated 80 degrees to starboard—and lives to tell about it—perhaps the first vessel in the history of the sea to survive such a roll.

At 1300 the barometer drops to an estimated 27.30 inches—the needle off the scale—one of the lowest readings in the long narrative of storms.

But the typhoon has done its worst; at 1340 the barometer registers a slight rise, and at 1439 the wind slackens to about eighty knots.

The storm curves on into the wide open spaces of the Pacific the rest of that day—the eighteenth. The winds still howl; the ships still heave, the ocean is confused, and even on the nineteenth the seas are huge and horrid, but the great typhoon is over. Behind it, it leaves the fleet scattered and broken, with more unrequited damage, as Admiral Halsey later noted, than at any time since the First Battle of Savo Island. Survivors of *Monaghan* and *Hull* and *Spence* are pitifully few; destroyer escort *Tabberer,* herself demasted, picks up the first survivors from *Hull* at ten that night, and others—including Lieutenant Commander Marks—who had lost his first command— the next day. *Tabberer* also rescues ten survivors from *Spence* aboard a liferaft on the twentieth; other ships—scouring the ocean now that news of the sinkings is widely disseminated—find a handful of spent and injured sailors, who will forever comprehend, more fully than any living men, the meaning of the fury of the sea.

The great typhoon of December 17 and 18, 1944, cost 790 dead or missing—202 from the *Hull,* about 256 from the *Monaghan* (only six were saved), 317 from the *Spence,* three dead in the *Monterey,* others killed or missing from other ships. More than eighty men were injured; 146 planes were blown overboard or damaged beyond repair. The battleships lost planes and gear, but sustained no major damage; the large carriers suffered damage to radars and to the hangar deck roller curtains. But the small ships were battered and spent. Of the light carriers, *San Jacinto, Monterey, Cowpens, Cabot,* and *Langley* suffered badly; the list of *Monterey's* damages covered nine closely-typed legal pages. The cruisers *Miami* and *Baltimore;* the escort carriers *Cape Esperance, Anzio* and *Altamaha,* and the destroyers and destroyer escorts *Aylwin, Dewey, Buchanan, Hickox, Benham, Donaldson, Melvin R. Nawman,* and *Dyson* required major repair, while nine other vessels sustained more minor damage. The strikes against Luzon were canceled and the Third Fleet straggled—cockbilled and askew—into the atoll of Ulithi.

A Navy Court of Inquiry, summoned to solemn postmortem, found that "large errors [had been] made in predicting the location and path" of the typhoon. Admiral Halsey called the typhoon a "disaster." Admiral Chester W. Nimitz pointed out that the damage done "repre-

sented a more crippling blow to the Third Fleet than it might be expected to suffer in anything less than a major action"; and the Commander-in-Chief of the Pacific Fleet noted his determination to
inculcate his officers with "the necessity of understanding the Law
of Storms. . . ."

The damaged ships were repaired; the typhoon warning service and
meteorological forecasts were improved; the war continued toward its
triumphant finale.

Yet on June 5, 1945—just six months later, with the end not far
off—Third Fleet was again lashed, though with no ships lost and lesser
damage, by a typhoon. Fleet Admiral "Ernie" King, the hard-bitten
"sun-downer," who chivvied and harried the Navy to global victory
from his Washington command post, was caustic; he noted the Third
Fleet had been "involved" in a similar situation during the great
typhoon of December 1944, and declared that "on each occasion,"
there had been sufficient information to avoid the worst damages, had
officers "reacted to the situation as it developed with the weather-wise
skill to be expected of professional seamen."

And . . . from Commander Service Force, a sobering comment
from Man—arrogant in his victory against Man:

". . . there is no ship afloat that cannot be capsized in a seaway."

        NOTES   The great typhoon of 1944 was the real-life
genesis for the fictional typhoon which formed the climactic denouement of *The Caine Mutiny*.

Responsibility for the damages and losses sustained in the typhoon
of December, 1944, was placed squarely upon the Commander Third
Fleet (Admiral William F. Halsey), and to a "lesser degree" upon
some of his subordinate commanders, but in "view of the valuable
services rendered by these officers in prosecution of the war against
our enemies" no action was taken. The mistakes made were "errors
in judgment resulting from insufficient information committed under
stress of war operations and stemmed from the firm determination to
meet military commitments."

The second typhoon of June 5, 1945, which caught the fleet committed to support of the Okinawa battle, did less damage but caused even more ire in Washington, since to Admiral Ernest King it was redundant evidence of the lack of a seaman's "weather eye." Actually, the fleet's commitment to Okinawa permitted somewhat less discretion and gave it less maneuvering flexibility than it had had in December, 1944. Nevertheless, the records and endorsements of the second Naval Court of Inquiry show that Admiral King was quite angry and rightly so. Some of his remarks singed even three-star and four-star admirals.

The June 5, 1945 (Okinawa) typhoon caused serious damage to the carriers *Hornet, Bennington, Windham Bay,* and *Salamaua;* the cruisers *Pittsburgh* (which lost her bow), *Baltimore,* and *Duluth* were seriously damaged, and twenty-six other vessels sustained minor damage. Seventy-six planes were destroyed, seventy damaged, six officers and men were killed or lost overboard and four were seriously hurt.

Admiral King noted that the "gravity of the occurrence was accentuated by the fact that the senior officers concerned were also involved in a similar and poorly handled situation during the typhoon of Dec. 1944." But Admiral Chester W. Nimitz, Commander-in-Chief of the Pacific Fleet, noted that Admiral Halsey and other officers concerned had "rendered invaluable service to [their] country. . . . [Their] skill and determination have been demonstrated time and again in combat with the enemy."

The destroyers lost in the December, 1944, typhoon were not, by any means, the only ships that have capsized in a seaway.

The destroyer *Warrington* was lost in an Atlantic hurricane in 1944 and other smaller ships have similarly foundered. A few of our pre-war destroyers had bad names as "top-heavy," a criticism that was oversimplified but that contained a definite kernel of truth. The addition of heavy top-side weights in the form of radar and anti-aircraft armament after the war started made it imperative that fuel tanks be ballasted as fuel was used.

The two typhoons led to improvements in ship design, particularly in quick-pumping arrangements for fuel and ballast tanks, in electrical panels more protected against flood water, and in the lightening of top-side weights. They also speeded the development of the modern system of "hurricane-hunters" and storm forecasting, and renewed the traditional emphasis of the Navy—too much neglected during the war and, indeed, minimized in the age of steam and plane—on seamanship.

ACKNOWLEDGMENTS   The principal sources for this account of one of the most famous typhoons in history are the records of the Naval Court of Inquiry, and log books and reports of the ships concerned. I also consulted *Admiral Halsey's Story* (with Lt. Comdr. J. Bryan III), Whittlesey House, New York, 1947; and *Battle Report, Volume V—Victory in the Pacific* by Captain Walter Karig, USNR (and others), Rinehart & Co., New York, 1949. I am indebted to the Public Information Office of the Navy Department for statistical, and other aid, and to the Office of Public Information, Department of Defense.

This account, in somewhat briefer form, was first published in the *New York Times Magazine,* and is republished with the permission of the editor.

1852

"The *Birken'ead* Drill"—

WOMEN AND CHILDREN, FIRST!

> *To take your chance in the thick of a rush, with firing all about,*
> *Is nothing so bad when you've cover to 'and, an' leave an'*
> *likin' to shout;*
> *But to stand an' be still to the Birken'ead drill is a damn tough*
> *bullet to chew,*
> *An' they done it, the Jollies—'Er Majesty's Jollies—soldier an'*
> *sailor too!*
> *Their work was done when it 'adn't begun; they was younger*
> *nor me an' you;*
> *Their choice it was plain between drownin' in 'eaps an' being*
> *mashed by the screw,*
> *So they stood an' was still to the Birken'ead drill, soldier an'*
> *sailor too!*
>
> Rudyard Kipling—*Soldier an' Sailor Too*

The wreck of H.M.S. *Birkenhead* in 1852 was the genesis of Kipling's tribute to the Royal Marines (" 'Er Majesty's Jollies—soldier an' sailor too"). But the *Birkenhead's* loss also helped to establish—or at least to confirm—an Anglo-Saxon tradition of the sea—women and children, first. J. G. Lockhart in his book *Peril of the Sea* declares, "the story of the *Birkenhead* has become a tradition—a tradition of

which succeeding generations are justly proud . . . it established a
law which has become embodied in the unwritten maritime code . . .
that . . . in the moment of danger at sea the weak must not be
allowed to go to the wall, nor the fittest claim the right to survive . . .
and that . . . women and children must first be saved."

It was Britain's imperial era; never had the jewels of Empire glit-
tered so brightly as in the reign of Victoria, that beloved Queen.

The White Ensign and the Red Duster fluttered from gaffs and
flagstaffs to the winds of all the seas; the sun never set upon Her
Majesty's ships and armies.

In South Africa, where the Queen's forces under Sir Harry Smith
were fighting for dominion and glory against the Kaffirs, Her Majesty's
Steam Ship *Birkenhead,* transporting much-needed drafts (replacements) for ten regiments, stood into Simon's Bay on Feb. 23, 1852,
forty-seven days out of Cork.

Birkenhead was a 1,400 ton paddle steamer, which carried canvas
(as did nearly all steamers in those days). She was laid down in 1845
as the Royal Navy's first iron steamer; she was designed as a frigate
but used as a transport. And it was as a transport that she steamed to
the Cape of Good Hope in 1852, with men—many of them raw
recruits—from ancient British regiments.

Birkenhead lay in Simon's Bay for two days, provisioned, coaled,
discharged some fifty of her passengers, embarked a few officers'
horses and fodder for them, and stood out at four bells in the "fine
and calm" evening of the twenty-fifth. Her master, Commander Robert
Salmond, had his orders for Algoa Bay and Buffalo Mouth, where he
was to land the drafts of the different regiments. Embarked were 630
souls—130 in the ship's company including a file of Royal Marines;
seven women and thirteen children, the families of some of the soldiers;
and 480 officers and soldiers from the Queen's Regiment, the 6th
Royal Regiment, the 12th Lancers, the 60th Rifles, the 74th Highlanders, and other units serving in the Kaffir War.

At eight bells, as the evening watch was set and the bright stars of
the Southern constellations gleamed in the sky, *Birkenhead's* position
was picked off on the chart and the course was set for the night to
give Cape Hanglip a "berth of about four miles." John Haines, A.B.,

relieved the wheel at four bells (10 P.M.) and repeated the course—
S.S.E. ½ E. Mr. Spear, who was Second Master, was the Officer of
the Watch, and checked the steersman frequently.

"Don't let her go to eastward of the course; keep her a quarter
point to windward," he cautioned Haines.

The watch was uneventful and gradually the crowded ship, hot and
sultry with its packed humanity, settled down.

The mid-watch started with dragging feet. Mr. Davis, the officer of
the watch, checked the course intermittently by the glowing light of
the binnacle, as *Birkenhead* logged about 7½ knots, her paddle wheels
chunking rhythmically. Captain Salmond and the sailing master, Mr.
Brodie, had turned in; no other officer except Mr. Davis, the officer
of the watch, kept the deck. Thomas Daly, A.B., and John Butcher,
A.B., were lookouts, stationed on either bow of the fo'c'sle, and Able
Stone was the leadsman in the chains. Sometime before four bells (2
A.M.), Thomas Cuffin who had the wheel watched Mr. Davis take
bearings on a light ashore. At ten minutes of two Able Stone, the
leadsman, heaving the lead from the chain on the after sponson of the
port paddle box, sang out the sounding:

"By the mark thirteen . . ."

Before he could cast again, the ship struck forward, scrunching
aground with a rolling, ripping jar on a pinnacle rock or reef off
Danger Point, several miles from shore.

Soundings were made as the ship woke and stirred to slow fright—
two fathoms by the impaled bow, seven alongside, and eleven by the
stern.

William Culhane, the Assistant Surgeon, rushed to the deck and
asked Davis what was the matter.

Davis: "Unfortunately it is my watch and she is gone on shore and
I steered the course I was ordered by Mr. Spear at eight bells."

Back in the gunroom, Mr. Culhane, reassured by Mr. Davis' matter-
of-fact manner, was horrified when a clerk rushed in:

"Good God! Doctor; all the people who were down in the cockpit
in the forward part of the ship are drowned in their hammocks; the
water rushed in so fast I barely got out through a hatch ahead of it."

Aft on the poop the captain had come up in his bathrobe to ask
what the noise was and where the ship was.

"She's ashore, sir," some of the men said.

"Mr. Davis, what course are you steering?" the captain asked sharply.

"S.S.E. ½ E., sir," Mr. Davis responded.

"That is right," the captain said simply.

And then—

"Let go the bower anchor and call the boats away. . . ."

"Aye, aye, sir."

Men ran about the ship to carry out the command, as John Drake, the *Birkenhead's* Colour Sergeant, acting on the captain's orders, called all officers up on deck. The officers stood by as Captain Salmond gave a fatal command; he called for a "back turn." The engine was reversed; the paddle wheels chunked backward for a few revolutions; the ship struggled on the rock—the gouge and rent in her hull was opened wide, and she backed off into deep water.

There was not much time after that; *Birkenhead* was gone completely in twenty to thirty minutes after striking.

John Archbold, the gunner, heard the chief engineer report to Captain Salmond that the rising water "was making" three or four feet a minute and had put out his fires. Archbold tried to "fire away" some guns, at the captain's orders, but he could not get to the magazines for powder; the lower decks were flooded to the hatches. The gunner got some "blue lights" and rockets from the passage leading to the captain's cabin and sent them fiery, sizzling, high into the night.

Up from the lower decks, half-dressed, some clad only in thin shirts, the troops streamed as the ship's crew struggled with the boats, and the water rose in the hold and the fires died beneath the boiler.

"Major Seton of the 74th Highlanders called all the officers about him and impressed on them the necessity of preserving order and silence amongst the men."

The troops stood in seried, silent ranks at quarters awaiting orders. Captain Edward R. Wright of the 91st Regiment was directed to receive, transmit, and have executed Captain Salmond's commands.

"Get the men aft on to the poop," the captain ordered hoping to ease the damaged bow.

The soldiers moved smartly as ordered, and then Captain Wright sent men to lead the plunging, kicking horses out of the port gangway over the side and into the sea.

As soon as the horses were over and well clear of the wreck, where they could do no damage to the boats, seven soldiers' wives and their thirteen children (all the dependents that were aboard)—some of them tearfully clinging to their husbands and fathers—were passed down into the cutter, manned by a few seamen and in charge of Mr. Richards, Master's Assistant. Mrs. Spruce; Mrs. Nesbit; Mrs. Montgomery and other wives struggled to stay with their soldier-husbands and some of them had to be torn away—sobbing—to be put into the boat. The cutter with its helpless cargo was almost swamped by a large roller as it pulled clear. But the men left on the wreck breathed more freely as the cutter pulled away; "it is hard to describe the sensation of oppression lifted from one's mind on knowing the utterly helpless part of the ship's living cargo had been deposited in comparative safety."

Thirty soldiers were sent atop each paddle box to aid the seamen trying to cant and launch the paddle box boats, and sixty more under two officers were detailed in three shifts to man the chain pumps on the lower afterdeck. This was scarcely done when *Birkenhead's* flooded bow, to aft of the foremast, broke off with a sharp crack, rose to the perpendicular, with the bowsprit pointing toward the stars and with the foremast jabbing and raking the rest of the hulk. The stays to the funnel parted; the stack fell crashing across the starboard paddle box, crushing some of the men working on the boat; and Mr. Brodie, the Sailing Master, was knocked from the bridge into the sea. But there was no panic; the men carried out orders as if embarking on a routine voyage, instead of facing death; most of them stood silently waiting, "as if on parade."

Ensign Lucas of the 73rd Regiment shared with another officer the duty of supervising the men at the chain pumps. Lucas had dressed carefully in his uniform after the ship struck; his men, some of them only half uniformed, were disciplined, quiet, and obedient. The troops toiled at the pumps, but the futility was obvious now.

There was not much more that could be done; the second cutter with the women and children; the first cutter with seamen and some troops; the gig with about nine men had been lowered and were standing by—filled to virtual capacity—about 100 to 150 yards away. Three boats with 60 to 70 people, and save for those drowned in their hammocks when the ship struck, or killed by the falling stack, the rest of the 630 souls were still aboard. Still drawn up in ordered ranks—most of them; still standing silent facing danger. . . .

There were other boats aboard and crew and soldiers struggled in these last minutes to free them. The starboard paddle box boat was damaged and partly carried away by the falling funnel; the port boat was jammed and ultimately capsized; the long boat, or pinnace, had to be hoisted with a complicated system of tackles—and there was no time. There was another gig, too, and a dinghy (but there were no davits in those days as we know them now), and it took time and back-breaking labor to launch boats—and there was no time.

But still the "orders were implicitly obeyed and perfect discipline maintained," as the stern part of the ship slowly sank.

The men found it hard to hold their footing and to remain in ranks, for the hulk—deep in the water, and lifted by the long swell—was rolling heavily, dipping her yardarms under.

The last moments of *Birkenhead* were distinguished by the same simple courage and "utmost order"; there "was not a cry or murmur from soldiers or sailors."

Under the dark, starlit sky, the three loaded boats lay near by, lifting and falling on the long swells. The dull boom of the surf, break-ing on the shore several miles away, the creak of cordage as the hulk lifted heavily, the straining efforts of the men working on the un-launched boats, and an occasional quiet word from the officers broke the stillness. Wreckage, a few bodies—the horses swimming far away —and men who had been washed overboard clinging to a truss of hay or a hatch cover surrounded *Birkenhead*. But no ship had come in answer to the blue lights and the rockets. . . .

Toward the end, Captain Salmond despairing, as the stern sank deeper and deeper, gave his final order:

"All those who can swim, jump overboard and make for the boats."

But Major Seton, Captain Wright, and other officers, standing in the stern in front of their men, saw the danger instantly:

"Stand fast!"

They "begged the men not to do as the captain said, as the boat with the women must be swamped. Not more than three" jumped overboard; hundreds stood fast in disciplined ranks.

Just before the end, the ship broke in two again—just abaft the engine room, washing large numbers of men into the sea. In the final minute or so before the after portion sank, Ensign Lucas of the 73rd Regiment, saw the dark sea "alive with men"—some drowning, some swimming strongly, some struggling toward bits of wreckage. The shrouds and rigging of the mainmast were lined with men from deck to trucks. The poop and extreme after-portion—still crowded with troops, some fully uniformed, some half-dressed, still in ranks—slowly up-ended until the heel of the rudder was "completely out of water." Lucas, with Major Seton beside him, stood looking out over the up-ending stern in those final seconds.

Lucas "shook hands with Seton and expressed the hope we would meet ashore."

Seton: "I do not think we shall, Lucas, as I cannot swim a stroke."

Those were probably Seton's last words; the final plunge of the wreckage swept the officers apart and Seton was never seen again. Captain Salmond, too, disappeared; he was swimming strongly in the water near Colour Sergeant Drake when something struck the commander, and he went under.

With them died most of the ship's company and most of the soldiers bound for the Kaffir War. About 210 were saved—some were in the boats; thirty to forty exhausted survivors were rescued by the schooner *Lioness* the next day from the main topmast which remained above water when the after part of *Birkenhead* sank. Still others clinging to wreckage, or hanging to a makeshift raft, made it to shore, and four were found alive after thirty-eight hours in the water. But hundreds, stalwart to the last, went down with *Birkenhead;* others died in the pounding surf after almost reaching shore, and many were entangled and drowned in the thick kelp which rimmed Danger Point.

But not a woman or child was lost and the surviving officers were unanimous in their judgments:

". . . the resolution and coolness of all hands . . . in a moment of extreme peril . . . was remarkable. . . .

"The order . . . that prevailed on board from the time the ship struck until she totally disappeared far exceeded anything that . . .

could be effected by the best discipline, and is more to be wondered
at, seeing that most of the soldiers were but a short time in the service.
. . . Everyone did as he was directed and there was not a murmur
or cry among them until the vessel made her final plunge."

The tragedy of the *Birkenhead* excited the pride of England; Queen
Victoria erected a marble memorial to the dead in the colonnade of
Chelsea Hospital, London. The King of Prussia had the record of the
wreck read to his regiments, as an example of the best meaning of
discipline.

And the name *Birkenhead* became a nautical and military tradition,
a tradition which has lived brightly in the century since her stranding
—a tradition of order and obedience in the face of imminent peril, a
tradition of women and children, first.

NOTES   Estimates of the *Birkenhead* dead differ. Lockhart, depending apparently chiefly upon Captain Wright's report and
the report from Commodore Wyvil, says 445 were drowned and 193
were saved. However, this writer believes there were only 630 souls
aboard when *Birkenhead* was wrecked, and figures presented to the
Portsmouth courts-martial indicate 210 were saved and 420 lost.
Among those saved were Captain Wright, senior surviving military
officer, and R. B. Richards, Master's Assistant, senior surviving officer
of the ship's company. Fifty-nine of the ship's company, including six
officers, forty-two seamen, five boys, and six Marines were saved; of
the passengers five army officers, 126 soldiers, seven women, and
thirteen children—a total of 151—were rescued.

The courts-martial at Portsmouth exonerated completely all the
survivors; the proceedings found "no blame imputable" to any of the
survivors, "but on the contrary the court sees reason to admire and
applaud the steadiness shown by all in most trying circumstances."
It declared, however, that though it might "be unjust to pass censure
upon the deceased [Captain Salmond and, presumably, his sailing
master, Mr. Brodie], whose motives for keeping so near the shore
cannot be explained," nevertheless, the "fatal loss was owing to the

course having been calculated to keep the land in close proximity. . . ."

The court added "praise of the departed for the coolness displayed at the moment of extreme peril and for the laudable anxiety shown for the safety of the women and children to the exclusion of all selfish consideration."

The court specifically ignored or rejected inferences by Commodore Wyvil that the failure of Captain Salmond and Sailing Master Brodie to come on deck between 10 P.M. and the time the ship struck inferred "extreme neglect of duty." It also rejected contentions that the boats might have saved more survivors from the water and that the rescue operations were not well organized. It specifically praised the "conduct of those who were first in the boats" and endorsed their judgments.

Read a hundred years later, the eye-witness testimony in the courts-martial and the questions asked leave, however, some room for doubt about the judgment of Captain Salmond and the conduct and judgment of all of those in the boats. And the list of survivors seems to include a disproportionate number of the ship's company and too few troops.

It seems indeed probable that the story of the *Birkenhead* has been embellished somewhat with the years and that the few discreditable events which probably occurred have been forgotten and the general discipline, courage, and steadiness somewhat, though not greatly, magnified. It is almost certain that the imaginative painting "The Wreck of the *Birkenhead*," by Henny (London) represents an heroic generalization of the final scene.

Ensign Lucas, in his letter, suggests that the soldiers did not know the ship was foundering; he states he asked the ship's carpenter after *Birkenhead* struck the reef what the trouble was and was told:

"We have struck a rock and we are going down fast."

Lucas says he asked "the carpenter not to tell the men, fearing panic."

Captain Wright in his letter-report of March 1, 1852, included with the court-martial papers, states that the perfect discipline and excellent conduct of the men "struck me as being one of the most perfect instances of what discipline can effect, and almost led me to believe that not a man on board knew the vessel was likely to go down."

It is indeed possible that many of the young soldiers did not realize their peril until the very end, but many in the ship's company certainly understood the danger, and after the bow broke off few in the *Birkenhead* could have had many illusions. And, in any case, the great majority of the men held steady until the very end—refusing to leap into the water and swamp the boats.

It is curious—in view of Kipling's utilization of the *Birkenhead* incident in his tribute to the Royal Marines—that one of the few criticisms of the conduct of any of the *Birkenhead* personnel to be found in the courts-martial proceedings was directed against a Marine survivor in one of the boats, who was alleged to be impudent and surly. Kipling's poem, indeed, leaves a false impression—the impression that the glory of the *Birkenhead* was chiefly the glory of the Royal Marines. There were a handful of Marines aboard attached to the ship's company— (six were saved)—and probably their conduct as well as that of the great majority of all aboard was courageous and disciplined. But the principal glory of the *Birkenhead* must go to the young soldiers and their officers who were passengers in an alien environment, yet who stood "an' [were] still to the *Birken'ead* drill"—the drill of discipline, obedience, and courage.

ACKNOWLEDGMENTS   The principal source for the *Birkenhead* story is the "Sessional Papers"—House of Commons, 1852, Volume 30, pages 219–249. These papers contain the proceedings of two courts-martial of the surviving officers and crew of H.M.S. *Birkenhead* held aboard H.M.S. *Victory* at Portsmouth, England, on 5 and 7 May, 1852, under the Presidency of Henry Prescott, Esq., C.B., Rear Admiral of the Red and Second Officer in Command of Her Majesty's ships and vessels at Spithead and in Portsmouth Harbor. Included in these papers are eyewitness reports of survivors, official reports, a letter to the Admiralty from Commodore C. Wyvil at Simon's Bay, describing the wreck, and a letter report from Captain Edward R. Wright of the 91st Regiment, dated March 1, 1852. I have drawn liberally upon these documents, and quotations in this account are chiefly from these papers.

J. G. Lockhart, *Peril of the Sea,* Frederick Stokes, 1925, is another important source consulted. Lockhart quotes from a letter written by a survivor, Ensign Lucas, and in turn I have utilized some of the Lucas material in this account.

Other sources of secondary importance are *Notes and Queries, London*—"Loss of Her Majesty's Steamship *Birkenhead,*" Jan.–June, 1921; "The Loss of the *Orion,* the *Amazon* and the *Birkenhead*"— a letter by William S. Lacon to the President of the Board of Trade, London, Parker, Furnival and Parker—Military Library, 1852; and *Ships and South Africa,* by Marischal Murray, Oxford University Press, London, 1933.

1912

R.M.S. *Titanic*

The White Star Line *Titanic,* largest ship the world had ever known, sailed from Southampton on her maiden voyage to New York on April 10, 1912. The paint on her strakes was fair and bright; she was fresh from Harland & Wolff's Belfast yards, strong in the strength of her forty-six thousand tons of steel, bent, hammered, shaped, and riveted through the three years of her slow birth.

There was little fuss and fanfare at her sailing; her sister ship, the *Olympic*—slightly smaller than the *Titanic*—had been in service for some months, and to her had gone the thunder of the cheers. But the *Titanic* needed no whistling steamers or shouting crowds to call attention to her superlative qualities. Her bulk dwarfed the ships near her as longshoremen singled up her mooring lines and cast off the turns of heavy rope from the dock bollards.

She was, moreover, not only the largest ship afloat, but was believed to be the safest. Carlisle, her builder, had given her double bottoms, and had divided her hull into sixteen watertight compartments, which made her, men thought, unsinkable. She had been built to be a gigantic lifeboat. Her designers' dreams of a triple-screw giant, a luxurious, floating hotel, which could speed to New York at twenty-three knots in absolute safety, had been carefully translated from blueprints and mold loft lines at the Belfast yards into a living reality.

The *Titanic's* sailing from Southampton, though quiet, was not wholly uneventful. As the liner moved slowly toward the end of her dock that April day, the surge of her passing sucked away from the quay the steamer *New York,* moored just to seaward of the *Titanic's* berth. There were sharp cracks as the manila mooring lines of the *New York* parted under the strain. The frayed ropes writhed and whistled through the air and snapped down among the waving crowd on the pier; the ship swung toward the *Titanic's* bow, then was checked and dragged back to the dock barely in time to avert a collision. Seamen muttered, thought it an ominous start.

Past Spithead and the Isle of Wight the *Titanic* steamed. She called at Cherbourg at dusk and then laid her course for Queenstown. At 1:30 P.M. on Thursday, April 11, she stood out of Queenstown harbor, screaming gulls soaring in her wake, with 2,201 persons—men, women, and children—aboard.

Occupying the Empire bedrooms and Georgian suites of the first-class accommodations were many well-known men and women: Colonel John Jacob Astor and his young bride; Major Archibald Butt, military aide to President Taft, and his friend, Frank D. Millett, the painter; John B. Thayer, vice-president of the Pennsylvania Railroad, and Charles M. Hays, president of the Grand Trunk Railway of Canada; W. T. Stead, English journalist; Jacques Futrelle, French novelist; H. B. Harris, theatrical manager, and Mrs. Harris; Mr. and Mrs. Isidor Straus; and J. Bruce Ismay, chairman and managing director of the White Star Line.

Down in the plain wooden cabins of the steerage class were 706 immigrants to the land of promise, and trimly stowed in the great holds was a cargo valued at $420,000—oak beams, sponges, wine, calabashes, and an odd miscellany of the common and the rare.

The *Titanic* took her departure on Fastnet Light and, heading into the night, laid her course for New York. She was due at quarantine the following Wednesday morning.

Sunday, the third day out, dawned fair and clear. The *Titanic* steamed smoothly toward the west, faint streamers of brownish smoke trailing from her funnels. The purser held services in the saloon in the morning; on the steerage deck aft the immigrants were playing games, and a Scotsman was puffing "The Campbells Are Coming" on his bagpipes in the midst of the uproar.

At 9 A.M. a message from the steamer *Caronia* sputtered into the wireless shack:

CAPTAIN, *Titanic*—WESTBOUND STEAMERS REPORT BERGS GROWL-ERS AND FIELD ICE IN 42 DEGREES N. FROM 49 DEGREES TO 51 DEGREES W. 12TH APRIL.

COMPLIMENTS

BARR

It was cold in the afternoon; the sun was brilliant, but the *Titanic*, her screws turning over at seventy-five revolutions per minute, was approaching the Banks.

In the Marconi cabin Second Operator Harold Bride, earphones clamped on his head, was figuring accounts; he did not stop to answer when he heard MWL, Continental Morse for the nearby Leyland liner *Californian*, calling the *Titanic*. The *Californian* had some message about three icebergs; he didn't bother then to take it down. About 1:42 P.M. the rasping spark of the wireless of those days spoke again across the water. It was the *Baltic*, calling the *Titanic*, warning her of ice on the steamer track. Bride took the message down and sent it up to the bridge. The officer of the deck glanced at it and sent it on to the bearded master of the *Titanic*, Captain E. C. Smith, a veteran of the White Star service. It was lunch time then; the captain, walking along the promenade deck, saw Mr. Ismay, stopped, and handed him the message without comment. Ismay read it, stuffed it in his pocket, told two ladies about the icebergs, and resumed his walk. Later, about 7:15 P.M., the captain requested the return of the message in order to post it in the chart room for the information of officers.

Dinner that night in the Jacobean dining room was gay. It was bitter on deck, but the night was calm and fine; the sky was moonless but studded with stars twinkling coldly in the clear air.

After dinner some of the second-class passengers gathered in the saloon, where the Reverend Mr. Carter conducted a "hymn sing-song." It was almost ten o'clock and the stewards were waiting with biscuits and coffee as the group sang:

"O, hear us when we cry to Thee
For those in peril on the sea."

On the bridge Second Officer Lightoller—short, stocky, efficient—was relieved at ten o'clock by First Officer Murdoch. Lightoller had talked with other officers about the proximity of ice; at least five wireless ice warnings had reached the ship; lookouts had been cautioned to be alert: captains and officers expected to reach the field at any time after 9:30 P.M. But at 22 knots, its speed unslackened, the *Titanic* plowed on through the night.

Lightoller left the darkened bridge to his relief and turned in. Captain Smith went to his cabin. The steerage was long since quiet; in the first and second cabins lights were going out; voices were growing still, people were asleep. Murdoch paced back and forth on the bridge, peering out over the dark water, glancing now and then at the compass in front of Quartermaster Hichens at the wheel.

In the crow's-nest, Lookout Frederick Fleet and his partner, Leigh, gazed down at the water, still and unruffled in the dim starlit darkness. Behind and below them the ship was a white shadow, with here and there a last winking light; ahead of them lay a dark and cold and silent ocean.

There was a sudden clang. *Dong-dong. Dong-dong. Dong-dong. Dong.* The metal clapper of the great ship's bell struck out 11:30. Mindful of the warning, Fleet strained his eyes, searching the darkness for the dreaded ice. But there were only the stars and the sea. In the wireless room, where Phillips, first operator, had relieved Bride, the buzz of the *Californian's* set again crackled into the earphones:

Californian: "Say, old man, we are stuck here, surrounded by ice."

Titanic: "Shut up, shut up; keep out. I am talking to Cape Race; you are jamming my signals."

It was 11:40.

Then, suddenly out of the dark it came, a vast white monstrous shape, directly in the *Titanic's* path. For a moment Fleet doubted his eyes. But it was a deadly reality. Frantically he struck three bells—*something dead ahead.* He snatched the telephone and called the bridge:

"Iceberg! Right ahead!"

The first officer did not stop to acknowledge the message: "Hard-a-starboard!"

The quartermaster strained at the wheel; the bow swung slowly to port. The monster was almost upon them now.

Murdoch leaped to the engine-room telegraph. Bells clanged. Far below in the engine room those bells struck the first warning. Danger! The indicators on the dial faces swung round to "Stop!" Then—"Full Speed Astern!" Quickly the engineers turned great valve wheels. . . .

There was a slight shock, a brief scraping, a small list to port. Shell ice—slabs and chunks of it—fell on the foredeck. Slowly the *Titanic* stopped.

Captain Smith hurried out of his cabin. "What has the ship struck?"

Murdoch answered, "An iceberg, sir. I hard-a-starboarded her and reversed the engines, and I was going to hard-a-port around it, but she was too close. I could not do any more. I have closed the water-tight doors."

Fourth Officer Boxhall, other officers, the carpenter, came to the bridge. The captain sent Boxhall and the carpenter below to ascertain the damage.

A few lights switched on in the first and second cabins; sleepy passengers peered through port-hole glass; one casually asked a steward: "Why have we stopped?"

"I don't know, sir, but I don't suppose it's anything much."

In the smoking room a quorum of gamblers and their prey were still sitting round a poker table; the usual crowd of kibitzers looked on. They had felt the slight jar of the collision and had seen an eighty-foot ice mountain glide by the smoking-room windows, but the night was calm and clear, the *Titanic* was unsinkable; they hadn't bothered to go on deck.

But far below, in the warren of passages on the starboard side forward, in the forward holds and boiler rooms, men could see that the *Titanic's* hurt was mortal. In No. 6 boiler room, where the red glow from the furnaces lighted up the naked sweaty chests of coal-blackened firemen, water was pouring through a great gash two feet above the floor plates. This was no slow leak; the ship was open to the sea.

In ten minutes there were eight feet of water in No. 6. Long before then the stokers had raked the fires out of the furnaces and had scrambled through the watertight doors into No. 5 or had climbed up the long steel ladders to safety. When Boxhall looked at the mail room in No. 3 hold, twenty-four feet above the keel, the mailbags were already floating in the slushing water. In No. 5 boiler room a stream of water spurted into an empty bunker. All six compartments forward of No. 4 were flooded; in ten seconds the iceberg's jagged claw had ripped a three-hundred-foot slash in the bottom of the great *Titanic*.

Reports were coming to the bridge. Ismay in dressing gown ran out on deck in the cold, still, starlit night, and climbed up the bridge ladder.

"What has happened?"

Captain Smith: "We have struck ice."

"Do you think she is seriously damaged?"

"I'm afraid she is."

Ismay went below and passed Chief Engineer William Bell fresh from an inspection of the damaged compartments. Bell corroborated the captain's statement, then hurried back down the glistening steel ladders to his duty. Man after man followed him, among them Thomas Andrews, one of the ship's designers, and Archie Frost, the builder's chief engineer, with his twenty assistants—men who had no posts of duty in the engine room but whose traditions called them there.

On deck, in corridor and stateroom, life flowed again. Men, women, and children awoke and asked questions; orders were given to uncover the lifeboats; water rose into the firemen's quarters; half-dressed stokers streamed up on deck. But the passengers—most of them— did not know that the *Titanic* was sinking. The shock of the collision had been so slight that some were not awakened by it; the *Titanic* was so huge that she could not be damaged by floating ice; the night was too calm, too beautiful, to think of death at sea.

Captain Smith half ran to the door of the radio shack. Bride, partly dressed, eyes dulled with sleep, was standing behind Phillips, waiting.

"Send the call for assistance."

The blue spark danced: "CQD—CQD—CQD—CQ—" Miles away Marconi men heard. Cape Race heard it, and the steamships *La Provence* and *Mt. Temple*.

The sea was surging into the *Titanic's* hold. At 12:20 the water burst into the seamen's quarters through a collapsed fore and aft wooden bulkhead. Pumps strained in the engine rooms, men and machinery making a futile fight against the sea. Steadily the water rose.

The boats were swung out—slowly; for the deck hands were late in reaching their stations, there had been no boat drill, and many of the crew did not know to what boats they were assigned. Orders were shouted; the safety valves had lifted, and steam was blowing off in a great rushing roar. In the charthouse Fourth Officer Boxhall bent above a chart, working rapidly with pencil and dividers.

12:25 A.M. Boxhall's position goes out to a fleet of vessels: "Come at once; we have struck a berg."

To the Cunarder *Carpathia* (Arthur Henry Rostron, Master, New York to Liverpool, fifty-eight miles away):

"It's a CQD, old man. Position 41–46 N.; 50–14 W."

The blue spark dancing: "Sinking; cannot hear for noise of steam."

12:30 A.M. The word is passed: "Women and children in the boats." Stewards finish waking their passengers below; life preservers are tied on; some men smile at the precaution. "The *Titanic* is unsinkable." The *Mt. Temple* starts for the *Titanic;* the *Carpathia,* with a double watch in her stokeholds, radios, "Coming hard." The CQD changes the course of many ships—but not of one: the operator of the *Californian,* nearby, has just put down his earphones and turned in.

The CQD flashes over land and sea from Cape Race to New York; newspaper city rooms leap to life and presses whir.

On the *Titanic,* water creeps over the bulkhead between Nos. 5 and 6 firerooms. She is going down by the head; the engineers— fighting a losing battle—are forced back foot by foot by the rising water. Down the promenade deck Happy Jock Hume, the bandsman, runs with his instrument.

12:45 A.M. Murdoch, in charge on the starboard side, eyes tragic, but calm and cool, orders boat No. 7 lowered. The women hang back; they want no boat ride on an ice-strewn sea; surely the *Titanic* will not sink! The men encourage them, explain that this is just a precautionary measure: "We'll see you again at breakfast." There is little confusion; passengers stream slowly to the boat deck. In the steerage the immigrants chatter excitedly.

A sudden sharp hiss—a streaked flare against the night: Boxhall sends a rocket toward the sky. It explodes, and a parachute of white stars lights up the icy sea. "God! Rockets!" The band plays ragtime.

No. 8 is lowered, and No. 5. Ismay, still in dressing gown, calls for women and children, handles lines, stumbles in the way of an officer, is told, "Get the hell out of here." Third Officer Pitman takes charge of No. 5; as he swings into the boat Murdoch grasps his hand. "Good-bye and good luck, old man."

No. 6 goes over the side. There are only twenty-eight people in a lifeboat with a capacity of sixty-five.

A light stabs from the bridge; Boxhall is calling in Morse flashes, again and again, to a strange ship stopped in the ice jam five to ten miles away. Another rocket drops its shower of sparks above the ice-strewn sea and the dying ship.

1 A.M. Slowly the water creeps higher; the fore ports of the *Titanic* are dipping into the sea. Rope squeaks through blocks; lifeboats drop jerkily seaward. Through the shouting on the decks comes the sound of the band.

The "Millionaires' Special" leaves the ship—boat No. 1. With a capacity of forty people, it carries only Sir Cosmo and Lady Duff Gordon and ten others. Aft, the frightened immigrants mill and jostle and rush for a boat. An officer's fist flies out; three shots are fired in the air, and the panic is quelled. . . . Four Chinese sneak unseen into a boat and hide in its bottom.

1:20 A.M. Water is coming into No. 4 boiler room. Stokers slice and shovel as it laps about their ankles—steam for the dynamos, steam for the wireless spark! As the water rises great ash hoes rake the flaming coals from the furnaces. Safety valves pop; the stokers retreat aft, and the watertight doors clang shut behind them.

The rockets fling their splendor toward the stars. The boats are more heavily loaded now, for the passengers know the *Titanic* is sinking. Women cling to each other and sob. The great screws aft are rising clear of the sea. Half-filled boats are ordered to come alongside the cargo ports and take on more passengers; but the ports are never opened, and the boats are never filled. Others pull for the lights of a steamer, clear but miles away. They never reach it; the lights disappear, the unknown ship steams off.

The water rises and the band plays ragtime.

1:30 A.M. Lightoller is getting the port boats off; Murdoch the starboard. As one boat is lowered into the sea a boat officer fires his gun along the ship's side to stop a rush from the lower decks. A woman tries to take her Great Dane into the boat with her; she is refused and steps out of the boat to die with her dog. Millet's "little smile, which had played on his lips all through the voyage" plays no more; his lips are grim, but he waves good-bye and brings wraps for the women.

Benjamin Guggenheim, in evening clothes, smiles and says, "We've dressed up in our best and are prepared to go down like gentlemen."

1:40 A.M. Boat No. 14 is clear, then 13, 16, 15, and C. The lights still shine, but the *Baltic* hears the blue spark say, "Engine room getting flooded."

The *Olympic* signals, "Am lighting up all possible boilers as fast as can."

Major Butts helps women into the last boats and waves good-bye to them. Mrs. Straus puts her foot on the gunwale of a lifeboat, then she draws back and goes to her husband: "We have been together many years; where you go I will go." Colonel John Jacob Astor puts his young wife in a lifeboat, steps back, taps cigarette on fingernail: "Good-bye, dearie; I'll join you later."

1:45 A.M. The foredeck is under water, the fo'c'sle head almost awash; the great stern is lifted high toward the bright stars; and still the band plays. Mr. and Mrs. Harris approach a lifeboat arm in arm.

Officer: "Ladies first, please."

Harris bows, smiles, steps back: "Of course, certainly; ladies first."

Boxhall fires the last rocket, then leaves in charge of boat No. 2.

2 A.M. She is dying now; her bow goes deeper, her stern higher. But there must be steam. Below in the stokeholds, the sweaty firemen keep steam up for the flaring lights and the dancing spark. The glowing coals slide and tumble over the slanted grate bars; the sea pounds behind that yielding bulkhead. But the spark dances on.

The *Asian* hears Phillips try the new signal: SOS.

Boat No. 4 has left now; boat D leaves ten minutes later. Jacques Futrelle clasps his wife: "For God's sake, go! It's your last chance; go!" Mme. Futrelle is half-forced into the boat. It clears the side.

There are about 660 people in the boats—and 1,500 still on the sinking *Titanic*.

On top of the officers' quarters men work frantically to get the two collapsible boats stored there over the side. Water is over the forward part of A deck now; it surges up the companionways towards the boat deck. In the radio shack Bride has slipped a coat and life jacket about Phillips as the first operator sits hunched over his key, sending, still sending—"41–46 N., 50–14 W. CQD—CQD—SOS—SOS—"

The captain's tired white face appears at the radio-room door: "Men, you have done your full duty. You can do no more. Now, it's every man for himself." The captain disappears—back to his sinking bridge, where Painter, his personal steward, stands quietly waiting for orders. The spark dances on. Bride turns his back and goes into the inner cabin. As he does so a stoker, grimed with coal, mad with fear, steals into the shack and reaches for the life jacket on Phillips' back. Bride wheels about and brains him with a wrench.

2:10 A.M. Below decks the steam is still holding, though the pressure is falling—rapidly. In the gymnasium on the boat deck the athletic instructor watches quietly as two gentlemen ride the bicycles and another swings casually at the punching bag. Mail clerks stagger up the boat-deck stairways, dragging soaked mail sacks. The spark still crackles. The band still plays, but not ragtime:

> *Nearer my God to Thee,*
> *Nearer to Thee. . . .*

A few men take up the refrain; others kneel on the slanting decks to pray. Many run and scramble aft, where hundreds are clinging above the silent screws on the great uptilted stern. The spark still signals and the lights still flare; the engineers are on the job. The hymn comes to its close. Bandmaster Hartley, Yorkshireman violinist, taps his bow against a bulkhead, calls for "Autumn" as the water curls about his feet and the eight musicians brace themselves against the ship's slant. People are leaping from the decks into the nearby water

—the icy water. A woman cries, "Oh, save me, save me!" A man answers, "Good lady, save yourself. Only God can save you now." The band plays "Autumn":

> *God of Mercy and Compassion!*
> *Look with pity on my pain. . . .*

The water creeps over the bridge where the *Titanic's* master stands; heavily he steps out to meet it.

2:17 A.M. "CQ—" the *Virginian* hears a ragged, blurred CQ, then an abrupt stop. The blue spark dances no more. The lights flicker out; the engineers have lost their battle.

2:18 A.M. Men run about blackened decks; leap into the night; are swept into the sea by the curling wave which licks up the *Titanic's* length. Lightoller does not leave the ship—the ship leaves him; there are hundreds like him, but only a few who live to tell of it. The funnels still swim above the water, but the ship is climbing to the perpendicular; the bridge is under and most of the foremast; the great stern rises like a squat leviathan. Men swim away from the sinking ship; others drop from the stern.

The band plays in the darkness, the water lapping upwards:

> *Hold me up in mighty waters,*
> *Keep my eyes on things above,*
> *Righteousness, divine atonement,*
> *Peace and everlas . . .*

The forward funnel snaps and crashes into the sea; its steel tons hammer out of existence swimmers struggling in the freezing water. Streams of sparks, of smoke and steam, burst from the after funnels. The ship upends to fifty, to sixty degrees.

Down in the black abyss of the stokeholds, in the engine rooms where the dynamos have whirred at last to a stop, the stokers and the engineers are reeling against hot metal, the rising water clutching at their knees. The boilers and the engine cylinders rip from their bed plates and crash through the bulkheads—steel against steel.

The *Titanic* stands on end, poised briefly for the plunge. Slowly she slides to her grave—slowly at first, and then more quickly— quickly—quickly.

2:20 A.M. The greatest ship in the world has sunk. From the calm dark waters where the floating lifeboats move there goes up, in the white wake of her passing, "one long continuous moan."

The boats that the *Titanic* had launched pulled safely away from the slight suction of the sinking ship, pulled away from the screams that came from the lips of the freezing men and women in the water. The boats were poorly manned and badly equipped, and they had been unevenly loaded. Some carried so few seamen that women bent to the oars. Mrs. Astor tugged at an oar handle; the Countess of Rothes took a tiller. Shivering stokers in sweaty coal-blackened singlets and light trousers steered in some boats; stewards in white coats rowed in others. Ismay was in the last boat that left the ship from the starboard side; with Mr. Carter of Philadelphia and two seamen he tugged at the oars. In one of the lifeboats an Italian with a broken wrist—disguised in a woman's shawl and hat—huddled on the floor boards, ashamed now that fear had left him. In another rode the only baggage saved from the *Titanic:* the carryall of Samuel L. Goldenberg, one of the rescued passengers.

There were only a few boats that were heavily loaded; most of those that were half-empty made but perfunctory efforts to pick up the moaning swimmers, their officers and crew fearing they would endanger the living if they pulled back into the midst of the dying. Some boats beat off the freezing victims; fear-crazed men and women struck with oars at the heads of swimmers. One woman drove her fist into the face of a half-dead man as he tried feebly to climb over the gunwale. Two other women helped him in and stanched the flow of blood from the ring cuts on his face.

One of the collapsible boats, which had floated off the top of the officers' quarters when the *Titanic* sank, was an icy haven for thirty or forty men. The boat had capsized as the ship sank; men swam to it, clung to it, climbed upon its slippery bottom, stood knee-deep in water in the freezing air. Chunks of ice swirled about their legs; their soaked clothing clutched their bodies in icy folds. Colonel Archibald Gracie was cast up there, Gracie who had leaped from the stern as the *Titanic* sank; young Thayer who had seen his father die; Lightoller who had twice been sucked down with the ship and twice blown to the surface by a belch of air; Bride, the second wireless operator, and Phillips, the first. There were many stokers, half naked; it was a shivering company. They stood there in the icy sea, under the far stars, and sang and prayed—the Lord's Prayer. After a while a life-boat came and picked them off, but Phillips was dead then or died soon afterwards in the boat.

Only a few of the boats had lights; only one, No. 2, had a light that was of any use to the *Carpathia,* twisting through the ice field to the rescue. Other ships were coming hard too; but one, the *Californian,* was still dead to opportunity.

The blue sparks still danced, but not the *Titanic's; La Provence* to the *Celtic:* "Nobody has heard the *Titanic* for about two hours."

It was 2:40 when the *Carpathia* first sighted the green light from No. 2 boat; it was 4:10 when she picked up the first boat and learned that the *Titanic* had foundered. The last of the moaning cries had just died away then.

Captain Rostron took the survivors aboard, boatload by boatload. He was ready for them, though only a small minority of them required much medical attention. Bride's feet were twisted and frozen; others were suffering from exposure; one died; seven were dead when taken from the boats, and were buried at sea.

It was then that the fleet of racing ships learned they were too late; the *Parisian* heard the weak signals of MPA, the *Carpathia,* report the death of the *Titanic.* It was then—or soon afterward, when her radio operator put on his earphones—that the *Californian,* the ship that had been within sight as the *Titanic* was sinking, first learned of the disaster.

And it was then, in all its white-green majesty, that the *Titanic's* survivors saw the iceberg, tinted with the sunrise, floating idly, pack ice jammed about its base, other bergs heaving slowly nearby on the blue breast of the sea.

It was not until later that the world knew, for wireless then was not what wireless is today, and garbled messages had nourished a hope that all of the *Titanic's* company were safe. Not until Monday evening, when P. A. S. Franklin, vice-president of the International Mercantile Marine Company, received relayed messages in New York that left little hope, did the full extent of the disaster begin to be known. Partial and garbled lists of the survivors; rumors of heroism and cowardice; stories spun out of newspaper imagination, based on a few bare facts and many false reports, misled the world, terrified and frightened it. It was not until Thursday night, when the *Carpathia* steamed into the North River, that the full truth was pieced together.

Flashlights flared on the black river when she stood up to her dock. Tugs nosed about her, shunted her toward Pier 54. Thirty thousand people jammed the streets; ambulances and stretchers stood on the pier; coroners and physicians waited.

In midstream the Cunarder dropped over the *Titanic's* lifeboats; then she headed toward the dock. Beneath the customs letters on the pier stood relatives of the 711 survivors, and relatives of the missing— hoping against hope. The *Carpathia* cast her lines ashore; stevedores looped them over bollards. The dense throngs stood quiet as the first survivor stepped down the gangway. It was a woman. She half staggered, led by customs guards, and stopped beneath her letter. A moan came from the crowd; fell, grew in volume, and dropped again.

Thus ended the maiden voyage of the *Titanic,* the greatest ship in the world.

NOTES   The aftermath of weeping and regret, of recriminations and investigations, that followed the *Titanic's* sinking dragged on for weeks after the tragedy. Charges and countercharges were hurled about; the White Star Line was bitterly criticized; Ismay was defended by those who had been with him on the sinking *Titanic* and by the Board of Trade investigation in England.

It was not until weeks later, when the hastily convened Senate investigation in the United States and the Board of Trade report in England had been completed, that the whole story was told. The Senate investigating committee, under the chairmanship of Senator William A. Smith, who was attacked in both the American and British press as a "backwoods politician," brought out numerous pertinent facts, though its proceedings verged at times on the farcical. Senator Smith was ridiculed for his lack of knowledge of the sea when he asked witnesses, "Of what is an iceberg composed?" and "Did any of the passengers take refuge in the watertight compartments?" The Senator seemed particularly interested in the marital status of Fleet, the lookout, who was saved. Fleet, puzzled, growled aside: "Wot questions they're arskin' me!"

The report of Lord Mersey, Wreck Commissioner in the British Board of Trade's investigation, was tersely damning:

The *Titanic* had carried boats enough for 1,178 persons, only one-third of her capacity. Her sixteen boats and four collapsibles had saved but 711 persons; 467 people had needlessly lost their lives. The boats had been but partly loaded; officers in charge of launching them had been afraid the falls would break or the boats buckle under their rated loads; boat crews had been slow in reaching their stations; launching arrangements were confused because no boat drill had been held; passengers were loaded into the boats haphazardly because no boat assignments had been made.

But that was not all. Lord Mersey found that sufficient warnings of ice on the steamer track had reached the *Titanic,* that her speed of twenty-two knots was "excessive under the circumstances," that "in view of the high speed at which the vessel was running it is not considered that the lookout was sufficient," and that her master made "a very grievous mistake"—but should not be blamed for negligence.

Captain Rostron of the *Carpathia* was highly praised. "He did the very best that could be done." The *Californian* was damned. The testimony of her master, officers, and crew showed that she was not, at the most, more than nineteen miles away from the sinking *Titanic* and probably no more than five to ten miles distant. She had seen the *Titanic's* lights; she had seen the rockets; she had not received the CQD calls because her operator was asleep. She had attempted to get in communication with the ship she sighted by flashing a light, but vainly.

"The night was clear," reported Lord Mersey, "and the sea was smooth. When she first saw the rockets the *Californian* could have pushed through the ice to the open water without any serious risk and so have come to the assistance of the *Titanic*. Had she done so she might have saved many if not all of the lives that were lost.

"She made no attempt."

The following excerpts from a letter written to me by Karl Baarslag, a radio operator and author of *SOS to the Rescue* and other books, are of interest:

The German SS Frankfort *was the first to respond to Phillips' CQD, but he merely conveyed the information to his Captain, wanted more details and succeeded only in exhausting Phillips' patience, who by this time was working the* Carpathia. . . .

As a non-radioman it seems to me you did not quite understand Phillips' irritability with the Californian's *operator. Phillips had been up all day repairing a burned-out secondary of his transformer, and but for his skill and success the* Titanic's *wireless would have been mute that fateful night. Bride, the junior, was to relieve his chief at 2 A.M., but because Phillips had been up all day he got up instead before midnight, intending to relieve him at 12 P.M. Bride testified that he felt no impact but awakened presumably because the ship had stopped.*

In the days of crystal receivers notes were feeble and hard to copy and a broad spark alongside, such as the Californian *had, broke into and utterly jammed the important messages Phillips was trying to copy from Cape Race. He had received a number of ice messages that day and they did not seem to have made much impression on the bridge. Also it is not known whether Evans informed Phillips that he was stopped by ice or merely called him with the resultant interference. Phillips curtly told Evans to keep out as he was busy with Cape Race.*

Evans, in my opinion the world's most unfortunate radio operator in that he might have saved 2,200 lives had he stayed up 15 minutes longer, had been up and continuously on duty from 7 A.M. until 11:20 P.M., long past the usual time for him to go off watch. His ship was stopped by ice for the night, the crew, except a few on watch, were turned in, and there was no reason for him to continue on any longer. Even a $20 a month radioman is entitled to some sleep. Evans went to bed with the tragic consequences the world now knows. . . .

Bride, a green man, seems to have been an unreliable witness and his story of the grimy coalpasser who tried to steal Phillips' lifebelt was in all probability a piece of pure imagination. . . .

The firemen were ordered out at 1:40 A.M., after all forward fires had been drawn. Those that remained in the boiler and engine rooms were all licensed engineer officers. They died to a man although many were guarantee engineers merely making the first trip to break in apparatus and whose presence in the engine room was therefore entirely voluntary. There is an inspiring and beautiful monument to their imperishable memory in Southampton, England. . . .

The band at no time played "Nearer My God to Thee," as the pious would have us believe. [Some survivors testified that it did, according to reports immediately after the disaster.] *To have done so would have wrecked the excellent morale and discipline that was maintained throughout the disaster and have frightened and demoralized the passengers. The last piece played was the Church of England hymn, "Autumn," as you correctly relate. . . .*

ACKNOWLEDGMENTS   This chapter is republished from *Harper's Magazine* with the permission of the editors.

The primary and indispensable sources on the loss of the *Titanic*—sources which I have consulted, referred to, and quoted—are the records of the British Board of Trade investigation, which was conducted by Lord Mersey, Wreck Commissioner, and the proceedings of the United States Senate investigating committee. I have supplemented the data therein contained from personal reminiscences and the stories of passengers as related in books such as Lawrence Beesley's *The Loss of the SS Titanic* and in contemporary newspaper files. Wherever possible, all facts have been checked and rechecked, and the story, as published in *Harper's,* was read and approved by a number of survivors and others who have made a study of the disaster.

1816

"Sauve Qui Peut!"

THE HORRIBLE WRECK
OF THE FRIGATE MEDUSA

> *Les annales de la Marine n'offrent pas d'example d'un*
> *naufrage aussi terrible que celui de la frégate la Méduse.*
>
> *Naufrage de la frégate la Méduse—*
> Savigny et Correard

The hundred days had ended, the days that shook the world. The *Armée du Nord* was scattered and broken; the bodies of the veterans of the Napoleonic wars lay rotting on the ridge of Waterloo. Murat rode no more, and on a lonely South Atlantic isle Bonaparte was imprisoned.

Peace had come, and with it Louis XVIII, *le désiré:* fat and gouty, "a clever, hardhearted man, shackled by no principle, very proud and false." The wars were over, and to defeated France a generous enemy had returned the colonies raped from her by force of arms.

It was June 17, 1816, and in the roadstead of Rochefort the forty-four-gun frigate *Medusa,* Captain La Chaumareys; the *Echo,* corvette; the flute *La Loire;* and the brig *Argus* were casting toward the sea.

Schmaltz, new Governor of Senegal, sent with a small expedition by Louis XVIII to take over the French colony from the British, stood upon the afterdeck of the *Medusa*. His hand, ruffed in its lace and velvet sleeve, tapped impatiently on the breech of a gun. Below and about him crowded soldiers, sailors, clerks, engineers, doctors, women —scoundrels and students, pimps and prostitutes, riffraff and respectability.

There were Napoleon's veterans—fresh from the wars, scarred, hard-bitten, rough, irascible, hating their officers. There were huge colonials, their black shining faces marred with bluish tattoo marks; swarthy Spaniards; stiff, tight-jacketed guardsmen with plumed shakos; and scarlet-coated officers, the dandies of the Restoration. The ladies were attired and garnished as befitted their stations in life; some—with elaborate coiffures and the great flaring bonnets popular with the return of royalty—wore redingotes, warm against the sea air. These were standing apart in a small group, already nervous at the thought of the great sea and the dangers it might bring. The others, the bourgeois women, were plainly dressed and obviously less nervous; while one or two *filles de joie,* painted, smiling, arch, were already looking about them, eager for a rendezvous. Through the press hurried the seamen in their flat hats and brass-buttoned pantaloons, pulling on lines, walking the capstan round.

Slowly the *Medusa* got under way; the winds of the narrows filled her canvas and she eased toward the open sea. Thus with a fair wind and an ebbing tide this company of knaves and villains and ordinary folk, more than four hundred of them crowded on the decks of the frigate, stood out to their fate.

From the first the expedition was a tragedy of errors. The *Medusa* nearly grounded in the Bay of Biscay, and diverged about a hundred miles from her course on the stretch to Madeira; but reaching there on June 27, she made Tenerife the next day. From Tenerife she set out in company with the smaller ships on a haphazard course to St. Louis, Senegal. Captain La Chaumareys, at best an indifferent sailor, bothered himself not at all with the navigation of the ship but enjoyed his mistress and his wines, locked in his cabin away from the scum of the forecastle. Governor Schmaltz, his pompous dignity buttressed by his fine linen and soft velvets, whiled away the tedium of the sea voyage with wine and food, and the navigation of the *Medusa* was entrusted to "a man who knew very little about the coast of Africa and apparently still less about the sea": Richefort, of the Philanthropic Society of Cape Verde, a passenger aboard the *Medusa* who had impressed the captain with his knowledge, took complete charge of the navigation of the vessel, though his incompetence seems to have been obvious to everybody except the captain.

The result was inevitable. The *Echo* (the other ships of the squadron had been outdistanced and left behind) set her own course toward St. Louis after her "desperate signals" to the flagship had been ignored, and the *Medusa* stood blithely and blindly on to ground, July 2, on Arguin Bank, a well-charted shoal reaching out into the Atlantic for about a hundred miles to the north of Cape Blanco.

The grounding was followed by wild disorder. "Terror and consternation were instantly depicted on every face." The crew stood motionless; the passengers, in utter despair, ran about the decks shrieking and searching for Philanthropist Richefort from Cape Verde. An officer struck Caroline Picard, daughter of one of the passengers; ". . . much time was lost in doing nothing"; there was no courage, no chivalry, no leadership.

The *Medusa* was not badly damaged; she had grounded but lightly. Governor Schmaltz, however, refused to allow his barrels of flour to be jettisoned; the captain, torn rudely from the arms of his mistress, would not permit some of the frigate's guns to be pitched overboard; in short, half measures only were pursued.

Even so, at high tide the frigate momentarily floated; but with an incompetent master to help her she gave up the fight and wearily settled her keel in the sand again. The next day the sea made up, and she was doomed. The great rudder swung half off its gudgeons, and sweeping to and fro smashed the stern to matchwood. Water leaked into the cabins; the decks bulged; the keel splintered. She would never sail again: it was time to leave her.

The six boats were large enough to hold only about two hundred and fifty of her four hundred, but the coast of Africa was barely sixty miles away. The fourth of July dawned clear with a gentle swell and an easy sea. There was plenty of food and no immediate danger that the *Medusa* would break up; rescue should be easy. But no one trusted anybody; the governor and the captain were interested only in their own safety, and "cared not a whit for the safety of anyone else." There was a rumor of mutiny on the night of the fourth; but somehow out of the chaos was evolved a plan: a raft was to be built capable of carrying two hundred people with provisions, and the boats were to tow it to shore. By daybreak of the fifth several feet of water had seeped into the *Medusa's* hold and the preparations to leave her were carried out in panic and disorder.

Topmasts, yards, booms, and timbers were lashed together in a rough triangle and boards were nailed, as a sort of crude deck, barely awash, to the heavy pieces. This rude contrivance had been thrown together the preceding evening amid wild excitement, and though the raft was about sixty-five feet long and twenty-three feet wide, it was so poorly constructed that even fifteen persons did not have sufficient space to stretch out on a float designed to support two hundred.

But onto this structure, together with several casks of flour, six barrels of wine, and two small casks of water, some 147 people— soldiers and officers, passengers, ten seamen, and one woman (the wife of a sutler, and long used to hardship around the campfires of the Napoleonic wars)—were driven by "threats and cajolery." Some of them were barely sober: men had smashed into the spirit room during the night, had stove open the casks of liquor, and many of the passengers and crew had collapsed dead-drunk about the littered decks or were still staggering blearily on deck amidst cordage, flapping canvas, piled baggage, and tearful women.

It was *sauve qui peut;* only the governor and the captain and their entourage left the wreck in comfort. The governor was lowered carefully over the rail in an armchair into his barge, where, surrounded by his wife and family, their luggage and an ample store of provisions, he lolled back comfortably while sailors rowed him away from the ship. The captain, with his mistress and his wines, also made off in a well-found half-filled boat. The rest of the four hundred were left to their own devices, without leadership except for a few gallant officers, without courage or nobility except for a few isolated individuals. The strongest fought their way into the four remaining boats; the rest swarmed onto the raft; sixty, including one Picard and the women and children (one of them yet at breast) in his family of eight were left marooned aboard the wreck. Picard, however, picked up a firelock from the deck and, leveling it at the occupants of a yawl which was rapidly making away from the frigate, forced them to return and take off his family. The long boat was sent back for others and took aboard all but seventeen men, who were either drunk and incapable or distraught with fear.

So on the bright morning of July 5, 1816, the motley convoy stood away from the hulk of the shattered frigate, bedded deep on Arguin Bank. There were a few cries of *"Vive le roi!"* and the white flag of the Bourbons fluttered from a musket barrel.

The boats were to have towed the crowded raft direct to shore; the officers in command had sworn they would not abandon it, and for a brief time they made their honor good. But the raft was unwieldy and cumbrous; with its huddled cargo it had sunk two or three feet beneath the waves; its people were crowded shoulder to shoulder; the sea was at times surging to their waists, and each wave that struck made them stumble in heaps on one another, their feet being entangled in the cordage and between the planks.

The convoy was barely two leagues from the *Medusa* when the tow rope to the raft was let go—cut or broken. Governor Schmaltz contended later that the rope had broken, but it is doubtful whether he and the captain ever intended to see the raft safe to shore. In any case, the boats made off. La Chaumareys was too deeply concerned with his mistress to worry about the wretches on the raft, and when the people in one of the badly stocked boats asked him for a little wine and food he leaned back comfortably in the stern, with a cup of wine in his hand, and refused to listen to them.

A sea breeze rippled across the tropic sea and dappled the ocean, green above the white sand of Arguin Bank. Far overhead white clouds rode across the sun. And around the thighs of the wretches on the raft white foam boiled as the 147—one a woman—jammed rump to rump, stared upon the sunlit sea.

Rage came first; then, later, prayer.

Their plight was hopeless. There were no mast, no anchor, no cable, no lines, no chart; they had canvas but no way to spread it; they were completely at the mercy of the sea. The coast of Africa was only fifty miles away, but it might as well have been two thousand. The casks of flour had been thrown overboard to lighten the overloaded raft;

they had a twenty-five pound bag of biscuits soaked with sea water, and the barrels of wine and casks of water. That was all.

The wreck of the *Medusa* was still in sight, but there was no way to return to it; the wind was off the sea.

Midshipman Coudin, with a bruise on his leg so terrible that he almost fell senseless each time he had to brace himself to the raft's motion, assumed his first command. With the help of his ten seamen and the officers of the stupefied, half-drunken soldiers, he put up a mast of sorts, jammed between the openings of the raft and braced with makeshift shrouds cut from the lashings of the raft. So they stretched a kind of sail.

The first meal was really the last; the salt-soaked biscuit, mashed to a paste in wine, provided little more than a mouthful apiece.

Then night came—the first night.

The sea made up. The raft creaked and groaned. The crowded men staggered back and forth; spindrift in their faces, swirling water about their legs. They clung to the mast, to the raft's lashings, to each other. Some were swept away and drowned; they were the lucky ones. The raft groaned and labored, changing its shape, opening and shutting like an accordion. Men slipped down between the openings and the great spars squeezed shut and held them there; they too were drowned, and they too were lucky.

July 6—SECOND DAY   By morning there were 126 left; twenty had gone, the bodies of some of them still trapped in the interstices of the raft, stumbling blocks to the living. They were all numb, bruised, half-drowned, and starving. They looked with dull eyes on the sea; like trapped animals they awaited death.

The last illusion of hope died with the sunset. "If the preceding night had been terrible; this was still more horrible." The wind again rose; the sea licked hungrily over the raft; boiling spume swept it bow and stern; only in the center could a man live. Those who could not get there perished, and there were many.

The press of bodies in the middle was so great that some men were actually stifled by the weight of their comrades. Officers at the foot of the mast tried to direct the men how to shift from side to side to keep the raft from being overturned. The night wore on in a black horror of darkness, to the sound of beating sea, howling wind, and the groans and shrieks of the dying. Men clung with broken and bleeding nails to the raft's lashings. The rich uniforms that once had graced the avenues of Paris were reduced to pulpy, filth-stained rags. The hours wore on.

Some time in the night Napoleon's veterans opened a cask and drank of its wine. There followed saturnalia. Crazed by suffering, maddened by drink, the soldiers started a frantic revolt. One man with a boarding axe rushed to the raft's edge and commenced to hack the ropes that bound it together. An Asiatic of hideous appearance and tremendous size, in the torn uniform of a colonial, advanced toward the group of officers. Alexandre Correard, an engineer, shouted the alarm:

"Aux armes! À nous, camarades! Nous sommes perdus."

An officer struck down the Asiatic with his saber, and he reeled bleeding into the sea. The axeman too was killed. Then the melee became general. The mutineers drew knives and rushed on the officers. They were repulsed, but withdrew to the bow and commenced to hack at the raft's bindings. The fight raged stamping over the foam-covered platform; the yawning holes in the raft, hidden by the sea, cost many their lives; others died beneath saber blows in the darkness. The Southern Cross—mariners' sign of hope—gleamed above the dark horizon, while the maddened mutineers hacked the mast stays and shrouds. The mast came crashing down upon a struggling group, and so injured a captain of foot that he fell senseless.

"He was seized by the soldiers, who threw him into the sea; but we perceived it, saved him, and placed him on a barrel, from which he was taken by mutineers who were going to cut out his eyes with a penknife. Exasperated by so many cruelties we no longer restrained ourselves, but charged them furiously."

The poor *vivandière* and her husband were pushed into the sea by the madmen, but were hauled out again by Engineer Correard and Chief Workman Lavillette. Seated on dead bodies, their backs against a barrel, they spat out the salt water and gasped their way back to life.

The moon came up and shone on the slain. At last the mutineers crawled to the feet of their officers and asked for pardon; but before midnight, again, like wild beasts, they were tearing with fists and nails and knives and teeth at the throats of the same officers. All things human seemed to have gone; there was left the ravening beast.

Midshipman Coudin, with his first command in chaos, sat bleeding on the foam-covered platform, holding in his arms a boy of twelve.

July 7—THIRD DAY . . . *they were tortured between the pieces of wood which formed the scaffold on which they floated. The bones of their feet and their legs were bruised and broken every time the fury of the waves agitated the raft; their flesh, covered with contusions and hideous wounds, dissolved, as it were, in the briny waves, whilst the roaring flood around them was covered with their blood.*

Sixty had died during the night, most of them soldiers. There was one barrel of wine left among the sixty-seven survivors; the water was gone. Delusions, thirst, and griping hunger—sharks nosing about the raft—but the mast was stepped again, and some of the men tried to catch fish—without success. Because of the loss of the water casks the sixty-seven were cut down to half their wine allowance.

The raft drove back and forth before the wind.

Famished men looked longingly on the bodies of the dead. Some gnawed at the leather of their sword belts and *cartouchières*. A few who still had hats ripped out the greasy sweat bands and chewed them. Finally one hacked at a stiffening body. In a moment, like a pack of wolves, dozens were at *"cette affreuse nourriture."*

"Seeing that this horrid nourishment had given strength to those who had made use of it, it was proposed to dry it in order to render it a little less disgusting."

The raft beat back and forth, drifting to wind and tide.

The day was calm and fine. The doomed men stood in little groups, the water lapping about their knees, unable to lie down, leaning one against the other.

That night twelve more died.

July 8—FOURTH DAY The forty-eight clung to life. A shoal of flying fish passed under the raft and about two hundred of them were caught in its interstices. The men devoured them; but their hunger was so great and the quantity so small that they were obliged to eat other food—strips of salted flesh from the one dead body not heaved overboard during the night.

The fourth night the cry of *"Aux armes, à nous!"* rang across the raft again. The Spaniards, Italians, and Negroes—most of whom had taken no part in the first mutiny—attacked their officers. Bleeding skeletons fought in the moonlight on the foam-covered raft. The loyal sailors threw the Spanish ringleader overboard; the poor *vivandière*, with great scabrous wounds upon her legs, was again heaved into the sea by the mutineers, but was again rescued, this time by Midshipman Coudin. Both sides fought desperately; by daylight eighteen more were dead, and the thirty left were nearly all hacked and broken from wounds.

July 9—FIFTH DAY *The sea water had stripped the skin from our feet and legs; we were covered with wounds and bruises which, constantly irritated by the salt water, gave us the most intolerable pain; only twenty of us were able to stand upright or move about; we had wine only for four days, and scarcely a dozen fish.*

The raft drifted and beat before the wind; the clean winds whispered across the great clean sea.

July 10—SIXTH DAY Two soldiers tried to tap the remaining wine cask; they were flung into the sea. "On this day died also the young boy named Leon," in M. Coudin's arms. Twenty-seven were left.

Far overhead the white clouds sailed, and at night the cold beauty of the stars looked down.

Twelve among the twenty-seven—among them the *vivandière*, her legs swollen and the skin peeling to her thighs—were dying. "They were covered with wounds and had almost entirely lost their reason. They might have lived long enough to reduce our stock [of wine] to a very low ebb, but there was no hope that they could last more than a few days; to put them on short allowance was only hastening their death, while giving them a full ration was uselessly diminishing a quantity already too low; after an anxious consultation we came to the resolution of throwing them into the sea, and thus terminating at once their sufferings."

Three sailors and a soldier—stronger than the rest—heaved the dying veterans of Napoleon and the sutler's wife into the waves, where the sharks waited greedily.

"This gave us the means of subsistence for six additional days."

The fifteen remaining cast into the sea after their victims all the weapons—which had already done their bloody work—except one saber.

There followed the rapid disintegration, the decomposition within a few days, of blood and bone and muscle and sinews, of bodies that Nature had taken decades to build. Such was the slow monotony of torture that there was nothing left of human impulses, nothing left of intellect; nothing left but instinct, the tenacious life spark, dwindling low, which bade them hold on.

They lived—but barely, while the raft drifted and the white clouds raced above the tropic sea. In the days the sun burned them, and their tongues gagged their puckered, dried-up throats. In the nights they took turns resting on a kind of platform, made from the raft's planks, clear of the water.

On the ninth day a white butterfly, "of the kind so common in France," settled on the listless sail. Hope.

Bastille Day in France—the barricades, the blood of Frenchmen running in the streets of Paris . . . for *Liberté, Egalité, Fraternité.*
"Allons, enfants de la patrie—"

One of the fifteen feebly stirred and squeezed between his cracked lips a drop of tooth-cleaning fluid from a small phial that had been found. Thirty cloves of garlic and a small lemon, together with tiny sips of wine, were keeping them alive; they sought refuge from the burning heat beneath the water which covered the fore part of the raft.

—*Bastille Day in France.* Thirst, thirst!

Even the smallest sips of wine produced intoxication in their wasted bodies; Coudin, Charlot, and others—despite the nosing sharks—tried to throw themselves into the sea.

The days wore on; the raft drifted, like the smiling clouds so far above.

Raging thirst; blazing, sunken eyes; bodies that stank. . . .

They were saved, the miserable fifteen, on July 17 by the brig *Argus* which had made Senegal and had been sent back to look for them.

They were more beasts than men then; their faces matted with tangled beards; their hair unkempt, bleached, and whitened; their legs raw to mid-thigh. They crawled whining to the edge of the raft when the boat put out to take them off; whimpering and gasping they were taken back to the world of men, back from horror which would leave its terror forever in their broken bodies and their shattered minds. In the short space of thirteen days they "had seen and taken part in such horrors as happily fall seldom to the lot of man."

Of the miserable fifteen, five died a short time after reaching St. Louis; the rest carried to their graves the memories of the raft.

The people in the boats all reached shore safely. Four of the boats landed along the coast, and their passengers made their way painfully to St. Louis. Governor Schmaltz and Captain La Chaumareys, traveling in style in their well-stocked, well-found boats, had their crews take them direct to St. Louis by sea, abandoning all pretense of leadership and all solicitude for the rest of the shipwrecked.

No attempt was made to rescue the seventeen left aboard the wrecked frigate until July 26, seven days after the survivors from the raft had been landed, and seventeen days after Schmaltz and La Chaumareys had reached Senegal. Then the governor "at length recollected that there was, on board, about five thousand pounds in specie and a quantity of provisions which it would be a great advantage to recover.

" 'In speaking of those things,' said M. Correard—one of the raft's survivors—to him, 'you make no mention of something infinitely more precious—the seventeen unhappy men who remained behind.'

" 'Pooh,' answered the governor, 'you may depend on it, there are not three of them surviving.' "

A schooner started for the wreck of the *Medusa* on July 26, but twice returned to port without reaching the broken frigate, because she was "badly equipped and ill-found." Finally, fifty-two days after the *Medusa* had been abandoned in disorder and fear, the schooner reached the sunbleached, weather-beaten wreck, and took off from its sagging decks three half-mad, shaggy creatures who had subsisted for days on tallow and a little bacon. Of the original seventeen, twelve had given up hope of rescue after six weeks aboard the wreck, had built a raft, and had tried to reach shore. The raft broke up and they were drowned. Another—half-crazed—entrusted himself to a hen coop and was never heard of again. Another had died just before the schooner arrived.

The three survivors had lived like rats on the rotting wreck, each man for himself. With knives and snarls and growls they had greedily scavenged from hogshead and slop barrel and bilges what nourishment they could find. The schooner's crew found them half naked, bestial, but slobbering with joy at the sight of the rescuing vessel.

Two of the three died soon after arriving at Senegal; the third, "who pretended to know a great many particulars relative to the desertion of the frigate, was assassinated in his bed at Senegal when he was just upon the eve of setting off for France. The authorities could not discover the murderer."

NOTES   The loss of the *Medusa*, with its frightful aftermath, is generally considered to be one of the most horrible—if not the most horrible—shipwrecks recorded in nautical history. For the purposes of publication, some of the worst details of suffering included in Savigny's and Correard's account have had to be deleted.

ACKNOWLEDGMENTS   Republished from *Esquire* with permission of the editor.

The author has studied the firsthand accounts and reliable translations for this story, and is also indebted to J. G. Lockhart's description of the wreck of the *Medusa*, published in his book, *Peril of the Sea*. A few of the quotations are from Lockhart; most of them are from the account written and published in 1817 by Jean Baptiste Henri Savigny, *ex-chirugien de la Marine,* and Alexandre Correard, *ingenieur-geographe,* who were two of the fifteen saved from the raft. I am also indebted to Mme. Dard's (formerly Mlle. Picard) account of the wreck, as translated and published in *The Mariner's Chronicle,* published by Durrie and Peck, New Haven, 1834. Another source consulted was *The Shipwreck of the Alceste;* also *The Shipwreck of the Medusa,* Dublin, Thomas I. White, 1831. The *Encyclopaedia Britannica* furnished material for the introduction.

1942

Saga
of a Stout Ship–

THE U.S.S. HOUSTON

She was a stout ship, *Houston,* with the "finest trained crew in the Navy," men who had worked together and played together for one and a half years. The men "worshiped" the skipper; "they prayed to two gods—God and the captain."

She was a stout ship, *Houston,* and she had left her mark on the Imperial Japanese Navy in several bruising scrimmages before she died in Sunda Strait on Friday, February 28, 1942, in one of the most gallant actions in the history of the sea.

A stout ship, *Houston,* and her name is immortal; as of Sir Richard Grenville and the *Revenge,* men will sing of the cruiser *Houston* long after her last survivor is dead:

> *God of battles, was ever a battle like*
> *this in the world before?*

The U.S.S. *Houston* was not old, as ships go, when she met her end. She was launched, ironically enough, during the height of the disarmament era, September 7, 1929. She was built at Norfolk, Virginia, in accordance with the disarmament limitation treaty of 1922. A bottle of water, instead of the usual champagne, was used at her launching in deference to the prohibition law (Volstead Act).

A New York *Times* correspondent, reporting the ceremonies, commented:

"There was no excitement and little enthusiasm."

The commission pennant was hoisted to her main truck in June, 1930. She was long and slim and had a fast pair of heels which the years did not impair, and her nine eight-inch guns in three turrets gave her reach and punch. The cruiser was a comfortable ship and a great favorite of the late President Roosevelt, before she went out to the Asiatic station for her second cruise in the exotic seas of the Orient. That was in August, 1940, when much of the world was already locked in a death grapple. Capt. Albert H. Rooks, the skipper whom the men came to "worship," took command in the summer of 1941, and he had as his executive officer and second in command another popular officer, Comdr. D. W. Roberts.

The ship was a taut ship and a happy one and pretty well prepared for action at the time of Pearl Harbor. Some needed changes in fire control installations had not been made; she had not been in dry dock for months, for she was too far from base in the United States, and her anti-aircraft guns and ammunition were not of the latest type, but as fighting ships went at that time *Houston* was in fair trim. The first months after war were a rat race. Captain Rooks took *Houston* all over the Eastern Seas, shepherding merchantmen and convoys here and there, driving through the narrow straits, guns manned day and night and lookouts all over the tops and bridge. By early February, 1942, the Japanese had leapfrogged down the Philippines and were in Borneo; the tide of their empire was surging all over the East, leaving in its wake a bloody froth of disaster and defeat.

The *Houston's* crew, red-eyed and tired, knew little of the big picture, but they were proud of their ship and their skipper and anxious for a go at the enemy.

But first blood went to the Japs.

February 4, 1942 The U.S.S. *Houston* and U.S.S. *Marblehead* with two Dutch cruisers, the *DeRuyter* and the *Tromp,* four American and three Dutch destroyers, steamed east past Bali to intercept a Japanese convoy, heading southward down the slot of Macassar Strait. It was an ill-fated attempt. Fifty-four enemy planes, bombing from high level with great accuracy, intercepted and attacked the formation.

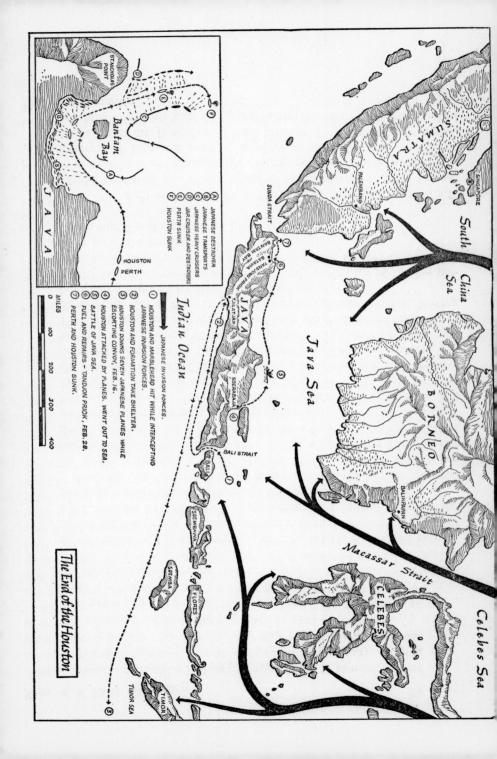

The End of the Houston

Indian Ocean

Java Sea

South China Sea

Celebes Sea

Macassar Strait

SUMATRA

BORNEO

CELEBES

JAVA

PALEMBANG

SINGAPORE

BALIKPAPAN

SUNDA STRAIT

BANTAM BAY

BATAVIA

TANDJONG PRIOK

TJILATJAP

SOERABAJA

BALI STRAIT

BALI

SOEMBAWA

SOEMBA

FLORES

TIMOR

TIMOR SEA

① JAPANESE INVASION FORCES.

② HOUSTON AND MARBLEHEAD HIT WHILE INTERCEPTING JAPANESE INVASION FORCES.

③ HOUSTON AND FORMATION TAKE SHELTER.

④ HOUSTON DOWNS SEVEN JAPANESE PLANES WHILE ESCORTING CONVOY, FEB. 16.

⑤ HOUSTON ATTACKED BY PLANES. BATTLE OF JAVA SEA.

⑥ FUEL AND REPAIRS – TANDJON PRIOK, FEB. 28. WENT OUT TO SEA.

⑦ PERTH AND HOUSTON SUNK.

MILES
0   100   200   300   400

Inset:

Bantam Bay

St. Nicholas Point

JAVA

Ⓐ JAPANESE DESTROYER
Ⓑ JAPANESE TRANSPORTS
Ⓒ JAPANESE HEAVY CRUISERS
Ⓓ JAP CRUISER AND DESTROYERS
Ⓔ PERTH SUNK
Ⓕ HOUSTON SUNK

⚓ HOUSTON
⚓ PERTH

Marblehead was hard hit and later limped home to the States after an epic voyage. *Houston* turned and twisted frantically, driving through great geysers tossed up by near-misses which deposited tons of water on her decks and washed the shell-loaders off their feet.

After the first run, when *Houston* shot down a Jap bomber, the enemy planes flew high. But one of the first salvos straddled *Houston,* and the near misses shook the cruiser and lifted her bodily out of water. Plates were sprung and slow leaks developed and an anti-aircraft director was knocked off its tracks. Captain Rooks, the calm and able skipper, conned his ship through danger without serious damage, turning her violently as the bombs were released and dodging through bomb splashes and fragments. She took it for more than two hours, but the last bomb of the day got her clean. A stray 500-pounder—dropped out of pattern—smashed through two platforms of the mainmast and exploded just forward of Turret Three. The eight-inch guns were loaded; powder bags were in the hoists, and bomb fragments sieved through the thin turret armor and detonated the powder. "In one blazing instant all hands in the turret and in the handling rooms below were dead." The after repair party was also wiped out "almost to a man." Forty-eight men died and many were wounded. Turret Three was out of action, and the Japs pushed on to the south.

And aboard *Houston,* the hammers banged throughout the night as the crew built coffins for their dead shipmates. On February 5, the following day, at Tjilatjap, "that stinking fever-ridden little port on the south coast of Java . . . the brown poker-faced natives dressed in sarongs" watched as the band played a funeral dirge and the first dead of the cruiser were buried in a little Dutch cemetery.

February 16   More of the same in the Timor Sea. For nearly an hour *Houston,* shepherding a convoy, was the target of attacks from forty-five enemy bombers. The 5-inchers and the 1.1's barked and grunted; the score—seven enemy planes as "probables"; no damage to *Houston.*

February 25   The yellow tide of empire was still roaring to the south. *Houston* in Soerabaya Harbor was attacked from the air in morning and afternoon; the Jap planes were flying at so high an altitude that the cruiser's 5-inchers were the only guns that could reach the enemy. At night the cruiser, now operating as part of the short-lived and ill-fated "ABDA Command" (American-British-Dutch-Australian), made a sweep to sea, the crew at general quarters.

February 26   Back in Soerabaya; three air-raid alarms during the day and attack in the afternoon. Again *Houston's* guns the only ones firing in defense of Soerabaya. Splinters from near misses. *Houston's* band plays swing tunes on the quarterdeck after the "All Clear." . . . So far so good. *Houston* is lucky. The Japs have claimed her sinking so many times her crew now calls her "The Galloping Ghost of the Java Coast." . . . To sea, and general quarters that night.

February 27   Still at sea, *Houston* in company with other Allied ships, repelled torpedo plane attack in the morning.

In the afternoon the "ABDA" fleet made its greatest and final sweep to sea. The "fleet" was pick-up, extemporized, crippled, tired—the heterogeneous ships of four nations, with differing standards in com-munications, gunnery, tactics. The ships had been together only one day; they could not read one another's signals; liaison officers had to interpret the orders of Rear Admiral Karel W. F. M. Doorman of the Royal Netherlands Navy, who was in tactical command.

"ABDA" fleet was groggy before it fought; it had been under con-stant air attack and reconnaissance day and night, night and day for almost a month, with no "eyes" of its own, its ships damaged and wounded, and with naval base facilities at Soerabaya so primitive that *Houston's* Turret Three was still out of action. Yet "ABDA" fleet knew and the world knew that the time was now, the hour was crisis. The Jap tide was spilling over onto Java, last bastion of the Malay barrier, and Australia lay to the south. Time must be bought with the bodies of men, the wrecks of ships. So "ABDA" fleet steamed forth— a seeming brave show, the cruisers R.N.S. *De Ruyter,* H.M.S. *Exeter,* U.S.S. *Houston,* H.M.A.S. *Perth,* R.N.S. *Java* in column, three British destroyers on the bow, two Dutch destroyers to port, and astern four United States slow-speed destroyers that had trouble in keeping up with the battle.

They encountered in midafternoon not the tender-skinned enemy
transports which they hoped to attack, but a part of the Japanese
covering force for the eastern wing of the powerful Java Invasion
Forces. The Jap planes had picked up Doorman's scratch command
long before the cautious little Dutchman knew about the enemy; the
Japanese admirals had sent the transports scurrying for protection and
stood boldly ahead to seek action.

On paper, there was no great disparity between the opposing fleets;
on paper the Allies actually had an advantage in light cruiser fire
power. The Japanese had some eighteen ships in the opening action
against fourteen Allied vessels; both sides had two heavy cruisers;
the Allies three light cruisers against the enemy's two, and nine destroyers against the enemy's fourteen. But *Houston's* after turret was
still out of action; *Exeter,* the other heavy, was a thin-skinned ship; all
of the Allied vessels were in bad need of overhaul; it was a fleet—in
name only—drawn from "four different nations . . . manned by personnel exhausted by constant activity," with no air cover, and no
support.

What followed has come to be known in history as the Battle of the
Java Sea.

The battle opened at 30,000 yards, as "you shoot at a bobbing
cork." The *Houston,* firing rapidly from her two forward turrets,
straddled the rear enemy cruiser about the sixth salvo, and her spot-
ters observed what they thought was a hit soon afterwards. Black
smoke burgeoned from the Jap's sides—followed by scarlet flame; she
slowed and fell out of line. But the enemy fire was accurate. *Houston,*
splashed by near misses, was repeatedly straddled; and little *Perth,*
flying her great white battle ensigns—900 yards astern of *Houston*—
was straddled eight times with no damage. In the Jap line junior
officers aboard the heavy cruiser *Nachi* were terrified by the "huge
blood-red geysers" from *Houston's* shells—caused by the crimson dye
in the shell noses used to identify the "Galloping Ghost's" salvos.

At 4:30 P.M. *De Ruyter,* flagship, was hit by an eight-inch dud;
minutes later the Japanese launched forty-three torpedoes, but failed
to make a hit. But the "ABDA" fleet was living on borrowed time.

The *Exeter,* veteran of the *Graf Spee* battle, was severely damaged

when an eight-inch shell from *Haguro* pierced her vitals, exploded in
a powder chamber, and ruptured a main steam line. The *Exeter,*
breathing smoke and steam from her wound, was forced to slow and
turn; the Allied line was in disorder, and about 5:30—shortly after a
Dutch destroyer had blown up, jackknifed, and sunk like a stone—
Houston was pummeled. She took an eight-inch shell forward which
passed through the ship without exploding, and another eight-inch
shell aft, which ruptured some oil tanks and virtually wrecked the
ship's laundry. But the tough fists of Turrets One and Two still kept
smashing out at the enemy; the fire was so rapid that the grease on the
gun slides melted, and poured inches deep into the pits and loading
platforms; the guns were red-hot and men fainted from the terrific
exertion.

But *Houston's* eight-inchers were the main hopes of the Allied fleet
and she could not falter. Nor did she.

Ammunition in the forward magazine ran low—and there was no
more nearer than Hawaii—so in the midst of battle and blazing heat,
the crew man-handled and wrestled shells and powder out of the rear
magazines beneath useless Turret Three and worked it forward for
the active turrets.

The day battle broke off in the sudden, brief dusk of the tropics,
with enemy targets smoking, or out of sight. An inferior Allied force
had put up a good fight, and *Houston's* six guns still spoke with voice
of thunder, tongue of flame.

But Doorman, the tenacious little Dutchman in *De Ruyter,* returned
to the attack again in literal obedience to orders from "ABDA" fleet:
"You must continue attacks until enemy is destroyed."

But the night battle was disastrous—though not for *Houston.* The
diminishing Allied formation, some of its ships scattered, damaged,
or sunk in the day action, were illuminated by flares and float lights
laid by Japanese planes. One after another, *Jupiter, Java* and *De Ruyter* were torpedoed; the British destroyer *Encounter* fell out to pick
up survivors of R.N.S. *Kortnaer;* the United States destroyers had
expended all their torpedoes and were ordered back to Soerabaya.
Well before midnight Rear Admiral Doorman, who had been fated to

make so brief and tragic an entry upon the stage of history, sent out
his last command from the *De Ruyter,* his sinking flagship:

*"To Houston and Perth: Do not stand by for survivors: proceed
Batavia."*

It was the wreckage of a fleet that got away—*Houston* and *Perth*
the only heavy units. But aboard *Houston* there was neither fear nor
dejection. Despite the exhaustion of the crew, "tails were over the
dashboard"; the "battleship" *Houston,* as her men liked to call her,
claimed the sinking of one Jap cruiser, heavy damage to another,
lesser damage to a third.

It was well Captain Rooks and his crew could not actually know the
score. For despite their hopes, "the Japanese had not lost a single
ship," and "in one afternoon and evening, half the ships of Admiral
Doorman's Striking Force had been destroyed, and the Admiral had
gone down with his flagship." But *Houston* still lived; her luck still
held—even the two shells that had struck her failed to explode.

February 28   But it could not last. *Houston's* luck had
run out. The Japs were on Bali and Sumatra; the enemy was landing
troops on Java itself. The sea gates that give upon the Java Sea—
Sunda Strait and Bali Strait—were being closed by the enemy.
"ABDA" fleet had been virtually wiped out; it was time to go. Orders
came for *Houston* and *Perth* to proceed in company, via Sunda Strait,
to Tjilatjap on the south coast of Java.

They spent these last few hours in port—the men of the *Houston*—
as they had spent nearly all their hours for the past month, in work and
in alarms. More air raids chivvied them, and they sagged and dropped
under the back-breaking labor of shifting the rest of Turret Three's
ammunition forward to the good turrets. This ammunition had been
underwater in flooded magazines after the bomb hit of February 4,
but it had to be used, anyway; there was no more that would fit the
Houston's guns within five thousand miles.

"AA" ammunition was scarce, a patch had to be welded by the
ship's company over the eight-inch shell hole in the forecastle; the
ruptured oil tanks aft had to be pumped out. Neither of the *Houston's*
three remaining planes was serviceable; only two searchlights were in

commission; the ship had been racked and strained by near misses and minor damage; the concussion from her own guns had opened up the seams sprung by Jap bombs.

She took on a little oil that last day in Tandjong Priok (the port of Batavia) and Lieut. L. E. Biechlin supervised the last of a series of ship's crew emergency repair jobs. But what *Houston* really needed was a dry dock and the swarming shipfitters and mechanics of a first-class naval base. There was no first-class naval base in Allied hands west of Hawaii. And in all the vast stretch of sea from the Kuriles to the Malay barrier, from Midway to the China coast, *Houston* was the sole major American naval unit still afloat.

Captain Rooks knew this, perhaps his crew suspected it, but they were neither afraid nor downhearted. Exhausted, yes; for four days they had been virtually without sleep, for weeks under intense strain, eating when and what they could; all the crew were hollow-eyed— many had been treated for exhaustion at sick bay.

But the "old man" and the "exec"—Rook and Roberts—and the intense and flaring pride of unit which makes a ship or a regiment great in the annals of history sustained them; *Houston's* crew was confident, cocky, proud, and defiant.

And so they put to sea on their last voyage. They cleared the mine-fields off Tandjong Priok soon after dark—the deep dark of the tropics with the stars bright as fireflies in the sky and a full moon shining down upon the Java Sea. *Perth* was leading; her skipper was "SOP" (senior officer present). They headed west over a calm sea at twenty knots; aboard *Houston* Condition Two was set; half the batteries were manned and half the crew crawled to brief and exhausted sleep.

They had no illusions—the men of the *Houston*. In the words of Morison, they "expected trouble"; their chance of escape through Sunda Strait was a one-to-ten shot.

For the invasion of Java was in full stride and the Japanese Western attack group, with fifty-six transports and freighters, covered and protected by two heavy cruisers, an aircraft carrier, several light cruisers and two squadrons of destroyers, was landing troops on St. Nicholas Point—Java's northwestern extremity. The enemy's formidable fleet lay squarely across *Houston's* path to freedom.

About 2300 (11 P.M.) as *Perth* and *Houston* were drawing on toward the entrance to Sunda Strait and safety, the dark hulls of ships were sighted—enemy ships, for there were no other in those seas. His Majesty's Australian ship *Perth,* soon to die, opened fire first with her six-inchers, *Houston's* Turret One and then Turret Two joined in, and star shells burst high in the night sky and floated lazily toward the seas, bathing Bantam Bay and the entrance to Sunda Strait in an eerie white light.

The stabbing flash of gunfire flamed round the horizon as *Perth* and *Houston* headed south, then circled west and north again as the new course opened up many more Japanese ships. Fire was shifted from forward to after director, from starboard to port, from port to starboard; targets were appearing on all sides now. The *Houston's* crew counted a positive minimum of at least fifty major ships and an unknown number of planes, torpedo boats, and landing barges; but there were more than that, for the *Houston* had run squarely into a great Japanese convoy making one of the enemy's main landings on the western tip of Java. *Houston* switched on a searchlight (McKie notes), "and at the end of the cold blue shaft were the silhouettes of Japanese merchant ships packed close together against the Java shore like cattle sheltering against a windbreak." This was the hour and this was the moment; the U.S.S. *Houston* had made off Bantam Bay her rendezvous with history.

11:20 P.M.—The fight is a melee now, a barroom brawl with the enemy throwing punches from all over the horizon and the *Houston* firing indiscriminately on all bearings. The turbines spin a song of power as the skipper works her up to high speed; down in the gun pits, the slides of the eight-inch rifles, still hot from the battle of the day before, are spewing grease. The night is warm, and on the bridge and clustered around the five-inchers the gun flashes illuminate the crew, clad in dungarees or in strange rainbow-colored uniforms—all shades of blues, greens, purples, and yellows—the result of shipboard attempts to dye whites khaki. The gun ranges vary from 2,000 to 10,000 yards; Jap shellfire rings the horizon; *Perth* and *Houston* are trapped.

11:45 P.M. to 12:35 A.M.—*Perth* goes some time in this period, her skipper standing on her bridge and giving his final order:

"Abandon ship. Every man for himself."

Long before she sinks she is riddled by shellfire and blasted by torpedoes; *Houston* loses sight of her in the night scrimmage as the tracers arc across the sky and the unequal fight goes on.

Around *Houston,* the enemy is pressing in on all sides; motor torpedo boats are darting through smoke screens, destroyers are driving hard in torpedo attacks, cruisers ringing the horizon with their fire. Comdr. Arthur L. Maher, gunnery officer, up in the foretop with head phones strapped over his ears, keeps up a running fire of orders and information into the JA, JD, and JX circuits. It is impossible to control the ship's fire from one, or even two, directors; there are too many targets, the guns go to local control. *Houston* has one advantage; she knows, once *Perth* is gone, that every ship is an enemy and all objects sighted are targets; the Japs, mixed up and excitable, are firing at one another.

Captain Rooks, coached by lookouts and by Commander Maher, conns the ship at high speed, twisting and turning in and out among the white torpedo wakes. Miraculously, *Houston* is hitting and is not being hit; first blood is hers; fires flame briefly on Jap ships; several destroyers turn away smoking, one seemingly sinks close aboard, but the exact damage the cruiser's roaring guns are doing no one knows; the night and the constant blinding stab of shellfire hides it.

A Jap shell has started a fire in the paint locker about 11:30 and another shell gets her almost amidships a little later, but there's no great damage done until midnight. Jap destroyers pass close aboard astern, but *Houston's* heels are still good and the skipper's maneuvering is brilliant; the "tin fish" pass close on either side. Frequently, so short are the ranges, even the 1.1's and machine guns open up, but ammunition is getting low, and *Houston's* time has come.

About midnight a torpedo crashes into the after engine room; the main steam line is ruptured; high-pressure steam, hot enough to ignite broom straws, fills the engine room, and the rushing sea water drowns the men who are not instantly scalded. The bulkhead stop valves in the steam line jam; they are closed as far as possible, but the white-hot steam seeps out of the after engine room, up over the boat deck and Battle Two, and into nearby repair stations, forcing the weary men with the haggard eyes and the rainbow-colored clothes away from their stations.

Enemy searchlights stab on, trying to impale the wounded cruiser against the black velvet of the sea, but pick up their own transports inshore by the beach instead; *Houston* gets on rapidly with her eight and five-inchers, and a large ship is left on her side and sinking.

But *Houston* is losing speed; the inboard propellers are dragging now, turning over idly like the feathered prop of a plane, and the enemy is getting the range. Probably about 12:20 a whole salvo comes aboard, a great fire flares in the lifejacket locker, and Turret Two goes up in smoke and flame. The flame leaps high above the bridge; conn has to be abandoned temporarily; another torpedo crashes into the starboard side; the plotting room is wrecked.

Ensign Charles D. Smith 2d, turret officer of Turret Two, sees the brief flash through the windows of his turret booth. He pulls the sprinkler system and grabs a fire hose. Over the battle telephones, bridge and foretop and forward engine room hear the ominous reports: "Fire in Turret Two." "Flood Turret Two's magazines."

Only five men escape from Turret Two; Smith makes his way to the bridge.

The flooded magazines bury the last of the eight-inch ammunition under tons of water, but the small guns still are shooting; the ranges are down now to 500 to 5,000 yards.

But still *Houston* fights on, using her five-inchers with star shell and common, pouring out tracers from the 1.1's and 50-caliber. Until now she had forced the fight; hers had been the initiative of surprise and the advantage of night, but now she's afire fore and aft, transfixed in the gleam of searchlights. But she knows not despair and her crew fight her in fury. As the Jap searchlights flick on, a little gunner's mate serving the starboard 1.1 mount under the wing of the bridge screams above the roar of the fight:

"Get that son-of-a-bitch!"

The lights are shot out, but others come on; *Houston* afire and wreathed in smoke and flames and billowing clouds of escaping steam is, in any case, an unmistakable target. And now her great eight-inch fists are idle, her speed is dropping. Now she's at bay and fighting for her life. By 12:25 A.M. *Houston,* for almost two years the proudest ship on the China station, is a shambles, raked fore and aft, dead and wounded littering her decks, fires raging, bridge and upper works a twisted mass of broken metal, lower deck compartments flooded. She's been hit by salvo after salvo of all calibers up to eight-inch and by at least three torpedoes, and her decks have been shredded by fragments, and machine-gun and light automatic fire. The Japs are closing in now and ringed around her, cutting her off from the sea; the melee is at point-blank range, as it was in the days of old.

Captain Rooks, that skipper whom the men worship, knows it is the end. He has taken her through "hell and high water" these past months; tonight he has outguessed and outshot a great enemy fleet; twisting and turning, he has kept his ship afloat and concentrated on inflicting maximum damage on the enemy. Now he turns to Ensign Herbert A. Levitt, Signal Officer, and says in a "tremulous" voice:

"Have the word passed for all hands to abandon ship."

Those are probably Captain Rooks' last words. A salvo from enemy destroyers strikes near the communications bridge, where Captain Rooks "was saying good-bye to several of his officers and men outside his cabin," demolishes a 1.1 inch mount, curls the bridge metal up like crumpled paper, and kills the skipper who the men thought was "God." Ensign Smith and Ensign Levitt bend over him, but the "old man" is beyond help; his chest and backbone and stomach are riddled and Captain Rooks dies quickly, eased by the balm of morphine on the bridge of his flaming ship.

Buda, the captain's Chinese cook, faithful unto death, sits cross-legged outside the skipper's cabin, oblivious of the carnage about him, and refuses to be comforted:

"Captain dead; *Houston* dead—Buda die, too."

And (as Winslow tells us) he went down with the ship.

As Maher, the gunnery officer, climbs down from the foretop to the shambles of the decks, Roberts, the "exec," still miraculously alive, takes over. *Houston* still has way on, so the abandon ship order is temporarily rescinded. The drumfire of the guns opens again, as the ship loses headway, stops dead in the water and, afire brightly, cants steeply to starboard. Another torpedo smashes into her, and perhaps a fifth, and the Jap destroyers and torpedo boats—bolder now that the *Houston* is dying—swarm close like a pack of snarling hounds, and spray the cruiser's decks with automatic fire.

But the *Houston,* transfixed in the glare of searchlights and flame and gun flashes, answers back, until again, about 12:33 A.M., "abandon ship" is ordered.

. . . Seaman Stafford, standing on the careening fantail, sounded the call a second time on his bugle. . . . The men stood by their guns and fired every bit of ammunition they had, even star shell, until all was expended. . . . Japanese destroyers swarmed about her, machine-gunning the quarterdeck and the port hangar where many of the survivors from below had congregated. . . .

Then the men take quietly to the water—what is left of them, but some of them fire their machine guns and pom-poms until the end.

The *Houston* goes slowly, the Japs raking and searing her as she dies, until at 12:45 A.M., March 1, 1942, the cruiser sinks proudly away into the black waters of Sunda Strait.

A Japanese searchlight picks out the Stars and Stripes still flying from the gaff as she rolls over and disappears. Over the debris-littered waters, viscous with the scum of oil and aviation gasoline, dotted with survivors, a heavy tropical rainstorm passes—*Houston's* only threnody. *Houston* takes with her the body of her dead skipper; probably her exec., who was last observed going aft to see that all living men were clear, and five hundred of her crew, dead, wounded, and living. Over 150 more are drowned or die in their struggle to reach the beaches of Java, some miles distant. Only 368 survivors of the "finest-trained crew in the Navy" fall into Japanese hands; seventy-six of these die in prison camps and one—tragically—just after release.

One of the most gallant battles in the history of the sea ends in unmitigated tragedy, but the beaches of Java the next morning are littered with Japanese bodies, and the wrecks of enemy ships lie fathoms deep in Bantam Bay.

And Rooks and the *Houston* go marching down the pages of history. The Congressional Medal of Honor, awarded for "extraordinary heroism," is the epitaph of the skipper, whom the men "worshiped," and *Houston's* unit citation will forever speak for itself:

". . . Often damaged, but self-maintaining, the *Houston* kept the sea and went down, gallantly fighting to the last against overwhelming odds. . . ."

NOTES   Samuel Eliot Morison in *The Rising Sun in the Pacific* has bestowed upon *Houston* her finest epitaph:

"*Houston's* great fight, the last half hour of it waged singly against overwhelming odds, is one of the most gallant in American naval annals."

The exact details of this last action will never be clear; Japanese accounts were not available until after the war, and were undoubtedly colored then by defeat. Apparently *Houston* took four to six torpedo hits out of some eighty-seven Japanese torpedoes fired at *Houston* and *Perth* (some of these struck Japanese ships). Shell hits may have numbered from twenty to fifty, plus thousands of rounds from machine guns and light caliber weapons.

She did not die in vain. The night melee in Bantam Bay and the entrance to Sunda Strait cost the Japanese four loaded transports, one of which was sunk, three of which were beached. One of these ships bore the Japanese Army commander—General Imamura, who clung to a piece of driftwood for twenty minutes before he was picked up. "Once ashore," Morison reports, "the soggy General sat down on a bamboo pile and his aide 'limped over to him and congratulated him on his successful landing.' "

In addition to the transports a Japanese minesweeper was also sunk and three destroyers, and other transports, were damaged.

The Battle of Sunda Strait was the climax of a long and dark agony for the United States, unrelieved save for epic flashes of heroic tragedy—such as that provided by the *Houston*.

The United States was not well prepared for World War II, and the U. S. Navy was over-confident, prior to the war, in its judgment of Japanese naval capabilities. The U. S. Asiatic Fleet was greatly outnumbered and in a hopeless position when war started; nevertheless, its accomplishments did not measure up to pre-war expectations. The United States learned from its mistakes—the hard way—and Captain Rooks and the *Houston* and others of their ilk provided the brave examples which rallied the nation to ultimate victory.

ACKNOWLEDGMENTS   Navy records and the reports of *Houston* survivors have been consulted for this account. I have also consulted freely and quoted from Commander Walter G. Winslow's article, "The

Galloping Ghost," first published in the February, 1949 *U. S. Naval Institute Proceedings.* Commander Winslow was then an aviator (without any operable planes to fly) aboard the *Houston;* he survived her sinking and long years of Japanese captivity and is still on active duty in the Navy. Commander Winslow's article was reprinted as an appendix to Ronald McKie's *Proud Echo,* Angus and Robertson, Sydney and London, 1953, an account of the brief fighting life and dramatic death of H.M.A.S. *Perth.* Another primary source was Samuel Eliot Morison's *The Rising Sun in the Pacific,* the third volume of Morison's "History of United States Naval Operations in World War II," Little, Brown and Company, Boston, 1948. I have also quoted briefly from this book. Other sources include *The Campaigns of the Pacific War,* United States Strategic Bombing Survey (Pacific) Naval Analysis Division, U. S. Government Printing Office, Washington, 1946; a companion volume of the same U. S. Strategic Bombing Survey series entitled *Interrogations of Japanese Officials,* Volume II; and a wartime contemporary account—chiefly of propaganda value— *Holland Afloat,* by H. George Franks, the Netherland Publishing Co., London, 1942.

I also interviewed several survivors of the *Houston* for personal accounts of her last fight. These included, among others, Captain Thomas B. Payne—then a lieutenant and senior aviator of the *Houston*—Commander Winslow, and others.

1910

Number 6

It was the year 1910 when Tatsuta Sakuma died with his men in the foul air of the sunken submarine *Number 6.* Sakuma was already, at thirty-one, a veteran of danger. He had participated in the Russo-Japanese War five years before; as a pioneer in the development of submarines he had often been close to death.

His command, the *Number 6,* had been in service four years. Launched September 28, 1905, at Kawasaki Shipyards, Kobe, and completed at the submarine base at Kure six months later, she was one of the first, the most awkward, and the strangest of Japanese submarines; but she had never been in serious trouble, and her crew—struggling against difficulty, discouragement, and constant mechanical defects—had kept her running. She was the smallest of Japan's nine submarines: seventy-three feet long, beam seven feet, fifty-seven tons displacement, a great, ungainly bathtub of a "boat," a she-devil for crankiness. She was always having propeller trouble; she had only two feet freeboard and was no good in the open sea: even when running on the surface the smallest wave washed clean over her so her crew must always be imprisoned in the steel shell. During maneuvers she was usually left behind; she was too fickle and untrustworthy for offshore work except in a smooth and glassy summer ocean.

Number 6, like other contemporary Japanese submarines, was gasoline-powered for surface running, with some rather primitive electric motors for submerged propulsion. But the electric motors were slow and unsatisfactory; they could be used only a short time before the batteries were discharged, and so, sticking above the surface like a sore thumb, just aft of the crude conning tower and the periscope, was a great intake or ventilating pipe, to provide air for the gasoline engines both when the boat was running partially submerged, and during rough weather on the surface. The pipe could be closed by a sluice valve when its intake was completely below the surface, and the electric motors were being used.

The valve was open that spring day in 1910, when the cherry trees blossomed on the Japanese islands and Lieutenant Sakuma took his ship to her fate. *Number 6* had been ordered to join in the maneuvers on April 11, and under tow of the *Rekizan Maru,* her mother ship, she left port for the maneuver area in Hiroshima Bay. The exercises—as far as little *Number 6* was concerned—were to determine how long the submarine could remain completely submerged. On April 12 and 13 she operated successfully, though never much more than a hundred feet away from the *Rekizan Maru.* On the fourteenth she stayed under water for two and a half hours, a feat for those days; and on the fifteenth she began her fatal voyage.

She cast off her lines to the mother ship and got under way—slowly and awkwardly—at about nine-thirty in the morning. The sun was shining on the sea. Sakuma was in the conning tower; Engineer Lieutenant Harayama was in the engine room; Sublieutenant Hasegawa bent above gauges; the eleven members of the crew were at their posts by valve wheels or engines. Shortly before ten Sakuma gave the order to submerge. Slowly the conning tower, air-intake pipe, the periscope disappeared beneath the surface. . . .

Aboard the *Rekizan Maru* it was logged as another routine test.

Number 6 started down, as she had submerged so often before, with the water gurgling into the ballast tank and the green sea swirling and frothing up above the thick glass of the conning tower ports. She was cranky, but with a stern master she would obey. Then suddenly there came a lurch—unexplainable, unexplained, a last awkwardness of the "boat"—and the thing was done. She had gone too deep.

Water poured in through the air intake. Sakuma's crisp voice calmly uttered orders. A sailor tried to close the air-intake sluice valve, but the chain slipped off the sprocket wheel; the water gushed in. Frantically he shut the valve with his bare hands, but it was too late. Old *Number 6* was heavy with the water of the sea.

She had always had a tendency to nose down on submerging, so her bow had been kept up, her stern down. The flooding water, rushing in through the intake aft, added to their stern inclination; and she started down for the bottom like a rotted log, at an angle of twenty-five degrees.

The electric switchboard was close to the opening of the ventilating tube; and the salt water gushed over the copper contacts. There were flaring blue sparks and hissing arcs of flame, the stench of a short-circuited burning cable, and then the lights went out. To die in darkness. . . .

Sakuma's voice still gave sharp, precise commands; each of the fourteen stood to his post.

The power was gone, the water was reaching toward the batteries—the scourge of the submarine: chlorine!

Sakuma's quiet, calm voice continued.

The hand pump! The hand pump was their chance for life. Blow out the main ballast tank, pump out the sea, lighten ship to compensate for that flood water in the hull; shoot her to the surface! The pump began to wheeze and suck and sigh in the darkness as sailors found its handle and fumbled with the valve wheels of its manifold in that black hulk beneath the sea.

But down she went—down. Water ruffled past the thick glass peepholes in the conning tower; the needle of the depth gauge quivered slowly around the dial—20 feet—30—40—50. . . .

She struck stern first in the mud of Hiroshima Bay, and the needle of the gauge settled at 52. She was planted solidly at a thirteen-degree tilt: lifeless, inert, solid. Already there was that fearful, faint tickling in the throat; already the men's nostrils seemed to flare wider to suck for air. The pump still heaved and sighed.

There was no need now for further orders. The men took their appointed turns at the hand pump, bending and straightening there in the dark, with the insulation of the burning cable fusing noxiously in the blackness, and the sweet stench of the chlorine tickling their tiny nostril hairs.

They worked, each in his own appointed turn, and then they felt their way back to their posts, forward by the torpedo, aft by the engines, amidships by the controls. Sakuma had come down out of the conning tower to see what could be done. There was not much, and they were doing it there in the dark; but still—with the slow pump wheezing and the tide of their lives ebbing on swift minutes—the needle of the depth gauge did not flicker. It pointed motionless to the measure of their fate, the boundaries of their grave—fifty-two feet. Sakuma left Sublieutenant Hasegawa in charge at the pump and returned, stumbling in the blackness, to the conning tower. Here the dim gray-green light, filtered through the water, filtered through the glass, shed a kind of sepulchral twilight over gauges and valve wheels and the cold, painted steel. Tatsuta Sakuma, conscious of his duty, sat down to report to his Emperor and to Japan.

He started to write—vertical columns from right to left, the well-remembered characters he had learned so long ago:

"I am sorry—" (first an apology from one so humble, one who had failed). "I am sorry that my carelessness sank the Emperor's submarine and killed the Emperor's sailors."

(He knew then that there was no hope. The unmoving needle pointed with awful finality to 52.)

"But every man of the crew has bravely done his duty until death."

(They still were doing it, and death not far, still holding death and fear at arm's length from their inner consciousness. The pump still sucked and wheezed, and the gasping lungs of fourteen men heaved now like bellows in the dark.)

"We are willing to die for our country, but I regret one point, that our deaths might discourage the people of the nation."

(He could not know it, but their names were to live far more in death than they would have done in life.)

"My sincere hope, gentlemen, is that this accident will give you material to study diligently the problems of submarine design and construction, and thus insure future submarine development. If this be done, we die without regret."

Sakuma paused—still the slow sucking of the pump, and in his throat the thinning air. Hurry; his pencil now must race to scribble out this last message, to tell the world how they had died, so that others might live.

"When we started on the gasoline-submarine exercise the ship went too deep, so we tried to close the sluice pipe valve. But the chain gave way, and before we could close the valve by hand, water flooded in, the stern filled; we tilted to 25 degrees and sank."

Recapitulation of disaster; these things he wrote seemed centuries past, yet they had happened so brief a time ago. Each breath now was a heavy period in time; each character he formed, each phrase he wrote, an eternity of effort. But quickly: the world must know.

"Stern inclination is 13 degrees. Switchboard wet, lights gone. Telegraph cable burned. Bad fumes came out, began to be hard to breathe. Sank on April 14, about 10 A.M.

He was fumbling now; the date was wrong. His mind was hazy, confused with images of the past, filled too with the insistence of little details that must be set down while he still could write.

"Breathing bad fumes we tried to drain the water with hand pumps. When the sinking began we immediately commenced to drain the main ballast tank. The lights are out; I cannot see the gauge, but I think we have blown the main ballast tank empty."

But still the needle stood inflexible at 52; still *Number 6* stuck in the mud of Hiroshima Bay, inert and unmoving, like the skeleton of a ship long sunk. The ballast tank was empty—empty, what could yet be done? The pump wheezed futilely. . . . Sakuma laid down his pencil, picked it up again.

"Cannot use current at all. Battery fluid is slightly flooded. No more sea water is coming in. No more chlorine gas is being produced. About 500 pounds of air left. Only thing we depend on is hand pumps. (The above note I wrote in the control room 11:45.)"

Five hundred pounds of air in the air tanks, but it was hissing swiftly out in the dark to keep fourteen pairs of lungs moving and fourteen hearts throbbing. The main ballast tank was clear; what else could be done to lighten her? The gasoline! Sakuma gave orders to pump out the gasoline. Valves were opened and closed in the darkness; the pump soughed to a stop briefly, and then sucked again, this time at the gasoline. Sakuma once more began to write.

"The flooding water wet our clothes and we are cold. . . . I think that a submarine's crew should always be calm and pay strict attention, and at the same time they must be brave. Otherwise we cannot hope for progress."

Progress, progress . . . they must not die in vain.

"Overstrict attention sometimes causes fear."

No fear was in Sakuma's soul, and those others in the dark below gave no sign.

"But I told them not to be afraid."

The code of the Samurai was triumphant still.

"People may laugh at this philosophy after this failure, but I am confident that my words are right."

In the darkness the pump still sucked at the gasoline.

"The depth gauge in the control room shows 52 feet. Efforts to drain continued until twelve o'clock, but no movement was made. Depth of the location around here is 58, so I think 52 is the right figure."

It was twelve o'clock now; and what would they be thinking on the surface, on the *Rekizan Maru,* and on the shore where the spring blossoms had come? Twelve o'clock; the air was fouler; hurry, hurry.

"The crew of a submarine should be a carefully selected crew, for you may have difficulties such as this. Fortunately my crew have done their duty to the best of their ability, and I am fully satisfied."

Obituary enough for Hasegawa and Harayama, for Chief Petty Officer Kadota, for Seaman Endo and those gasping in the black, dead hull. They would want no higher praise than this.

"I always expected death whenever I left home."

It was close upon him now—his lungs were like leather, his mouth open wide.

"Therefore my will is already at Karasaki. (This, of course, refers only to my private affairs, and it is not necessary to mention it. Messrs. Taguchi and Asami, please hand my will to my humble father.)"

In the blackness there is a sudden sharp crack aft of the main ballast tank and forward of the engines, and *Number 6* fills with the fumes of gasoline. They could not read the gauges in the darkness; they could not tell the pressure on the line; it had broken, and now more deadly fumes fill the fetid air. The pump stops wheezing; its work is done. Hasegawa and Kadota feel their way to the break in the pipe line, fumble futilely about the burst metal. The others stand stolid at their posts, Petty Officer Yokoyama in the bow by his torpedo, Harayama and Endo near him, not far from the pump; Warrant Mechanician Suzuki far aft, in the stern near the electric motor. This was the end; they all knew it. Sakuma picked up his pencil again, and traced wavering characters in the growing dark.

"Reverently I write to the Emperor; please do not let the bereaved families of my crew suffer. . . ."

It was hard to write; somehow his hand was heavy; the pencil dragged across the paper; his eyes blurred, his throat burned; he could feel the bulging veins in his neck and temples.

"Do not let them suffer. This is the only thought in my mind now. My best regards to the following: Minister Saito—Vice-Admiral Shimamura—Vice-Admiral Fujii—Rear Admiral Nawa—Rear Admiral Yamashita—Rear Admiral Narita (air pressure so high that my ear drums feel they are breaking)."

Blood beating in his ears, congested in his brain, white specks leaping in the air before his eyes; hold on—hold . . . The pencil hastened, scribbling the names.

"Capt. Oguri—Captain Ide—Commander Junichi Matsumura—Lieutenant-Commander (Kike) Matsumura (my brother)—Captain Funakoshi—Professor Kotaro Narita—Professor Koinji Ikuta."

The list was almost done. "12:30 very hard to breathe, gasping—"

This then was death, this wracking gasp and flailing heart, this skin so cold and clammy, smeared with sweat; this body crying for air . . .

"I thought to blow out the gasoline, but I am befuddled by the fumes. Capt. Nakano . . ."

The characters grew broad and sprawling; the pencil faltered. Below was silence; long since the pump had stopped. The men stood by their posts in the loneliness of death. In the conning tower the green filtered light shone faintly upon Sakuma's barely moving hand. There was no sound from the world above down here, no temple bells, no sound at all save the gentle play of the water against the peep-hole glass—and the roaring in his ears.

"It is now 12:40. . . ."

Within, the needle pointing to 52; without, the fluted ripples weaving patterns on the dead steel hulk of *Number 6,* mud-bound, waterlogged, drowned, at the bottom of Hiroshima Bay.

The *Rekizan Maru* was not concerned until eleven o'clock, an hour after *Number 6* had disappeared beneath the surface of the bay. Then the search began—the search that did not end until the sunken submarine was found next day, April 16, at 3:38 P.M. She was raised less than five hours later, but they could not open the conning-tower hatch; she was half towed, half carried, to a shallow inlet not far away. At 10 A.M. on the seventeenth, two days to the hour after her fatal plunge, she was opened; the water was pumped out of her; scavenging air was pumped in. It rushed in freshly, the pure spring air; but long too late to help those gasping lungs.

Commander Yoshikawa and First Lieutenant Nakajo went in together. All others were kept out; these first must ascertain how Sakuma and his men had died; at all costs the honor of the Empire must be saved. But there was no need to fear; they found the bodies calm and peaceful in their death—no signs of panic or disorder, each at his post save Lieutenant Hasegawa and Kadota, who had died by the break in the gasoline pipe they had tried to mend.

The honor of the Japanese Navy was proved.

They found the notes Sakuma had written; they have become part of the heritage of the old Japan. They brought the bodies to Kure aboard the *Toyohashi,* and there at the torpedo station the families wept proudly for their dead. The Grand Chamberlain of the Emperor Matsuhito came to Kure to pay his tribute; and at Kure on the twentieth, twenty thousand people, breathing the fragrance of spring flowers, hearing the tolling of the bells, mourned at the funeral.

It was the end—and a beginning. The nation gave 57,000 yen: 35,000 for the families of the victims, 22,000 for a memorial at the Kure naval station. And years later *Number 6* was lifted out of water and placed on land at the submarine school, in commemoration of one of the proud episodes of Japan's navy.

NOTES   The loss of *Number 6* created a national sensation in Japan, and at least until World War II Sakuma was a well-known naval hero there.

To lose a submarine and its crew at a depth of fifty-two feet seems

absurd today when "frogmen" and skin divers—without benefit of
steel hulls—dive far deeper. But the art of underwater navigation was
primitive in 1910, and the submarines of those days—particularly the
submarines of Japan, a budding naval power—were ungainly, awkward monsters.

The design of *Number 6* was obviously faulty in many particulars,
but even so, it is interesting to note that she utilized a clumsy form of
the modern "schnorkel" or breathing tube—a Dutch invention, utilized
by the Germans in the closing phase of World War II, and now standard in all modern submarine fleets. But the Japanese used it in conjunction with a gasoline engine, and volatile gasoline fumes in the
tight hull of a submerged submarine seem stupid and suicidal today.

It was this home-made "schnorkel" or ventilating pipe, with its in-
effective valve, that was the undoing of *Number 6*. But it was the
gasoline that led to the *coup de grâce*. When Sakuma tried to pump
out the fuel to lighten the submarine and bring her to the surface, the
gasoline had to be pumped out against the pressure of fifty-two feet
of water. The fuel line was not built for any such pressure, and parted
to bring quicker death to the trapped crew.

Number 6 had no escape hatch, no "lungs," or other rescue equipment. Even so, had there been a means of egress, or had the men been
"shot" from the torpedo tube one by one, many of them might well
have survived. "Free escapes"—that is escapes without "lungs" or
oxygen mask or any rescue device—have been made repeatedly from
100-foot depths in the training tower at the Submarine Base in New
London, Conn. And during wartime many trapped "submarin(e)ers"
(the official spelling in the U. S. Navy) made free ascents through
many fathoms of water. A few men of a German crew probably hold
the world's record; they rose in a "free escape" from about a 400-foot
depth. Some were dead when they reached the surface but two or three
survived.

Sakuma in death typified the stiff code of old Japan—the code of
the Samurai, the code of bushido. Despite the passage of time and the
undeniable modernization of Japan by Western thought, despite defeat
in World War II and the influence of the American occupation, much
of this same frightening devotion to the past, this same rigid accept-

ance of discipline, the same cult of the warrior spirit dominates the Japanese subconscious today.

ACKNOWLEDGMENTS Tamon Yamagushi, formerly Captain, I.J.N., naval attaché to the Japanese Embassy in Washington, in the days before World War II furnished the author with Japanese documents describing the sinking of *Number 6,* and with the last letters of Lieutenant Sakuma. I have compared a translation of these documents, specially made for this chapter, with one which appeared originally in the Kobe *Herald* and which was reprinted in incomplete form in the *Scientific American* of July 6, 1912. I have also referred to the *Encyclopaedia Britannica* and to various works on Japan.

As far as the author has been able to ascertain, this story gives for the first time in English the complete account of the disaster to *Number 6* and the complete text of Lieutenant Sakuma's notes.

1870

The Cruise
of the *Saginaw* Gig

The yellow glow of the sperm-oil hurricane lamp flickered over the open logbook. Ensign Garst, officer of the deck of the *Saginaw*, thumbed the pages, read the brief record of Robinson's watch:

From 8 to Midnight—Cool and pleasant, with light breezes from Nwd. and Ewd. Moon set at 9 P.M. Engine making 5 revolutions. Ship rolling heavily. Moderate swell from Nwd.

G. H. Robinson
Mate, U.S.N.

Garst took up a pencil, turned a page to start a new twenty-four hours. The slow plump of the paddle wheels, the sighing surge of long Pacific combers licking up against the laurelwood strakes of the little *Saginaw,* the creaking of blocks, the sharp rataplan of the halyards against the mainmast, mingled in that strange but distinctive medley of a ship at sea.

"Log of the United States Side Wheel Steamer *Saginaw,*" he scribbled, filling in the blanks. "4th Rate—6 guns. Making passage from Midway to Ocean Island under the command of Lt.-Comdr. Montgomery Sicard, U. S. Navy. Sat., Oct. 29th., 1870. Commences and until 4 A.M. Weather cloudy but pleasant; moderate breeze from Nt. Ewd. At 1 A.M. clewed up topgallant sails; furled them at 2——"

Garst laid down his pencil; he would have to complete his log later, when his watch was over.

At 3:22 A.M. the *Saginaw* stranded on the coral reefs surrounding Ocean Island, tiny mid-Pacific atoll, and started to go to pieces almost immediately. Garst had heard the booming of the surf and sighted the creaming line of breakers a few minutes before she struck. Captain Sicard had hurried to the hurricane deck; the engines had been backed, the jib taken in, and the topsails clewed up. But the steam had been low and the current setting in toward the island strong; she had ridden high on the reef, and the lacy spume of the breakers had shrouded the fourth-rate ship *Saginaw* in a white pall of foam.

For a few moments there was confusion; then the strong voice of Captain Sicard roared out, and ninety-three officers and men on the *Saginaw* began to salvage what they could from the wreck, and prepared to abandon ship.

The sharp coral outcroppings of the reef bilged the *Saginaw* in ten minutes; the sea washed through jagged wounds into her holds; her launch carried away, and her smokestack crashed over the lee side. Great rollers broke in a smother of foam over the wreck; aft, the colored steward, locked in irons and with the key lost, sang mournfully:

"Way down upon de Swanee ribber———"

A marine was washed overboard; the same comber threw him high upon the reef. As a scarlet sun bulged above the eastern horizon some of the crew scrambled onto the reef, standing knee-deep in the boiling surf. The boats were launched to leeward—just in time; the forward half of the ship broke off and was heaved high upon a coral ledge. Axes flashed in the morning sunlight; the mainmast was cut away and fell splashing into the sea. Across the still lagoon beyond the reef tired men rowed back and forth in cutter and captain's gig, from wreck to sandy shore, saving what the sea had left of the *Saginaw*.

Soon after the "necessaries of life" had been saved from the wreck and the crew had started to establish a permanent camp, Lieutenant John G. Talbot, sailing master of the *Saginaw* and second in command, volunteered to take a boat to the Sandwich Islands, eleven hundred miles away, to summon help for the castaways. Captain Sicard and Talbot and other officers held a conference.

A small boiler, supplemented by brass speaking tubes salvaged from the wreck of the bridge, had been fashioned into a rude distiller which, with the rain caught in sails, had solved the water problem until by accident a fresh-water well had been tapped. Enough salt pork, hardtack, flour, and canned goods had been saved (some of it dried out in the sun) to feed the crew on quarter rations for almost three months. A storehouse had been rudely constructed on stilts to keep out the rats; tents of sailcloth had been set up, and the scant diet of staples had been supplemented by the tough flesh of the gonies or brown albatross which nested on the island, by oily but rich seal steaks, and by an occasional catch of a few yellowtails. The one match saved from the wreck had started a fire which was kept burning day and night until some lanterns and a barrel of sperm oil were eventually salvaged.

But Sicard knew that Ocean Island was far from the steamer track; the *Saginaw* had come there—ironically enough—only to look for castaways. Uninhabited Midway, where the *Saginaw's* crew and her contractor's party had been attempting to blast a harbor entrance through the coral reef, lay fifty-five miles to the eastward, but there was no succor there, no help nearer than Hawaii, eleven hundred miles in a direct line to the east-sou'-eastward, but almost eighteen hundred miles with sail and oar by the usual sailing route at that season.

"God-a-mighty," one of the men said, "we might rot on this blarsted shoal and niver the world know."

Sicard and Talbot and the rest knew that this was true. Already the men were sick with dysentery and its griping pains. They were a hard-bitten lot; the water-spotted log recorded a list of punishments for fighting, for disrespect, for insolence. Even William Halford, coxswain of the captain's gig, a large square-faced man with a walrus mustache, had been clapped in double irons under sentry's charge for disrespect to superior officer. The outlook was gloomy.

Captain Sicard directed each officer to file with him "an opinion on the feasibility and necessity of sending a boat to the Sandwich

Islands." The opinions were affirmative, and Captain Sicard decided that the attempt should be made.

On November 5, 1870, the gig was carried well up on the beach and set in a cradle to be prepared for the eighteen-hundred-mile cruise, a cruise that in the annals of the sea is in many ways unique in its revelation of character and heroism, of the stoic endurance of men against hardship.

Within two weeks—two weeks of varying winds and sun and rain, and toil—the gig, a double-ended, fine-modeled whaleboat, had been made ready. Her sides had been raised eight inches, tapering down toward bow and stern; she had been decked over with light wood and canvas; four hatches with waterproof covers had been cut in the decking; two small masts shipped and stayed; and she had been stocked with ninety gallons of fresh water in ten breakers, and twenty-five days' full rations "with some little provision extra."

Five were to go in her; Talbot, in command; Halford, her coxswain; Peter Francis, the quartermaster; and John Andrews and James Muir, members of the contractor's party which had been working on the Midway Island harbor entrance. Andrews, a granite-faced Yankee from Boston, and Muir, a dour Scot, had been especially enlisted for one month to make the trip, because they were "men of such fine qualities and endurance."

On November 18, a clear and pleasant Friday with a gentle breeze from the north and eastward, the gig sailed for Hawaii. The whole crew stood by the water's edge as Talbot checked off with Captain Sicard and the officer of the day the gig's equipment. Her boat ensign with its thirteen stars in a fluttering circle waved gaily at the stern as the voices of the two officers monotoned above the surf's boom:

"One chronometer"	"One chronometer"
"One barometer, aneroid"	"One barometer, aneroid"
"One sextant"	"One sextant"
"One compass, binnacle"	"One compass, binnacle"
"One boat compass"	"One boat compass"
"One nautical almanac"	"One nautical almanac"
"One chart"	"One chart"
"One parallel rulers"	"One parallel rulers"

"One ensign"	"One ensign"
"Three Caston's signals"	"Three Caston's signals"
"One log line—235 feet"	"One log line—235 feet"
"One 28-second glass"	"One 28-second glass"
"One deck lantern"	"One deck lantern"
"Four gallons lamp oil"	"Four gallons lamp oil"
"Two balls lamp wick"	"Two balls lamp wick"
"Half quire note paper"	"Half quire note paper"
"Three pencils"	"Three pencils"

The voices paused. In addition to the food and equipment, the homemade sails, oars, and oarlocks, the gig carried in a tin dispatch case letters from the crew to their relatives, a report on the wreck from Captain Sicard to the Secretary of the Navy, and a bill of exchange for two hundred pounds sterling. For his principal navigational instrument Talbot had a crude sextant constructed by Herschel Main, second assistant engineer. It was made of the face of the *Saginaw's* steam gauge, broken bits of a stateroom mirror, scraps of zinc, and other odds and ends.

At eight bells in the afternoon watch Captain Sicard, with the crew mustered behind him on the beach, prayed solemnly for the safety and success of Talbot and his men. Talbot jumped into the gig and took his place in the stern hatch by the tiller. The others waded out to the twenty-two-foot boat, climbed over the sides, raised the anchor, hoisted the miniature sails—and the gig stood for the western channel through the reef. Before sundown it had faded from sight on the horizon to the northward.

That night while Paymaster Read in his tent was trying to forget gnawing hunger pains by playing a game of chess, with pieces made of blocks of wood and gonies' bones, Bailey, the foreman of the contractor's gang, came to him with a Bible in his hand and a smile upon his face. He had opened the book by chance at the fifty-first chapter of Isaiah, and had read what he thought was a word of good omen:

"The isles shall wait upon me, and upon my arm shall they trust."

Talbot held the gig on a northerly course, beating into the wind, as the faint blur that was Ocean Island faded into the seascape. The boat climbed the slow rollers and sank gently into the troughs, the green water chuckling under her counter as the light breeze filled the hand-stitched sails.

The mood of tense elation, common to all men embarking on expeditions of danger, which had lifted up the spirits of the five men as the gig started on her voyage, died with the sunset. As the westering rays slanted across the sky, a feeling of depression settled over the cockleshell craft and its crew. Talbot—sensitive, young, devout, deeply grieved by the recent loss of his mother, and keenly aware of the heavy burden of responsibility that rested upon him as leader of a forlorn hope—felt it more deeply than his less imaginative companions. His heart pounded; his throat muscles tensed as, hand on tiller and feet dangling into the black hole of the afterhatch, he watched the sun set on an empty sea. Behind him, beneath the ocean's rim, lay Ocean Island, the shattered strakes of the *Saginaw,* and the hungry men of her crew. Ahead, eighteen hundred miles of open water.

"Halford," he ordered, "take the helm while I check over and re-stow these stores. Andrews, you stay on deck with Halford; Francis, you and Muir give me a hand aft here."

The three men, doubled up in the small space between the thwarts and beneath the low deck, shifted, counted, and secured tins, breakers, and bags. The flickering light of their sperm-oil lamp, to be kept forever burning because of their lack of matches, glimmered uncertainly, casting elusive shadows across the dark belly of the boat. Against the seams the slow Pacific rolled, murmuring.

The water breakers were distributed fore and aft and lashed as near the midship line as possible. The food was carefully checked over and re-stored well above the bottom boards—out of reach of bilge water and flying spray. Five days' rations of hardtack sealed in tins was jammed up in the eyes of the boat; it was practically imperishable. Ten days' ration of the same in a black canvas bag was stowed on the afterthwart. Talbot opened the bag and pulled out a biscuit. In the dim lantern light its sickly saffron gleamed here and there with a faint greenish tinge, where mold had begun to form. Tiny holes burrowed through the hard crust—weevils. Talbot made a wry face, rubbed the mold off on his shirt, and put the biscuit back.

"We'll have to get some sun on those tomorrow."

The three men worked quickly, lashing down all loose gear, shifting the oars, spreading spare canvas across the bottom boards to make rough beds. Besides the hardtack, they checked off and stowed away two dozen small tins of bully beef; five five-pound tins of desiccated potatoes—a dried-out, mealy, tasteless mass; two big cans of beans which had been soaked in sea water after the *Saginaw's* wreck, and then had been dried in the sun, cooked, and stowed in tins; three tins of boiled wheaten grits which had come through the same debilitating process; one soggy ham; six tins of preserved oysters rescued from the officers' mess; ten pounds of dried beef; a dozen cans of lima beans and peas; five pounds of rancid, highly salted butter in a small tub; a gallon of black molasses; twelve pounds of white sugar; four pounds of tea, and five pounds of coffee. A small tin cooking apparatus burning sperm oil had been contrived out of pieces of scrap metal, and this was set up and secured near one of the hatches.

When Talbot and his helpers stuck their heads up through the hatches the swift Pacific twilight had ended. A lingering line of daylight to the westward marked a faint horizon; stars twinkled in the zenith. Quickly Talbot divided his crew into two watches—Halford and Andrews; Francis and Muir. Then, as Muir went below to prepare the evening meal—a bit of ham, a couple of biscuits with the mold rubbed off, a spoonful of molasses and some weak coffee—Talbot, buttocks braced against the hatch coaming and feet planted firmly on the bottom boards, focused the homemade sextant. In the little mirror he caught the reflected twinkling beauty of Arcturus, and twisting the tangent screw he brought the heavenly glimmer down to the earth's sea rim. The familiar routine comforted him—"the stars in their courses."

Saturday, Sunday, and much of Monday the fair weather held. At suppertime Monday, Muir, who was acting as cook, prepared to dish out some of the cooked beans from one of the two large cans. As he stuck his clasp knife into the tin, there was a loud pop, a quick wheeze as of escaping steam—and a foul odor. Spoiled!

At Talbot's orders the other tin of beans and the three cans of boiled wheaten grits were brought out. As his shipmates watched, Muir jabbed the tins with his knife. From each tin there was a pop, a wheeze, and a stench. Francis turned his head, looked out to sea; Andrews, his face muscles taut and the cords on his neck straining, stared at the tins; Talbot and Halford were grim.

Muir swore slowly and with precision.

"I'm going to try it—damned mess, but better than going hungry. Without this we'll be out of food in two weeks."

Talbot and Muir dipped into the putrid mess. Andrews and the others reluctantly followed their example.

Controlling his almost involuntary retching, Talbot carefully chewed and swallowed two mouthfuls of the spoiled beans. He tried to force himself to eat some of the grits but his will revolted. Muir and Andrews bolted a few teaspoonfuls of the wheaten grits, which were not so badly spoiled as the beans; Francis and Halford each champed a mouthful of the fermented food. The men washed the taste from their mouths with sea water and swallowed long drafts of fresh water drawn from the breakers. The spoiled cans were covered and carefully stowed away.

Five minutes later Talbot, green and shuddering, was stretched out over the afterdeck vomiting his supper into the sea.

The next morning, holding their noses and closing their eyes, three of the five carefully munched and swallowed more of the beans and grits. Halford and Francis went hungry, chewing bits of ham fat and rind into mush, and biting off tiny bits of the weevil-riddled hardtack from the one biscuit apiece doled out in the morning ration. Talbot kept his breakfast down for only two minutes. Again he was sick, stretched prone on the afterdeck, his face wet with the spray of the gig's motion. He rose weak in body and spirit.

During the morning Muir and Andrews were taken with griping pains; doubled up with cramps, they lay on the piled canvas on the bottom boards, arms locked around their knees, faces twisted with pain. Francis too was ill; Halford alone seemed unaffected by the tainted provisions.

At noon Talbot ate the beans again; Muir and Andrews were too ill to move. Talbot was sick again—immediately; his stomach rejected the putrid stuff as soon as he had swallowed it.

"It's no use; I can't do it. Throw the damned stuff overboard," he

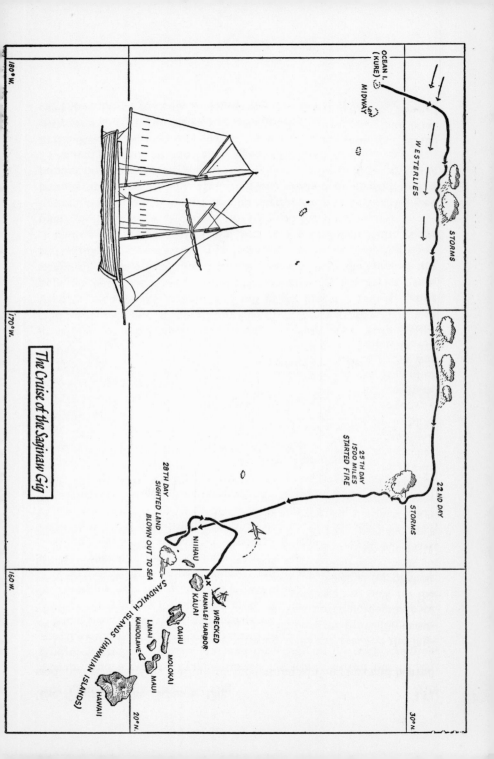

The Cruise of the Sagivaw Gig

said, pale and gasping. Halford rooted out the stinking tins and heaved them into the sea.

The gig held a course to the northward until she reached the latitude of thirty-two degrees. There she encountered the prevailing westerlies, and Talbot laid a course eastward toward the longitude of Kauai, one of the Sandwich Islands, where he hoped to pick up the northeast trades and shift course to the south on the final leg of their cruise.

For the first four days fair weather prevailed. Fickle but brisk southerly breezes filled the rags of the canvas draped from the gig's two masts, and she bowled along through scorching sun-filled days and starlit nights. For four days the little boat carried all her canvas— a jib, fore and main sails, a main tops'l, and a fore squaresail. Halford and Francis and Talbot held her on her course by the quivering needle of the boat compass; Andrews and Muir doggedly stood their watches for'd despite their griping pains and the acute dysentery that followed.

On Wednesday, five days out of Ocean Island, it came on to blow hard from the westward. Storm rack scudded across the heavens; a gony soaring on stiffened wings fled before the wind. The sea made up; spray splayed from the gig's forefoot and wet her decks. Rag after rag her canvas was stripped from her, until before nightfall she was running under her reefed fore squaresail. Halford and Talbot shared the watch in the cockpit, canvas drawn tightly about their waists. Forward the hatch covers were on, but the deck leaked; Francis and Andrews and Muir, stretched out beneath the thwarts, their joints wedged against hard wood, moved fitfully to escape the leaks. Their sunken cheeks covered with stubbles of beard, their red-rimmed lids and pain-racked faces were now in shadow, now in flickering light, as the flame of the ever-burning lantern shifted with the motion of the boat.

Talbot and Halford—the one slight, pale, almost spectral, buoyed up only by his indomitable will; the other tall, husky, square-jawed, a profane Viking—stood shoulder to shoulder in the afterhatch, minding the tiller, watching the hissing waves sweep up astern.

Black walls of water crested with foam rode endlessly out of the east, roared down on the cockleshell, tossing it first stern, then bow, skywards, passed beneath the straining strakes, and swept on. Toward morning as the gale reached its height a towering roller, its black ebony furrowed and roweled by the sharp spurs of the wind, howled up from astern. The gig lifted, but not quite quickly enough; the crest broke and thundered down on the decks in a deluge of green water. The sea cascaded off the turtleback deck and ran down the canvas loosely fitted about the waists of the two men in the stern.

Talbot licked the salt from his lips; Halford shook the water from his eyes and wrung out the drenched sleeves of his jacket. Below the glimmering lantern revealed spurts of water sluicing through leaky deck seams. Muir and Andrews swore and started to shift the canvas bread bag to a drier place. As their hands moved they were suddenly groping in blackness. A gush of water through a leaky deck seam over the afterthwart had extinguished the ever-burning lantern.

A second storm followed hard upon the first one. The winter gales had come, and the winds—with only brief intervals of shining days or peaceful nights—howled steadily out of the west, bringing with them a smother of foam. With no flame the tin cooking apparatus was useless. Time and again Muir, weak and haggard, his body still racked with griping pains, struck flint and steel together; but there was no dry tinder in the boat and nothing combustible could be found. The gig streamed with water; she had to be bailed once each watch; the men's clothing was soaked; salt-water sores formed on their legs; cracks in the skin opened between their fingers and toes; their joints stiffened and throbbed from the continual wet. Braced against the stanchions or curled around the masts, they tried to sleep, but the constant skittering of the small boat in the harrying sea gave them no rest. Water sluiced through the leaky deck seams; pain tore at their bowels; hunger enervated their bodies but left their minds keen and clear to note with exquisite perception the slowly mounting torture of the sea.

Without flame the coffee and tea were useless; for a time the rancid butter made the hardtack bearable, but within ten days, despite their utmost care, the mold had spread like a horrid fungus throughout the bread in the black canvas bag, and it was inedible. They lived on bits of dried beef or ham rind, a spoonful of molasses or sugar—most of it salt-soaked—and two spoonfuls a day of the desiccated potatoes.

Between their pitiful meals they sucked on tea leaves or coffee grounds and swilled gulps of water from their plentiful supply.

For days the sea did its worst. There were only short intervals when they could lie in weak sunlight, half-naked on deck, clinging to the rigging. Breathing stertorously through salt-cracked lips they soaked in the momentary warmth and tried to dry their tattered garments. At first, in the few periods of windless calm, they tried the oars; but their strength was soon gone; they made but pitiful progress. It was during one of these periods that Andrews discovered the loss of the last of their molasses. A black sticky sweetness was mixed with the bilge water below the bottom boards: the keg had leaked. They took this new misfortune without comment. There was nothing to say, nothing to do, and all of them had long ago thought all. They were tied to sanity and buoyed up only by the spirit of collective discipline, now merely a reflex from the past.

The gig sailed on eastward across the parallels of space, slowly approaching the goal of all their hopes—the Sandwich Islands. Talbot took sights when he could, but the frequent storms, clouds, rain, and mist obscured the heavens, and the heaving of the small boat on the restless ocean made accuracy difficult. During the second and third weeks—still making their easting—the gig all but foundered in a succession of storms. Again forced to heave to, the men fashioned a primitive sea anchor by lashing three of their five oars into a rude triangle and weighting it. The drag did its work well for hours, but finally the constant straining of the gig loosened the lashings, the contrivance disintegrated, and the oars were swept away. The deck leaked more seriously; Muir and Andrews did their best to calk the seams with ripped-up shirts and oakum plucked from the bow painter, but as fast as one leak was plugged other seams opened.

The masts working in their steps strained the strakes, and tiny leaks started in the bottom. A great sea which swept into the afterhatch half flooded the boat and washed away what was left of the sugar.

The little company of five men had hoped to reach the islands during the third week; twenty-four or twenty-five days would be the maximum time required for the passage, they had estimated. But it was not until the twenty-second day that Talbot, after a shaky sight of the sun, shifted the gig's course to southward. The winds had blown out of the north during the latter part of the trip, and again the boat was running before the breeze. Halford held her on her course most of the time now; he was still strong, though his skin had shrunken and his eyes glared out of deep hollows. Francis too was fairly strong, though failing rapidly. Talbot had been ill from diarrhea for eight days; he was better now, but weak and tottering—only his spirit was strong. Muir and Andrews were still locked in the groaning misery of dysentery, but their starvation diet had perforce relieved them; their pain was ending, though their exhaustion was extreme.

As the boat made its southing on the last leg of its cruise the men lived on the dried potatoes—all that was left: a spoonful a day moistened with a draft of water. Halford mixed his scanty ration with sperm oil; the rest tried it, but "were so weakened they could not retain it." The rest of the time they lay, all but the men on watch, chewing on bits of leather, and dreaming distorted dreams.

During the last of the storms the gig had a close call. Halford was crouching in the afterhatch steering. Under his armpits, to keep out the water, was a reeving string of the canvas cover nailed around the coaming. A nasty sea was running; the gig leaped forward on the combers' backs as they came up astern. Suddenly there was a shock; the boat listed, nearly capsized, then another sea swept her on. Halford looked astern: they had glanced against a water-soaked log forty or fifty feet long and as thick as the *Saginaw's* smokestack. It had almost done for them.

Once during a calm spell on a clear moonlit night Francis, who had stood his watch at the tiller and was crawling forward on deck, slipped overboard. As the boat glided past him he caught a fishing line which had been trailing astern all the voyage (though it had never caught a fish). It held; but it took all the strength of Halford and the rest to haul him back aboard.

On the twenty-fourth day, when the boat had logged some fifteen hundred miles, Halford at last succeeded in starting a fire. A bit of oakum and canvas dried in the sun burst into flame as the coxswain focused the sun's rays upon it with a glass taken from the binoculars. Quickly the lantern was relighted and a flame kindled in the cooking apparatus. But it was too late; there was nothing to cook. The men solaced themselves by mixing their spoonfuls of evaporated potatoes in water and heating the pasty substance.

On one of these interminable days Francis cracked. It was just before the noon spoonful of potatoes. The storms had left them, and the gig's tattered sails—most of them half torn from their boltropes—were drawing her gently over a calm and sunlit sea. Halford was steering and all except Francis were stretched, more dead than alive, on the turtleback deck.

As Talbot painfully lowered himself down the afterhatch to get his sextant, a gagging scream halted him. High-pitched, awful, it went from a crescendo of terror to the throaty yammering of an idiot.

The men on deck lay rigid, horror staring from their eyes. Talbot, shaken, crouched down beneath the deck and looked forward. Francis sprawled amid-ships, on hands and knees, his head wagging.

Again he screamed.

Halford now came below; then Andrews and Muir, almost too weak to move. Together with Talbot they got Francis over on to his back on the bottom boards and pillowed his head on a ragged shirt. The man looked at them out of burning eyes and muttered meaningless phrases.

They gave him double rations—two spoonfuls of the dried potatoes —and as much water as he would drink, and one of the four watched him until he returned slowly to sanity.

On the twenty-fifth day their food—the mealy mass of evaporated potatoes—gave out completely. So too did all but a slim, slim hope. Talbot had almost given up faith in his navigation (but never in the God of his fathers); he still kept his dead reckoning, but he found himself too weak to work out his position by observation. He told Halford—again—what to do and how to steer in case he died, for he was the officer still. Halford the Viking, with occasional relief from Talbot, Muir, and Andrews, and later from Francis, held the course slightly east of south. The sun blazed its patch across the sky; the cockleshell rode on.

On the evening of the twenty-sixth day, as the men lay with suppurating sores, their bellies bulging inelastic and dead-fish-white from famine, a "booby" lighted on the gunwale and stared curiously at

Halford at the tiller. The bird was almost within reach of the coxswain, but Halford's hand was weak and trembling. A slow stealthy shifting of position—a quick movement, a sudden squawk—and he had it by the neck. Holding the tiller pressed between elbow and ribs he wrung its neck, roughly tore off its feathers, and half cut, half tore it into five rudely equal parts. Raw and bleeding as it was, the men ate it with relish.

Thirty-six hours later at daybreak of the twenty-eighth day Halford held the tiller again. Round and beneath him lay a crew of dying specters. Something wet and cold brushed against his cheek, plopped on deck. It was a tiny flying fish. He grabbed the wiggling creature and crammed it, still alive, down his throat. In a moment a school of the fish came skipping along. He brushed five or six of them down the afterhatch and the men ate them raw. It was the last meal of the crew of the *Saginaw's* gig.

At sunup on the twenty-eighth day out—Friday, December 16—Halford sighted land. It rose as a dim blur to the northeast; another cloud, he thought at first. He altered course, but made no report to the living skeletons below. The cloud persisted, took shape, mounted out of the blue of the sea, was outlined against the sunlight—*land!* He shouted, his heart pounding. They had almost passed it in the night.

Talbot staggered on deck; the gig steered north by east, beating back against the wind. The men below stirred uneasily with the news; those who had been about to die were saved; but they were too far gone to cry aloud. Hope returned slowly to their numbed minds, but they could do little to trim the sails. Halford and Talbot managed; Halford usually at the tiller, a gaunt giant now, nourished on sperm oil.

All that day the gig reversed its course, the land taking shape out of the sea. Talbot, propping the binoculars on the hatch coaming, tentatively made it out as Kawaihua Rock on the southern end of Niihau, Sandwich Islands. He thanked God; he had talked often of God in those last days for he was a devout, believing man.

That night and all day Saturday the sea played with them as a cat teases a mouse. The wind—with them for a thousand miles—was against them now, coming off the land. They were blown out to sea again, yet kept the land in sight. Almost they despaired, but not quite. Saturday night they headed the buffeted gig as much into the wind as the creaking masts would stand, and held her on an east-sou'east course. Sunday, thirty days out of Ocean Island, the famished men, the wind permitting, put her on a sou'east course with the island of Kauai in sight. The sun sank with the features of the land clearly distinguishable Sunday night, and again Talbot thanked God.

As the quick twilight faded into dusk, he gave Halford instructions once more as to what to do in case something happened to him. Halford nodded and went below to stretch out on the bottom boards, while Francis, recovered but weak, held the gig hove to with head to the northwest. At eleven Halford came on deck again to take his trick at the tiller. The boat had drifted closer to shore, and the night was clear. Halford called Talbot to say he could distinguish the entrance to Hanalei harbor. Talbot ordered the boat to be kept away and steered for the entrance.

But the sea was not through with them yet. At one o'clock Monday morning, as Halford's watch was ending, the sky clouded over, and the outline of the land was dimmed. Talbot, who came on deck with Andrews and Francis, Halford's reliefs, again ordered the boat hove to. Halford went below, but tossed restlessly on the bottom boards— sound sleep had long been impossible to them all. Twice more, he knew from the gig's motion, the boat was kept away toward the land, then hove to. At two o'clock he felt long rollers surge beneath the keel and lick on toward the land; their dull boom as they broke was a sound ominous and new after a month of slatting sails and raging winds. He called Muir, weak and cracking, and joined the others on deck. Muir stayed below. Just as Halford crawled aft to the cockpit and stuck his head up through the hatch, a sea broke aboard aft. The gig was in the breakers!

"Put your helm down; haul aft your main sheet and get out of this!" Talbot's feeble voice shouted his last commands.

Halford hauled aft the main sheet; Francis put the tiller hard over, and slowly the boat's bow swung round into the wind. Just as it was swinging a roaring roller broke aboard. The cockleshell was snatched and flung landward and skyward—bottom up. End of all hopes. Foam-blinded, feeble, Andrews and Francis were hurled into the sea and disappeared in the smother. Riding the backs of the rollers the gig was swept shoreward, Talbot clawing feebly at its bilge, Halford clinging to the bow, Muir trapped under the deck beneath the overturned boat. Talbot—weak arms trembling, weighted down by the drag of his clothing—tried to pull himself to the stern and climb up on the slimy boat's bottom. Almost he succeeded. But the curling ringlets of foam from the waves' crests washed over his head; salt spume filled his nostrils. Dim dreams of faraway Ocean Island, of Captain Sicard, of the hardships past, swept through his mind. His crooked fingers loosed their hold. Slowly he sank.

The gig was righted by another wave. Halford scrambled on deck; Muir, gasping and purple in the face, stuck his head up the afterhatch. Halford helped him out.

Succeeding breakers capsized the boat again, twirling her over and over, flinging Halford and Muir shoreward in a flume of foam. The masts of the gig snapped off; a hole was smashed in the bow which had breasted eighteen hundred miles of blue water. With a last rush of water the boat was righted, the two men still clinging to the hatch coaming. The sea had finished; past the worst of the breakers the gig floated gently, half full of water, toward the beach.

So she came into port—dismasted, waterlogged, stove in; three of her five gone, and of the two remaining one naked, blood streaming from a deeply gashed leg, panting, but still unbeaten; the other a wreck of a man, head battered, face purple, crazily muttering. Thus the *Saginaw's* gig ended her cruise at 2:30 A.M., Monday, December 19, 1870, thirty-one days out of Ocean Island.

Halford slipped breast-high into the shallow water and waded to shore, taking with him the tin dispatch case. He returned again to the silently drifting gig and half hoisted, half dragged Muir, muttering and groaning, to the beach. Muir collapsed on the sand; Halford pillowed his shipmate's head on a coat and waded back to the boat, again, and again, and again, bringing ashore what was left of the precious paraphernalia of the cruise: the chronometer, the binoculars, the compasses. Far overhead the tropic stars twinkled; to the east a faint gray dawned as, tottering with exhaustion, Halford made his last trip and sank to the beach.

He slept the sleep of utter weariness until the sun shone on the

beach of Kalihi Kai (Kalihiwai). Then, struggling to his feet, rubbing
the sleep from his eyes, he looked for Muir and found him gone from
the place he had left him. Halford walked a staggering walk—his legs
strange to the land—down the beach, looking for the last of his comrades. He found Muir soon, surrounded by natives; "but he was dead
and very black in the face."

Christmas Day, 1870, on the sandy wastes of Ocean Island, the
crew of the *Saginaw* spent in somewhat gloomy contemplation. The
officers donned their best uniforms—salt-soaked and faded—to stroll
among the sand dunes. Assistant Engineer Blye cut up into bits three
cigars, all that remained of his store, and gave them out as Christmas
presents. Some of the men stuffed leaves and dried bark in the com-
munity clay pipe and had their after-dinner smoke.

The next ten days passed with work on a schooner, whose stark
wooden frames were rapidly taking shape out of the debris from a
previous wreck, supplemented by timbers saved from the *Saginaw*.
It was a morose period. The seals were fast being depleted; the staples
were practically exhausted; the albatross were wary. Help should have
arrived before.

On the evening of January 3 a steamer was sighted standing toward
the island. It was soon recognized as the *Kilauea*, "a vessel belonging
to the King of the Sandwich Islands," Captain Thomas Long commanding. The steamer stood away from the dangerous coral reef that
night, while ashore around a great bonfire the shipwrecked mariners
celebrated. The gig had gone through! Captain Sicard and his men ate
their last supper on the island—a holiday ration of salt pork, gonies'
flesh, flour, and beans.

The next morning, with the crew, bearded and bronzed, lined up in
front of the flagpole, their tattered uniforms patched and motley,
Captain Sicard advanced to the water's edge to meet Captain Long,
who was rowed ashore in his whaleboat from the *Kilauea*. The two
captains greeted each other, and conversed earnestly for a few moments. Then, with heads down, they walked slowly up the beach
toward the waiting company. Captain Sicard raised his hand, took off
his salt-crusted, faded uniform cap, and said:

"Men, I have the great sorrow to announce to you that we have been saved at a great sacrifice. Lieutenant Talbot and three of the gig's crew are dead——"

His voice trailed off, and Captain Sicard bowed his head. "A low murmur of grief passed along the line."

NOTES   The chapter is strictly factual in all essential details. I have tried, knowing something of the characters of the brave men who comprised the crew of the *Saginaw's* gig, to describe their reactions, as they might have been, to each recurrent hardship; and have supplied occasional phrases of conversation in the language they might have used. Each incident in the wreck of the *Saginaw* and in the epic journey of her gig is history, vouched for and attested by Halford and those shipmates who were rescued from Ocean Island because of his bravery and hardihood. Halford died at the age of 77 in 1919, one of the last links to the age of slatting sails and muzzle-loaders. It is to his daughter, Miss Alice Halford of Piedmont, California, who transcribed the story as her father had often told it, that I am indebted for this firsthand account of a boat voyage unique in the history of our navy.

ACKNOWLEDGMENTS   This chapter is republished from *Esquire,* with the permission of the editor.

The principal sources for the narrative are the reports of Captain Sicard to the Navy Department, and the personal narrative of Halford, sole survivor of the gig's crew, and of Paymaster Read of the *Saginaw*. These accounts have been supplemented by contemporary articles in newspaper files, in the *Army and Navy Register,* and in the *United States Naval Institute Proceedings*.

1918

"Remember Always to Dare"

It was the fall of 1918, and the Austrian army was being crushed in the climax of the battle of Vittorio Veneto. The Austrian fleet had been weakened by heavy losses, and its morale undermined by sedition which finally culminated in open mutiny.

The reckless efficiency of the Italian MAS boats (motor torpedo boats) whose motto was D'Annunzio's *"Memento Audare Semper"*—Remember Always to Dare—had swept the Adriatic clean of enemy craft; the great ships of Austria were immured behind formidable obstructions in Pola and other harbors, and the entrances to these bases were well protected by a strengthened series of complicated nets and chains and floating booms, which it was impossible to pierce and which no MAS boat was now able to jump.

But the Italians were still uneasy; those great ships—*Viribus Unitis, Prinz Eugen,* and their consorts—remained a mighty fleet and a menace to the Italian army's flank along the Adriatic. And so Major (later Lieutenant Colonel) Raffaele Rossetti, a naval constructor, and Surgeon Lieutenant (later Captain) Raffaele Paolucci, Royal Italian Navy, achieved their immortality in the dying days of the war.

It was at 1 P.M. on October 31, 1918, that Rossetti and Paolucci boarded an Italian torpedo boat at Venice. The sea was "dead, dark, and dull in autumnal dreariness." The flat sandy coast and the skyline they knew so well dropped astern, and at about eight in the evening they arrived off Brioni Island, peace-time playground for the wealthy, opposite Pola Harbor. Here they transferred to a MAS boat, and, towing a torpedo-like object astern, proceeded to within two-thirds of a mile of the mole of Pola.

In perfect silence they prepared for death: stripped, were injected with camphor against the cold, and dressed in special watertight rubber suits, with air pouches at chest and back. These gloved them snugly, all except their eyes. Rossetti hung a watch in a watertight glass case about his neck; both fitted to their heads weird headgear, shaped to look like wine casks; and they were ready.

The phosphorescence in the water glowed fitfully about the drifting boat. The enemy searchlights wheeled in the distance. It all seemed strangely dreamlike, but to Rossetti, suddenly buoyant with the beginning of adventure, the chances for life appeared greater than before. Some days previously, during the end of their months of preparation, he had estimated the odds at three to two against their return; now his spirits rose with the sight of the harbor lights, and mentally, like all who hold life dear, he grew more confident in the actual face of danger.

The "torpedo" was hauled alongside; with a whispered farewell and final instructions to the crew of the MAS boat Rossetti and Paolucci slipped into the water, and half sitting upon, half clinging to their strange mechanism, disappeared into the dark.

The forward part of their "torpedo" consisted of two detachable metal barrels, each filled with four hundred pounds of T.N.T., and each fitted with clockwork mechanism, time-firing devices, and gear to fix the mines to the side of a battleship. The long slim cylinder aft, reclaimed from a German torpedo which had failed to explode, housed a great flask of air compressed to a pressure of thirty-nine hundred pounds per square inch; this motivated a small engine driving two screws. There was supply enough to keep them moving at slow speed for many hours. Their queer craft was nine yards long, weighed a ton and a half, and made a speed of two miles an hour; it could be lowered or raised in the water, but normally ran fully awash. It was, in fact, a torpedo; but a torpedo controlled by men, an animate thing, a centaur of the sea.

Paolucci and Rossetti steered by using their arms and feet against the water. They had trained faithfully for this night; Paolucci had swum for hours night after night in the waters of Venetian lagoons; Rossetti had perfected the mechanism after more than two years of work; both together had tested it against obstruction after obstruction, had manhandled it through miles of sea. But the water was far colder off this harbor of Pola than in Venice. The men shivered as spray spurted down the necks of their rubber suits.

The dull gleam of a few lights and the dark blur of the mole grew plainer. It had been 10:13 when they started the engine and shoved off. Their comrades believed they were headed for certain death, but Rossetti felt curiously calm and comfortable now; he found himself looking upon the whole adventure with a detached air, like a scientist performing an uncertain experiment. Paolucci, riding the bow of their contrivance, with his rubber-gloved body bent to the waves like some strange sea god, experienced more fully the sensory perceptions of great but subdued excitement. Yes, the Istrian water was certainly colder than that of the lagoons of Venice, but nevertheless he found himself almost sweating with emotion.

Closer and closer as the minutes passed the two men rode toward Pola. The shape of the mole grew and defined itself out of the dark; the soft, blurred edges sharpened. To starboard loomed that headland they so often had studied on the chart. They edged their craft toward the barrage opening. . . . Then suddenly, stunningly, they felt the glare of light. The wheeling searchlights from the harbor fort had picked them out. Was this so soon the end? They felt naked, exposed, in the searchlight's beam; their eyes were dazzled by the glare; but they hung, inert and motionless, to their slowly drifting craft, their heads bobbling on the surface like empty wine casks, floating shoreward with the tide—— The searchlight passed them by.

They came soon afterward to the outer barrage, a mass of floating metal cylinders, linked and interlaced with looped wires and chains. The mole was close by now; they could hear the slow slap of the sea against its base. The tiny whir of their propellers, the faint, muffled chug of the engine seemed like roaring in their ears. They stopped the engine and approached the barrier. There was a new worry now: what if the barrier cylinders contained T.N.T.?

They soon had their answer; they approached the chains, touched them, and there was no explosion. They made their torpedo as buoyant as they could, and pushed and hauled it over the first barrier. Metal rasped on metal with a tiny shriek that cut the silence deeply. They paused, startled, but no one heard.

"Guard the propellers."

They nursed the stern into the water, keeping it safe from the looped chains and wires: if the propellers were damaged, then their task was in vain.

For a time now they swam, dragging their torpedo through the water toward the next obstruction (there were seven). But they made too slow progress; even at the risk of discovery from the mole hard by, they must start the engine. It coughed—and started, purring silently. They proceeded, sometimes blundering off the course in the darkness, shivering, half blinded by the salt water, at times swimming beside their torpedo to lighten her; dragging and pushing here; lifting gently there, struggling on the barriers.

All at once Paolucci gasped. Hard by, and moving toward them, they saw a black mass. Rossetti stopped the engine and they slid silently into the water, pressing their torpedo beneath the waves. The mass took shape, sliding softly nearer. A conning tower—a submarine, running without lights. She came so close that Paolucci had his hand on the control valve, ready to fire the mines—but she passed on into the night.

At last they reached the mole; the outer barriers were behind. While Rossetti floated, waiting, Paolucci swam forward, exploring cautiously, his hands scarcely rippling the surface. It was past midnight. The concrete wall of the mole went sheer down into deep water. The two brought their machine close into the shadow of it. They swam like frogs, silently and with elaborate care; the gleaming phosphorescence of disturbed water could mean their death and the failure of their great plan.

It was after midnight, and more and more, as they fended their ton and a half of death off the concrete with bruised tired hands. This seemed a fantastic dream. Their heads floated like wine casks in the waves; the tongues of the searchlights licked through the black night overhead.

Paolucci pulled himself ahead, softly, softly, in the water by the mole, a few feet from its top where sentries kept their watch. A noise overhead! He stopped and glued himself tight to the concrete wall like some great sea leech. Then slowly, slowly, he pushed himself out from the wall, the sea to his mouth. There was a shadow on the mole— motionless. Perhaps now a gun was pointing at his head. He put the thought from him, and rolled his head slightly, as a wine cask might move in a seaway. Nothing happened. Still slowly he turned and went back to Rossetti and their machine, heart pounding, arteries throbbing from the rush of blood, but the cold of the Istrian waters creeping up his numbing legs.

They went on, pushing gently, guiding carefully. They came to the inner barriers, and found a gate in the barrage—closed. It was formed by long floating timbers, joined to one another with intersecting beams. From these protruded steel-tipped spikes three feet long, with their points turned outwards. To some were fixed petrol cans for the obvious purpose of giving sound warnings. The barrier looked formidable, and beyond it a trawler lay, about whose deck a red light moved for a time; but soon this went out.

The tide had turned; by the time Paolucci had finished his inspection the strong ebb was carrying Rossetti and the machine back toward the sea. Struggling, they were scarcely able to tow it back beyond the mole's end. Twice they tried to reach the barrier and failed; the thing was beyond their strength. At last Rossetti started the motor again, and the torpedo swung about and headed for the center of the gate.

Now certainly they must be heard; to their alert ears that loud-seeming engine roared the end of hope. But it had commenced to drizzle, and the sentry on the mole must have heard nothing and seen nothing; nothing except, perhaps, two wine casks, dim in the wet mist, and the slap of little waves.

They pushed and hoisted their torpedo over the gate, and exhausted, panting, rested at last; but briefly. It was 1 A.M. by Rossetti's watch: three hours in the water, three hours of ceaseless struggle— had life been always struggle?

Rossetti's blood froze in sudden terror; Paolucci had coughed, again, and again, and again—and the guard ship only a few meters away! That uncontrollable fit of coughing was the most terrifying moment yet—but the gods were with them: no one heard.

They swam on, now turning over the motor briefly to give them aid, now swimming silently past some ship moored hard by. They came upon more inner obstructions: stout wire submarine nets armed with explosives set to detonate upon impact. A triple set of these lethal nets extended just off the tapering bowsprit of an anchored sailing ship, whose weather-beaten sides Paolucci saw dimly through the mist and night. They had not expected these nets; this was different from the defense plans as airplane photographs and the Italian intelligence service had compiled them. But they persevered. In the cold rain they wove their way through openings in the steel labyrinth, their bodies chilled, their minds numb with exhaustion and the ceaseless labor.

More hardships were to come, and near disasters. Once the strong ebb took the torpedo in charge and nearly washed it beneath the hull of a guard ship; as they struggled in the dark their weary splashings were almost reckless of discovery. At length they came to the last barrage—and pushed past it, past the guard ships into the dim obscurity of the harbor.

But there was no sudden exultation of accomplishment; it was three in the morning, and they were drained of emotion. They licked their salted lips, shifted their cramped limbs on their slowly moving steed, and set their teeth.

They were far behind schedule; by this time the attack should have been long delivered, and they should have been (if lucky) well on their way back to their rendezvous with the MAS boat on the open sea. But that, too, seemed a part of the dream—the MAS boat they had left so long, long ago.

Rosetti signaled to Paolucci that he wished to speak, and the bow man paddled back along the gleaming cylinder. The air was low! The gauge showed that less than half the supply remained; what was left was hardly enough for the return, even if they should give up the enterprise now. But they did not hesitate. Return was unthinkable.

The engine turned again; the waves slapped against its gleaming sides and broke in dabs of spume over the leaning hooded men astride it. The rain came down harder, mixed with hail.

And then they saw the lights, the lights of ships anchored in a row, the lights of the Austrian fleet, of the *Radetzky, Erzherzog Franz Ferdinand, Zriny, Prinz Eugen, Tegetthoff,* and, farthest shoreward, identified by its bulk, the great *Viribus Unitis,* flagship and pride. Now, with the engine wide, they rode awash—two men in rubber suits and strange headdresses upon a throbbing cylinder—in an enemy harbor, passing down the long line of the ships.

They were nearly at their goal, the great ship *Viribus Unitis* looming up in the foreground, the dawn graying in the east, and the cold rain falling with the hissing spatter of hail, when suddenly the torpedo began to sink. Desperately they fought, arms heavy with the hours of exertion, but its buoyance was going—going—a gasp came from Rossetti: he had found and closed an open intake valve which was admitting water in the cylindrical shell.

Relief came; relief accompanied by fatigue which was almost pain.

Twice they had to make that last painful hundred-yard approach toward the bow of the *Viribus Unitis,* for once the tide swept them away. It was past 4:30, and the east was brightening when they neared the end. They were close enough now; Rossetti detached one of the forward canisters of death and disappeared from Paolucci's gaze within the shadow of the ship.

They were separated—the two who had dared death together so often in that one night. Paolucci felt tired and utterly lonely as he spraddled the drifting torpedo with its single mine, and floated there in the wet dark—waiting.

Rossetti, with four hundred pounds of T.N.T. clutched to his chest, hurried, his heart sick within him as the light grew in the east. But his hands were numb with cold, the fingers bloodless from the long immersion in the sea. He hastened, but he could not see the clockwork mechanism as he floated there in the dark, clinging to the ship's side with his icy hands. The lever—ah, he had the lever. But careful; he must set it just so; pushed too far that mine, rocking so gently on the little waves, would explode in his arms. His fingers twitched, his tired face showed the agony of his restraint. He felt the dial—and gently, so gently, he pushed the lever to the left. At 6:30 the end would come. He turned a valve; the mine sank hard by the steel ship's side, and it was almost done. But not quite; the mechanism that attached the explosive canister to the ship's side jammed; a cord, wet and stubborn with the water, became tangled at this last moment.

Desperately he struggled as the light waxed and the dark grew gray with day. He (and Paolucci, drifting out there out of sight in the dark) stiffened with dismay as a bugle sang on the decks of the *Viribus Unitis* and lights were switched on and the voices of men rang across the waters. Discovery—— But no; they were still safe. And suddenly, as the dawn strengthened, the cord became disentangled, and the thing was done.

At last . . . the thing . . . was done.

Rossetti swam back slowly out of the shadow of the ship to Paolucci, this man he would always love; for had they not lived many lives, died many deaths this night together?

And Paolucci, struggling against the stream with the balky thing that had been their ship and their salvation, saw the broadening band of dawn, noted that it was 5:15, and then with a heart that had never experienced greater joy discovered the floating cask that was Rossetti's head moving toward him out of the shadow.

They turned toward the enemy shore to find rest, perhaps escape— but it was not to be. The phosphorescence in the water at last betrayed them as the dawn stretched its accusing fingers over the sea. A searchlight in the top of the *Viribus Unitis* flashed bright across the bay and pinioned them with its broad swathe of light. Men shouted; a boat shoved off from the ship's side; they braced themselves for the shock of bullets crashing into brain. But no bullets came; the boat flew with strong oars over the sea, and as it came they did their final duty. Paolucci detached the second canister of explosives and set it free in the swirling tideway. Rossetti opened the immersion valve and the "torpedo," gleaming bubbles marking its passing, sank deep into the waters of Pola harbor.

The men turned on their backs, the bright glare of the searchlight in their eyes, a great relief of mind and utter weariness of body their only sensation. They had done their jobs; the rest was in the laps of the gods.

A gutteral hail came from the boat:

"Wer da?"

It was a fitting query. In the searchlight glare Paolucci and Rossetti seemed strange creatures risen from primordial ocean—their heads obscured in their strange helmets, their bodies black and glistening in rubber.

"Italienische Offiziere."

They were hauled into the boat, gasping and tired, by men gibbering with excitement. Rest, at last.

But—O God, what was this? *They were being rowed back to the Viribus Unitis!*

It was 5:55 A.M. when they were brought aboard. About them on the upper deck crowded a throng of sailors, and Paolucci noticed with surprise that they were wearing the scrawled characters *Yugoslavia* on their cap ribbons. The crew watched the two men narrowly, like cats. And the clock crawled toward six.

They were taken below and informed that the Austrian admiral had been put ashore just a few hours before and the fleet command turned over to the Yugoslav National Council, by the Emperor of an Austrian Empire that was dying. Rossetti demanded to see the Commanding Officer.

He was taken to the cabin of Captain Ianko Vukovic de Podkapelski, a gallant gentleman. With a gesture genuinely dramatic and typically Italian Rossetti extended a dagger, their only arms, and surrendered as prisoners of war.

"Your ship is in serious and imminent danger. I urge you to abandon it and save your men."

The calm captain requested details and asked for an explanation of their presence in the fortified guarded harbor of Pola. Rossetti declined to answer, but urged the necessity of speed. The minutes crawled.

Captain Vukovic passed the word to his men, ordered the boats lowered. Panic spread.

"The Italians have put bombs in the ship!"

Half-clothed men, fresh from the hammocks, dived into the sea; scores worked frantically at the boats; the sailors, mad with mass panic, forgot their two prisoners and tried only to save themselves.

Paolucci and Rossetti, still in their rubber suits, seized the opportunity and dived back into the water, back into the sea in which they had lived the longest eight hours of their lives. But now at last they were surely safe; no longer would their leaping hearts expect each moment the lift of the deck, the crash of sound that meant death. Swim —for their lives.

They swam; but angry shouts followed them. There were those on the *Viribus Unitis* who disbelieved, and calmer minds quelled the panic. They were not a hundred yards away when a boatload of menacing seamen overtook them, and forced them *back to the Viribus Unitis again!*

On deck a threatening mob, some half-naked, some still dripping water, pressed close shouting and gesticulating. Some accused the Italians of deceiving them; others wanted to know where the bombs were. Paolucci edged aft and Rossetti followed him; moved aft again as the crowd surged about them, hemmed them in, aft, always aft, away from the bow. It was 6:27 A.M.

A shout arose from the mob:

"Take them to the hold! Lock them up!"

Angry hands tore off the rubber suits, searched the two prisoners. "To the hold!"

6:28 A.M.

The two doomed men backed against a bulkhead; Rossetti found a piece of chocolate and munched it. But he could almost hear the minutes tick and the thought of the hold drove terror into his brain. He appealed to the captain: they were prisoners of war and had done nothing not in accord with the rules of war. They had the right to proper treatment, etc., etc. . . . anything for time. The captain, his calm face grave, agreed, and ordered his men away. It was 6:30. . . .

The seconds ticked on, almost the two men counted them, waiting, waiting.

6:31 . . . 6:32. Rossetti looked at Paolucci with half-concealed dread. The minutes wheeled. . . . 6:33 . . . 6:35 . . . 6:40.

The crew, still sullen, milled and muttered; the two Italians slouched weakly against a stanchion. To have died so many deaths for nothing! Their thoughts swam feebly . . . something wrong with the mine . . . two years of work in vain . . . tired, so tired.

They stood there in their near-nakedness, and it was suddenly 6:44 . . . and the thing was done.

It was a "dull noise, a deep roaring, not loud or terrible, but rather light." But a great column of foaming water thundered from the wounded bow high toward the brightening sky, roared skyward and splashed down over the stricken decks. The *Viribus Unitis,* pride of the Austrian fleet, trembled. The sullen Slavs ran for the boats, dived into the sea. Some stayed long enough to shake their fists in the lined faces of two Italians who had created death. . . . The thing was done, successful after all . . . the dream.

The Italians shook hands with Captain Vukovic, slid down a rope into the sea, and swam away from the stricken ship. The captain hailed a boat and ordered them taken aboard. The glowering sailors wanted to leave them there to die, but one of Italian descent pulled them in bodily, weak and spent. And there in that small boat floating on the placid waters of Pola Harbor they saw the *Viribus Unitis* go down.

Slowly she settled; her list increased and she heeled more and more, the water racing over her decks, her great turret guns pointing toward the depths. Suddenly she turned over, with a slapping splash, and the green slime of her keel rose above the white water. Then Paolucci saw a man crawling on the slippery bottom; suddenly the black figure rose and stretched to his full height. It was Captain Vukovic, with his ship to the last.

The *Viribus Unitis* took a sudden plunge; screams died in the sea; there was a cascading whirlpool and a cloud of smoke and steam and jumbled wreckage where Captain Vukovic and the pride of the Austrian Navy had been. A sailor in the boat sobbed:

"My ship! My beautiful ship!"

The two Italians were taken to the hospital ship *Habsburg,* half-frozen and so exhausted that Paolucci almost fainted when a sailor struck him. But they staggered aboard, heads held high, like those Romans who once saluted Caesar only to die. It was then that they learned that their second mine had drifted in the fairway down the line of anchored ships, to explode against the thin steel sides of the auxiliary cruiser *Wien* and sink her. Their great adventure was doubly successful.

NOTES The work of the Italian motor-torpedo boats and light craft during World War I was both spectacular and effective. It was the kind of work—the quick and daring thrust, the alternatives, sudden death or great glory—for which the Italian temperament and psychology is ideally suited, and the Italian nation could find recompense in its glories at sea for the disasters on land. Against an alert and vigorous opponent such repeated and spectacular successes would probably not have been possible. The MAS boat of that day—forty feet or so in length, ten or twelve tons in displacement, twenty or thirty knots on gasoline motors; four or five knots on *silent* electric auxiliary motors; a considerable range, and an armament of two 18-inch torpedoes in brackets and several machine guns—was the ancestor of the motor-torpedo boats of today. That these little gnats of the sea are not new is shown by the fact that Italy built some four hundred of this type before the end of World War I.

The entry into Pola Harbor had been attempted many times before the gallant and dramatic venture of Rossetti and Paolucci. The Italians made fourteen raids into Austrian harbors during the course of the war. On May 13, 1918, the naval "tank" *Grillo* (Cricket)—strangest craft of its kind—climbed over three of the (then) four boom obstructions guarding Pola by means of moving spike-equipped steel chains, led around its bottom and actuated by an electric motor. It stuck on the fourth obstruction and was destroyed by its crew to prevent capture. On June 10, 1918, Luigi Rizzo, who had already distinguished himself in December, 1917, by forcing the booms of Trieste in a MAS boat and sinking an Austrian battleship, added to his laurels by torpedoing and sinking the Austrian battleship *Szent Istvan* some six and a half miles off Lutostrak in the Adriatic Sea. Motion pictures of the sinking ship were taken from an accompanying destroyer, and were recovered after the war in Vienna, thus providing the world with a most spectacular film.

The very night that Rossetti and Paolucci commenced one of the greatest adventures of all time, the crews of the Austrian dreadnoughts in Pola Harbor had mutinied. The mutiny—on the whole rather a peaceful affair—was but the culminating event of the dissolution of the Austro-Hungarian Empire and the beginning of the end of the war. The revolt had long been brewing, and that night most of the German and German-Austrian officers were expelled from the ships and the Yugoslav crews took charge. Although this does not detract from the credit due the two intrepid Italians, it does explain why some of the battleships were so brightly lighted and it also explains the laxness of the harbor patrol and boom defense guard.

Rossetti and Paolucci were not prisoners for long. The Austrian truce was signed November 4, 1918, and a day later units of the Italian fleet entered Pola. At once they were national heroes. They were presented with gold medals for valor, and in addition Rossetti received a gift of 650,000 lire from the Italian government. But he could not forget Captain Vukovic, the man he had killed. He had been deeply affected by his gallant conduct and resolved to return to Pola to seek his grave. On his arrival he learned that the body had never been recovered; and he thereupon quietly presented his 650,000 lire to the widow of the gallant officer—"a war adversary who, dying, left me an ineradicable example of generous humanity"—and to the widows and mothers of other war veterans.

ACKNOWLEDGMENTS   The principal sources for this chapter are the accounts of the two principals. Raffaele Paolucci's "The Fate of the *Viribus Unitis*" was published in *The Fortnightly Review* (New York), Vol. 105, 1919, pages 977–988, and has since been quoted and reprinted. Rossetti's story, "The Sinking of the *Viribus Unitis*" forms a chapter in an exciting book of true Adventures by Evan J. David: *Great Moments of Adventure,* Duffield and Co., 1930. These accounts furnished basic material and quotes. I also consulted *Their Secret Purposes,* by Hector Bywater; *Gallant Gentlemen,* by E. Keble Chatterton; "Italian Sea Power and the Great War," by Warren Whitney (a lecture); "The Work of the Italian Navy in the Adriatic during the War," by Charles D. Villarey, *Journal of the Royal United Service Institution,* 1919, Vol. 64, pages 175–197; *Italy and the World War,* by Thomas Nelson Page; and *The Italian Navy in the World War— 1915–1918,* compiled by the Italian Ministry of Marine, Rome. The references are listed in their approximate order of importance to this chapter.

1944

The *Shō* Plan–
The Battle for Leyte Gulf

In October, 1944, the greatest sea fight in history—perhaps the world's last great fleet action—broke the naval power of Japan and spelled the beginning of the end of the war in the Pacific. The Battle for Leyte Gulf, fought off the Philippine Archipelago, sprawled across an area of almost 500,000 square miles, about twice the size of Texas. Unlike most of the actions of World War II, it included every element of naval power from submarines to planes. It was as decisive as Salamis. It dwarfed the Battle of Jutland in distances, tonnages, casualties. But, unlike Jutland, there was no dispute about the outcome. After Leyte Gulf, the Japanese Fleet was finished. Yet it was a battle of controversy. . . .

The Empire was dying, and there were some who faced the fact. The long retreat was over, the great spaces of the Pacific had been bridged by the countless ships of the American "barbarians," and the enemy was knocking upon the inner strongholds of the Samurai. For Japan it was now the desperate gamble, the all-out stroke—to conquer or to die.

And so, the *Shō* ("To Conquer") plans were drawn; if the inner citadel—the Philippines, Formosa, the Ryukyus, the main islands— were penetrated by the U. S. Fleet all the remaining Japanese naval power that could steam or fly would be mobilized for a desperate assault.

In October, 1944, when U.S. troops in Europe were smashing into German Aachen street by street and the opposing armies faced a bitter winter of grudging gains, the time for *Shō* I—the defense of the Philippines—had almost come. Tarawa, with its bloody reef, was proud history; so, too, were the Gilberts, the Marshalls, the Marianas, New Guinea, Biak, Palau, and Morotai; B-29's were converging on the new fields in Guam, Saipan, and Tinian to bomb Japan; U.S. submarines were preying upon the enemy's commerce, the U.S. flag flew above palm-fringed islands once remote strongholds of the Emperor's power.

From August 31 to September 24 the fast carriers supported by the battleships of Admiral William F. Halsey's Third Fleet had raked over Japanese bases from Mindanao to Luzon, and on the twenty-first, while Radio Manila was playing "Music for your Morning Moods," naval pilots combed Manila Bay. The bag throughout the islands was large, the enemy opposition was surprisingly feeble, and Admiral Halsey reported to Admiral Chester W. Nimitz, commander-in-chief, Pacific:

". . . no damage to our surface forces and nothing on the screen but Hedy Lamar."

The weak Japanese reaction led to a change in American strategy.[A] The planned capture of Yap and step-by-step moves to Mindanao in the southern Philippines and then northward were eliminated; the amphibious assault upon the island of Leyte in the central Philippines was advanced by two months to October 20, 1944. . . .

It started, according to plan. A great armada of more than 700 U.S. ships steamed into Leyte Gulf at dawn on the twentieth; a lone Jap plane braved the skies. Initial Japanese opposition was weak; the vast American armada—the greatest of the Pacific war, with some 151 LST's, 58 transports, 221 LCT's, 79 LCI's, and hundreds of other vessels, may have overawed the defenders. By the end of A plus 2— October 21—103,000 American troops had been landed on Leyte with few casualties, and only three warships had been damaged.

Four hours after the first landing on Leyte, General Douglas MacArthur waded ashore; later Colonel Carlos Romulo, the little Filipino, who was with him, was to quip:

"There was the tall MacArthur, with the waters reaching up to his knees, and behind him there was little Romulo, trying to keep his head above water."

In front of a Signal Corps microphone on the beach just won and beneath rain-dripping skies MacArthur recalled the bloody epic of Bataan:

"This is the Voice of Freedom, General MacArthur speaking. People of the Philippines: I have returned. . . ."

But the Japs had not been fooled. At 0809, October 17, just nine minutes after U. S. Rangers had made preliminary landings on one of the smaller islands in the mouth of Leyte Gulf, Japanese forces had been alerted to carry out the *Shō* I plan. Admiral Soemu Toyoda, commander-in-chief of the Japanese Combined Fleet and leader of what he knew was a forlorn hope, had his last chance to "destroy the enemy who enjoys the luxury of material resources." From his head-quarters at the Naval War College just outside Tokyo, he sent the word "To Conquer" to his widely scattered units.

The *Shō* plan was daring and desperate—fitted to the last months of an empire strained beyond its capabilities. The Japanese Fleet had not recovered from its cumulative losses, particularly from the heavy blow it had suffered four months earlier in the Battle of the Philippine Sea,[B] when Admiral Raymond W. Spruance, covering our Marianas landings, had destroyed more than 400 Japanese planes, sunk three Japanese carriers, and broken the back of Japanese naval aviation. In mid-October, when Halsey—in a preliminary to the Leyte Gulf landing—struck heavily at Formosa, Toyoda had utilized his land-based planes and had also thrown his hastily trained carrier replace-ment pilots into the fight. The gamble failed. But the "pathology of fear" and the curious propensity of the Japanese for transforming defeats into victories in their official reports magnified the normally highly inflated claims of enemy aviators; Tokyo declared the Third Fleet had "ceased to be an organized striking force."

An enemy plane dropped leaflets over recently captured Peleliu:

FOR RECKLESS YANKEE DOODLE:

Do you know about the naval battle done by the American 58th [sic] Fleet at the sea near Taiwan [Formosa] and Philippine? Japanese

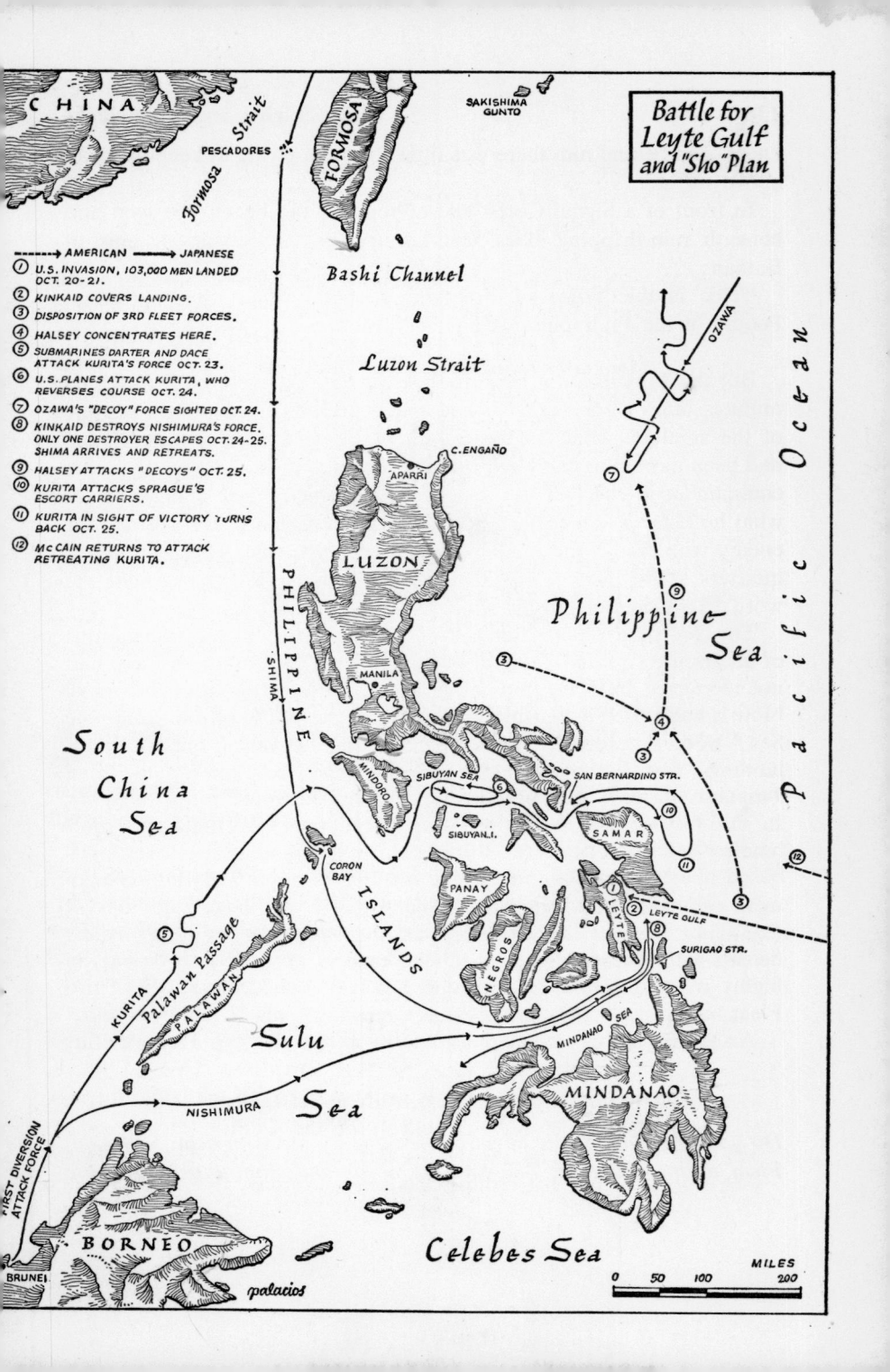

powerful Air Force had sunk their 19 aeroplane carriers, 4 battleships,
10 several cruisers and destroyers, along with sending 1,261 ship
aeroplanes into the sea. . . .

Actually only two cruisers—*Canberra* and *Houston*—were damaged; less than 100 U.S. planes lost; the Japanese were to have a rude awakening as the great invasion[1] armada neared Leyte Gulf.

But for Toyoda, the Battle of the Philippine Sea and his futile gamble in defense of Formosa had left the Japanese Fleet naked to air attack. Toyoda had carriers,[c] but with few planes and half-trained pilots. *Shō* I, therefore, must be dependent upon stealth and cunning, night operations, and what air cover could be provided chiefly by land-based planes operating from Philippine bases and working in close conjunction with the fleet.

Toyoda also confronted another handicap—a fleet widely separated by distance. He exercised command—from his land headquarters—over a theoretically "Combined Fleet," but Vice-Admiral Jisaburo Ozawa, who flew his flag from carrier *Zuikaku,* and who commanded the crippled carriers and some cruisers and destroyers, was still based in the Inland Sea in Japanese home waters. The bulk of the fleet's heavy units—Vice-Admiral Takeo Kurita's First Diversion Attack Force, of battleships, cruisers, and destroyers—was based on Lingga Anchorage near Singapore, close to its fuel sources. The Japanese Fleet was divided in the face of a superior naval force; it could not be concentrated prior to battle.

These deficiencies, plus the geography of the Philippines, dictated the enemy plan, which was hastily modified at the last minute, partially because of the Japanese weaknesses in carrier aviation. Two principal straits—San Bernardino, north of the island of Samar; and Surigao, between Mindanao and Dinagat and Leyte and Panaon—lead from the South China Sea to Leyte Gulf, where the great armada of MacArthur was committed to the invasion. The Japanese ships based near Singapore—the so-called First Diversion Attack Force—were to steam north toward Leyte, with a stop at Brunei Bay, Borneo, to refuel. There the force would split; the Central Group, Vice-Admiral Takeo Kurita, flying his flag in the heavy cruiser *Atago,* with a total of five battleships, ten heavy cruisers, two light cruisers,

and fifteen destroyers, would transit San Bernardino Strait at night;
the Southern Group, Vice-Admiral Shōji Nishimura,[2] with two battleships, one heavy cruiser, and four destroyers, was to be augmented
at Surigao Strait by an ancillary force of three more cruisers and four
destroyers under Vice-Admiral Kiyohide Shima, which was to steam
through Formosa Strait, with a stop in the Pescadores, all the way
from its bases in the home islands. All these forces were to strike the
great American armada in Leyte Gulf almost simultaneously at dawn
of the 25th of October and wreak havoc among the thin-skinned amphibious ships like a hawk among chickens.

But the key to the operation was the emasculated Japanese carriers,
operating under Vice-Admiral Jisaburo Ozawa from their bases in
Japan's Inland Sea. These ships—one heavy carrier and three light
carriers, with less than 100 planes aboard—"all that remained of the
enemy's once-great carrier forces"—were to steam south toward Luzon
and to act as deliberate decoys or "lures" for Admiral Halsey's great
Third Fleet, which was "covering" the amphibious invasion of Leyte.
The northern decoy force was to be accompanied by two hermaphro-
dites—battleship-carriers, the *Ise* and *Hyuga,* with the after-turrets
replaced by short flight decks, but with no planes, and by three cruisers
and ten destroyers. Ozawa was to lure Halsey's Third Fleet to the
north, away from Leyte, and open the way for Kurita and Nishimura
to break into Leyte Gulf.

At the same time all three forces were to be aided—not with direct
air cover, but by intensive attacks by Japanese land-based planes upon
American carriers and shipping. As a last-minute "spur-of-the-
moment" decision, the Japanese "Special Attack Groups" were acti-
vated, and the Kamikaze (Divine Wind) fliers commenced their suicidal attacks upon U.S. ships. As early as October 15, Rear Admiral
Masabumi Arima, a subordinate naval air commander, flying from
a Philippine field, had made a suicide dive and had "lit the fuse of
the ardent wishes of his men."[D] All of these far-flung forces were
under the common command of Admiral Toyoda far away in Tokyo.

Such was the desperate *Shō* I—perhaps the greatest gamble, the
most daring and unorthodox plan in the history of naval war.

It committed to action virtually all that was left of the operational
forces—afloat and in the air—of Japan's Navy—four carriers, two

battleship-carriers, seven battleships, nineteen cruisers, thirty-three destroyers, and perhaps 500 to 700 Japanese aircraft—mostly land-based.

But the opposing American forces were far more powerful. Like the Japanese forces which had no common commander closer than Tokyo, the U. S. Fleet operated under divided command. General MacArthur, as theater commander of the Southwest Pacific area, was in over-all charge of the Leyte invasion, and through Admiral Thomas C. Kinkaid, he commanded the Seventh Fleet, which was in direct charge of the amphibious operation. But Admiral Halsey's powerful covering force of the Third Fleet—the strongest fleet in the world— was not under MacArthur's command; it was a part of Admiral Chester W. Nimitz's Pacific Command forces, and Nimitz had his headquarters in Hawaii. And above Nimitz and MacArthur, the only unified command was in Washington.

The gun power of Kinkaid's Seventh Fleet was provided by six old battleships—five of them raised from the mud of Pearl Harbor, but he had sixteen escort carriers[3]—small, slow-speed vessels, converted from merchant hulls—eight cruisers and scores of destroyers and destroyer escorts, frigates, motor torpedo boats, and other types. Kinkaid's job was to provide shore bombardment and close air support for the Army and anti-submarine and air defense for the amphibious forces.

Halsey, with eight large attack carriers, eight light carriers, six fast new battleships, fifteen cruisers, and fifty-eight destroyers, was ordered to "cover and support forces of the Southwest Pacific [MacArthur's command] in order to assist in the seizure and occupation of objectives in the Central Philippines."[E] He was to destroy enemy naval and air forces threatening the invasion. He was to remain responsible to Admiral Nimitz, but "necessary measures for detailed coordination of operations between the . . . [Third Fleet] . . . and . . . the [Seventh Fleet] will be arranged by their . . . commanders."[F]

The combined Third and Seventh Fleets could muster 1,000 to 1,400 ship-based aircraft—thirty-two carriers; twelve battleships; twenty-three cruisers; more than one hundred destroyers and destroyer escorts and numerous smaller types and hundreds of auxiliaries. The Seventh Fleet also had a few tender-based PBY patrol planes (flying boats).[a] But not all of these forces participated in the far-flung air attacks and the three widely separated major engagements which later came to be called the Battle for Leyte Gulf.

Such was the stage, these the actors, and this the plot in the most dramatic and far-flung naval battle in history.

It opened with first blood for the submarines. At dawn on October 23 the U.S. submarines *Darter* and *Dace,* patrolling Palawan Passage, intercepted Admiral Kurita, bound for his rendezvous with destiny. The *Darter* put five torpedoes into Kurita's flagship, heavy cruiser *Atago,* at 1,000 yards range; damaged the cruiser *Takao.* *Dace*[4] hit the cruiser *Maya* with four torpedoes. The *Atago* sank in nineteen minutes as Kurita shifted his flag to the destroyer *Kishinani* and later to the battleship *Yamato.* The *Maya* blew up and sank in four minutes; *Takao*—burning and low in the water—was sent back to Brunei, escorted by two destroyers. Kurita steams on, shaken but implacable, toward San Bernardino Strait.

October 24 Aboard battleship *New Jersey,* flying "Bull" Halsey's flag, the plans are ready for this day as the sun quickly burns away the morning haze. In the carriers, bowing to the swell, the bull horns sound on the flight decks—"Pilots, man your planes."

At 6 A.M. the Third Fleet launches search planes to sweep a wide arc of sea covering the approaches to San Bernardino and Surigao straits. Submarine reports from *Darter, Dace,* and *Guitarro* have alerted the Americans—but not in time to halt the detachment of Third Fleet's largest task group—Task Group 38.1 commanded by Vice-Admiral John S. ("Slew") McCain with orders to retire to Ulithi for rest and supplies. The fleet's three other task groups are spread out over 300 miles of ocean to the east of the Philippines from central Luzon to southern Samar; one of them—to the north—has been tracked doggedly all night by enemy "snoopers." As the planes take off to search the reef-studded waters of the Sibuyan and Sulu seas and the approaches to San Bernardino and Surigao, Kinkaid's old battleships and little carriers off Leyte are supporting the "G.I.'s" ashore.

At 0746, Lieutenant (j.g.) Max Adams, flying a Helldiver above the magnificent volcanic crags, the palm-grown islands, and startling blue sea of the archipelago, reports a radar contact, and a few minutes later Admiral Kurita's First Diversion Attack Force lies spread out like toy ships upon a painted sea—the pagoda masts unmistakable in the sunlight.

The tension of action grips flag plot in the *New Jersey* as the contact report comes in; the radio crackles "Urgent" and "Top Secret" messages—to Washington, to Nimitz, to Kinkaid, to all task-group commanders. McCain, 600 miles to the eastward, enroute to Ulithi and rest, is recalled and Third Fleet is ordered to concentrate off San Bernardino to launch strikes against the enemy.

But at 8:20 far to the south, the southern arm of the Japanese pincer is sighted for the first time; Vice-Admiral Nishimura—with battleships *Fuso* and *Yamashiro,* heavy cruiser *Mogami,* and four destroyers—steaming toward Surigao. *Enterprise* search-attack planes attack[5] through heavy AA fire; *Fuso's* catapult is hit, her planes destroyed, and a fire rages; a gun mount in destroyer *Shiguro* is knocked out—but Nishimura steams on to the east, his speed undiminished. And Halsey continues the concentration of his fleet near San Bernardino to strike the Japanese Central Force.

There has been no morning search to the north and northeast, and Ozawa's decoy carriers, steaming southward toward Luzon, are still undiscovered.

The *Shō* plan now moves toward its dramatic denouement. Japanese planes flying from Philippine bases commence the most furious assault since the landing upon the Seventh and Third Fleets. To the north off Luzon, carriers *Langley, Princeton, Essex,* and *Lexington* face the brunt of the winged fury. Seven Hellcats from the *Essex,* led by Commander David McCampbell, intercept sixty Japanese planes—half of them Zeke fighters—and after a melee of an hour and thirty-five minutes of combat the Americans knock down twenty-four Japs with no losses. *Princeton* claims thirty-four enemy from another large raid; the *Lexington's* and *Langley's* "fly-boys" are also busy; over the air come the exultant "Tally-hos," and "Splash one Betty—Splash two Zekes" of the pilots.

But the Japs draw blood. At about 0938, as Third Fleet starts converging toward San Bernardino and the carriers prepare to launch deckloads to strike the enemy's center force, a Jap Judy dives unseen and unrecorded on the radar screen out of a low cloud. She drops a 550-pound bomb square on *Princeton's* flight deck; the bomb penetrates to the hangar deck, ignites gasoline in six torpedo planes, starts raging fires. The fight to save her starts, but at 1002 a series of terrific explosions split open the flight deck like the rind of a dropped melon, throw the after plane elevator high into the air, and by 1020 *Princeton's* fire mains have failed and she is dead in the water, with a 1,000-foot pall of smoke above her and hundreds of her crew in the water. The task group steams on southward to the San Bernardino rendezvous, while cruisers *Birmingham* and *Reno* and destroyers *Gatling, Irwin,* and *Cassin Young* hover about wounded *Princeton* in a day-long fight to save her.

But as *Princeton* flames and staggers, Kurita's Central Force of five battleships, accompanied by cruisers and destroyers, is running the gantlet. Carrier strikes start coming in against Japan's First Diversion Attack Force about 10.25 A.M., and the exultant U.S. pilots concentrate against targets none of them had ever seen before—the largest battleships in the world. *Yamato* and *Musashi,* long the mysterious focus of intelligence reports, lie beneath the wings of naval air power —their 69,500-ton bulk, 18-inch guns, 27.5-knot speed—dwarfing their sisters. *Musashi* is wounded early; oil smears trail on the blue water from her lacerated flank as a torpedo strikes home. But she is strong; her speed is undiminished. Not so *Myoko's.* This heavy cruiser is badly hurt in the first attack; she drops to fifteen knots and is left astern to limp alone into port; Kurita has lost four out of the ten heavy cruisers that sortied so gallantly from Brunei.

But he has no respite. At three minutes past noon another strike comes out of the sun. The Jap AA fire blossoms in pink and purple bursts; even the battleships' main batteries are firing. Several American planes are hit; one goes down flaming—but *Musashi* takes two bombs and two torpedoes; she loses speed and drops back slowly out of formation.

An hour and a half later *Yamato* takes two hits forward of her Number 1 turret, which start a fire—but her thick hide minimizes damages; the fire is extinguished. But *Musashi* is now sore-wounded; she takes four bomb hits in this attack and three more torpedoes; her upper works are a shambles, her bow almost under water, her speed down first to sixteen and then to twelve knots.

But Kurita's slow agony drags on during this long and sunlit day. He hopes in vain for air cover. *Yamato* is hit again in the fourth attack and the older battleship *Nagato* damaged.

At six bells in the afternoon watch (3 P.M.) Kurita orders the limping *Musashi* to withdraw from the fight. But not in time.

The final and largest attack of the day seeks her out as she turns heavily to find sanctuary. In fifteen minutes *Musashi* receives the *coup de grâce*—ten more bombs, four more torpedoes; she's down to six knots now, her bow is under water, and she lists steeply to port—a dying gladiator.

Kurita is shaken. He has had no air cover; he has been subjected to intense attack; his original strength of five battleships, twelve cruisers, and fifteen destroyers has been reduced to four battleships, eight cruisers, and eleven destroyers; all of his remaining battleships have been damaged; fleet speed is limited to twenty-two knots. There is no sign that Ozawa's northern decoy force is succeeding in luring the Third Fleet away from San Bernardino. At 1530 Kurita reverses course and steams away toward the West. And American pilots report the "retreat" to Admiral Halsey aboard *New Jersey*. . . .

To Admiral Halsey there is "one piece missing in the puzzle—the [Japanese] carriers."

The northern task group of Third Fleet has been under attack by enemy carrier-type planes, which might have been land-based—but none of the sightings has reported enemy carriers. Where are they?

At 1405 (2:05 P.M.), as Kurita's central force is pounded in the Sibuyan Sea, *Lexington's* planes take off to find out.[6] They are under orders to search to the north and northeast in the open seas untouched by the morning search.

The search planes fly through a cloud-speckled sky and intermittent rain squalls, leaving behind them a task group harassed by fierce, though intermittent Jap air attacks.

The flaming *Princeton,* billowing clouds of fire and smoke, is still afloat, with her covey of rescue ships around her. Despite intermittent explosions and singeing heat, cruisers *Birmingham* and *Reno,*

destroyers *Morrison, Irwin,* and *Cassin Young* have clustered alongside, pouring water from their pumps on the blazing carrier. Submarine contacts and enemy air attacks interrupt the fire fighting; the
rescue ships pull off. At 1523 (3:23 P.M.), about the time Kurita,
300 miles away, reverses course and heads to the westward in the
Sibuyan Sea, cruiser *Birmingham* comes alongside *Princeton's* blazing
port side again. The cruiser's open decks are thick with men—fire
fighters, line handlers, antiaircraft gunners, medical personnel, fire
and rescue squads, watch-standers. There is fifty feet of open water
between blazing *Princeton* and her salvor, *Birmingham;* a spring line
is out forward between carrier and cruiser.

Suddenly a "tremendous blast" rips off *Princeton's* stern and flight
deck; steel plates as big "as a house" fly through the air; jagged bits
of steel, broken gun barrels, shrapnel, helmets, debris rake *Birmingham's* bridge, upper works, and crowded decks like grapeshot; in a
fraction of a second the cruiser is a charnel house, her decks literally
flowing blood—229 dead, 420 mangled and wounded—the ship's
superstructure sieved.

Aboard *Princeton* all the skeleton fire-fighting crew are wounded.
Captain John M. Hoskins, who had been scheduled to take command
of *Princeton* shortly and had remained aboard with the skipper he
was relieving, puts a rope tourniquet around his leg, as his right foot
hangs by a shred of flesh and tendon. The surviving medical officer
cuts off the foot with a sheath knife, dusts the wound with sulfa
powder, injects morphine. . . . Hoskins lives to become the Navy's
first "peg-leg" admiral of modern times.

But still *Princeton* floats on even keel, flaming like a volcano,
manned by a crew of bloody specters. . . .

At 1640 the search to the north pays off. U.S. planes sight Ozawa's
decoy force of carriers. The contact reports electrify Third Fleet, but
mislead it, too; Ozawa's northern group of ships, which were sighted
about 130 miles east of the northern tip of Luzon, includes two hermaphrodite battleships but our fliers mistakenly report four.[7] Nor do
our fliers know Ozawa's carriers are virtually without planes.

The contact reports decide *Princeton's* fate; her weary crew of
fire fighters are removed, the day-long struggle is ended, and at
4:49 *Reno* puts two torpedoes into the flaming hulk and the carrier

blows up, breaks in two, and sinks. Mangled *Birmingham,* which lost far more men than the ship she was trying to save, steams with her dead and dying to Ulithi—out of the fight. . . .

Two hours later, near Sibuyan Island, the giant *Musashi,* pride of Kurita's Central Force, loses her long fight. Fatally wounded, she settles slowly deeper and deeper in the calm sea, and as the evening closes down, the greatest battleship in the world capsizes and takes with her to the depths half of her crew. But no American sees her passing. . . . And no American has seen Kurita, earlier in the afternoon, alter his course once more and at 1714 head once again with his battered but still powerful Central Force back toward San Bernardino Strait. . . .

At 1950, with the tropic dusk, "Bull" Halsey makes his decision and informs Kinkaid, commanding Seventh Fleet:

"Central force heavily damaged according to strike reports. Am proceeding north with three groups to attack carrier force at dawn."[8]

Third Fleet concentrates and steams hard to the north in what irreverent historians of the future are to call "Bull's Run." Night snoopers from *Independence* shadow the Jap northern force, and orders go to the carriers to launch planes at sunrise.[H] San Bernardino Strait is left uncovered—not even a submarine[I] patrols its waters; Kinkaid and Seventh Fleet, protecting the Leyte invasion, believe it is barred by Halsey; Halsey, banking too heavily on exaggerated claims from his pilots,[J] thinks Kurita's central force has been stopped by the day's air attacks and the battered Jap survivors can be left safely to Kinkaid. On such misunderstandings rest the course of history and the fate of nations.[K]

Surigao Strait is dark under the loom of the land. Since the morning there have been no sightings of the Japanese southern force; even its exact composition is not known. But Kinkaid and the Seventh Fleet have no doubts; the Japs will try to break through this night. Kinkaid and Rear Admiral Jesse B. Oldendorf, his "O.T.C." (officer in tactical command) have made dispositions for a night surface battle. They have provided a suitable reception committee, including PT boats deep in the strait and covering its southern approaches, three destroyer

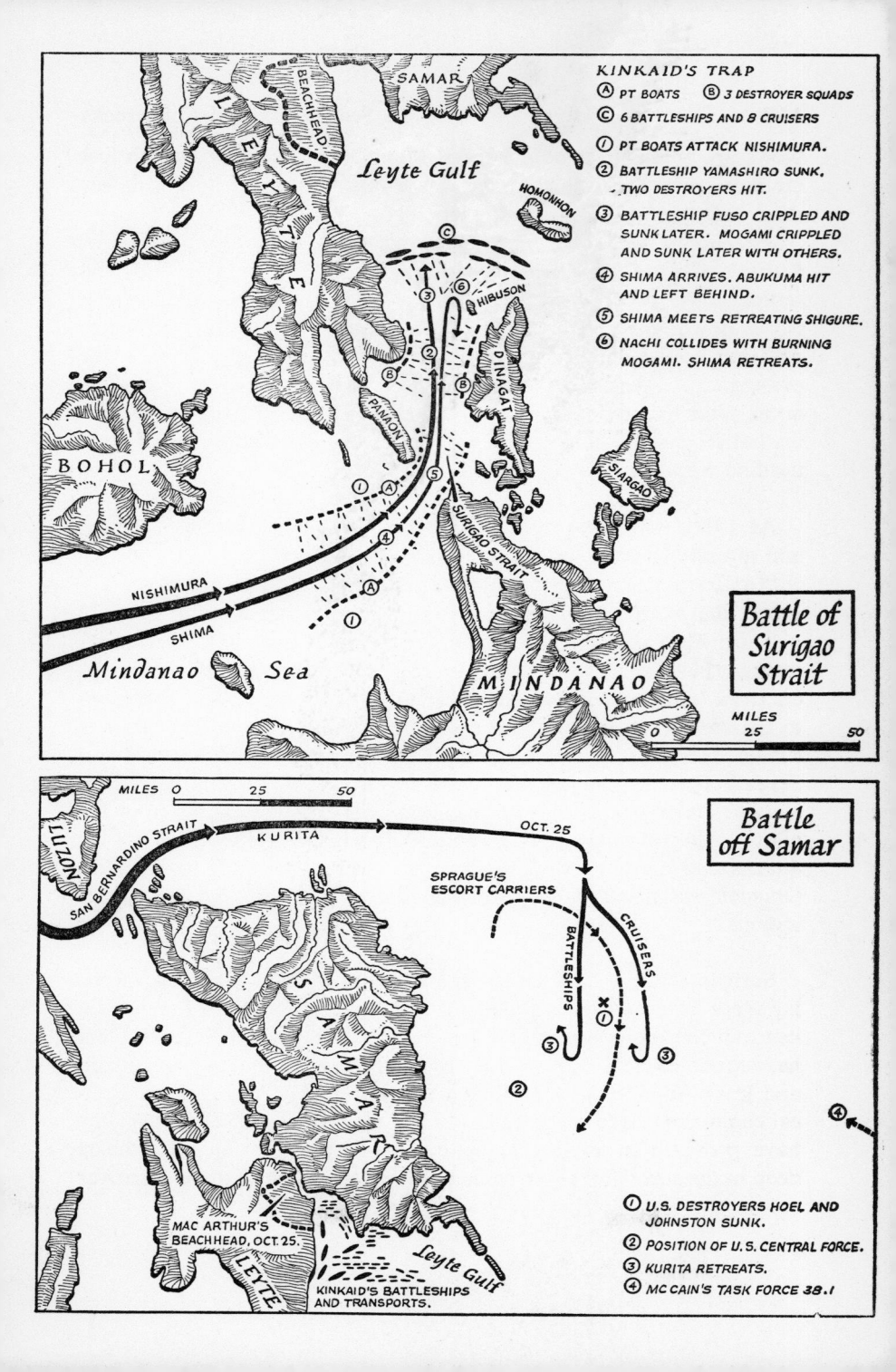

KINKAID'S TRAP

Ⓐ PT BOATS   Ⓑ 3 DESTROYER SQUADS
Ⓒ 6 BATTLESHIPS AND 8 CRUISERS

① PT BOATS ATTACK NISHIMURA.
② BATTLESHIP YAMASHIRO SUNK.
   TWO DESTROYERS HIT.
③ BATTLESHIP FUSO CRIPPLED AND
   SUNK LATER. MOGAMI CRIPPLED
   AND SUNK LATER WITH OTHERS.
④ SHIMA ARRIVES. ABUKUMA HIT
   AND LEFT BEHIND.
⑤ SHIMA MEETS RETREATING SHIGURE.
⑥ NACHI COLLIDES WITH BURNING
   MOGAMI. SHIMA RETREATS.

SAMAR

Leyte Gulf

HOMONHON

LEYTE

BEACHHEAD

BOHOL

PANAON

HIBUSON

DINAGAT

SIARGAO

SURIGAO STRAIT

NISHIMURA

SHIMA

Mindanao   Sea

MINDANAO

Battle of
Surigao
Strait

MILES
0   25   50

MILES 0   25   50

Battle
off Samar

LUZON

SAN BERNARDINO STRAIT

KURITA

OCT. 25

SPRAGUE'S
ESCORT CARRIERS

BATTLESHIPS

CRUISERS

S A M A R

① ③

② ④

MAC ARTHUR'S
BEACHHEAD, OCT. 25.

Leyte Gulf

LEYTE

KINKAID'S BATTLESHIPS
AND TRANSPORTS.

① U.S. DESTROYERS HOEL AND
   JOHNSTON SUNK.
② POSITION OF U.S. CENTRAL FORCE.
③ KURITA RETREATS.
④ MC CAIN'S TASK FORCE 38.1

squadrons near the center, and at the mouth—where the strait debouches into Leyte Gulf—six old battleships and eight cruisers.[9]

Into this trap the Japanese southern force blunders in two divisions —each independent of the other. Nishimura, with battleships *Fuso* and *Yamashiro,* cruiser *Mogami,* and four destroyers, lead the way. Cruising twenty miles behind Nishimura is Vice-Admiral Shima with three cruisers and four destroyers from Jap home bases. The two Jap forces attack piecemeal and uncoordinated; neither knows much of the other's plans. Shima and Nishimura were classmates at the Japanese Naval Academy; their careers have bred rivalry; Nishimura, formerly the senior, has been passed in the processes of promotion by Shima, who commands the smaller force but is now six months senior in rank to Nishimura. But Nishimura, a sea-going admiral, has seen more war. Neither seems anxious to serve with the other; there is no common command.

Radars on the PT boats pick up the enemy about 11 P.M. as "sheet lightning dim[s] the hazy blur of the setting moon and thunder echoe[s] from the islands' hills."

Thirty-nine PT boats, motors muffled, head for Nishimura and attack in successive "waves" as the enemy advances. But the Japs score first. Enemy destroyers illuminate the little boats with their searchlights long before the PT's reach good torpedo range; a hit starts a fire in *PT 152;* a near miss with its spout of water extinguishes it; *PT 130* and *PT 132* are also hit.[10] But Nishimura is identified; course, speed, and formation are radioed to Kinkaid's fleet and the harassing PT attacks continue.

Aboard destroyer *Remey,* flag of Destroyer Squadron 54, Commander R. P. Fiala, turns on the loud-speaker to talk to the crew:

"This is the captain speaking. Tonight our ship has been designated to make the first torpedo run on the Jap task force that is on its way to stop our landings in Leyte Gulf. It is our job to stop the Japs. May God be with us tonight."

The destroyers attack along both flanks of the narrow strait; their silhouettes merge with the land; the Japs, in the middle, can scarcely distinguish dark shape of ship from dark loom of land; the radar fuzzes and the luminescent pips on the screen are lost in a vague blur.

It is deep in the mid-watch—0301 of the twenty-fifth—when the first destroyer-launched torpedoes streak across the strait. In less than half an hour Nishimura is crippled. His slow and lumbering flagship, the battleship *Yamashiro,* is hit; destroyer *Yamagumo* is sunk; two other destroyers are out of control. Nishimura issues his last command:

"We have received a torpedo attack. You are to proceed and attack all ships."

Battleship *Fuso,* cruiser *Mogami,* destroyer *Shigure* steam on toward Leyte Gulf.

But before 4 A.M. a tremendous eruption of flames and pyrotechnics marks *Yamashiro's* passing; another American torpedo has found her magazine, and the battleship breaks in two and sinks, with Nishimura's flag still flying.

Fuso does not long outlive her sister. Up from the mud of Pearl Harbor, the avengers wait—six old battleships patrol back and forth across the mouth of the strait. This is an admiral's dream. Like Togo at Tsushima and Jellicoe at Jutland, Kinkaid and Oldendorf have capped the T; the remaining Jap ships are blundering head on in single column against a column of American ships at right angles to the Jap course. The concentrated broadsides of six battleships can be focused against the leading Jap, and only his forward turrets can bear against the Americans.

Climax of battle. As the last and heaviest destroyer attack goes home in answer to the command—"Get the big boys"—the battle line and the cruisers open up; the night is streaked with flare of crimson.

Fuso and *Mogami* flame and shudder as the "rain of shells" strikes home; *Fuso* soon drifts helplessly, racked by great explosions, wreathed in a fiery pall. She dies before the dawn, and *Mogami,* on fire, is finished later with the other cripples. Only destroyer *Shigure* escapes at thirty knots.

Into this mad melee, with the dying remnants of his classmate's fleet around him, steams Vice-Admiral Shima—"fat, dumb, and happy." He knows nothing of what has gone before; he has no cogent plan of battle. *Abukuma,* Shima's only light cruiser, is struck by a PT torpedo[11] even before he is deep in the strait; she is left behind, speed dwindling, as the two heavy cruisers and four destroyers steam onward toward the gun flashes on the horizon. About 4 A.M. Shima encounters destroyer *Shigure,* sole survivor of Nishimura's fleet, retiring down the strait.

Shigure tells *Shima* nothing of the debacle; she simply signals:

"I am the *Shigure;* I have rudder difficulties."

The rest is almost comic anticlimax. Shima pushes deeper into the strait, sees a group of dark shadows; fires torpedoes and manages an amazing collision between his flagship, the *Nachi,* and the burning stricken *Mogami,* which looms up flaming out of the dark waters of the strait like the Empire State Building. And that is all for futile Shima; discretion is the better part of valor; dying for the Emperor is forgotten and Shima reverses course and heads back into the Mindanao Sea and the obscurity of history.

The Battle of Surigao Strait ends with the dawn—debacle for the Japanese. One PT boat destroyed; one destroyer damaged for the Americans. The southern pincer toward Leyte Gulf is broken.[L]

October 25   Dawn of the twenty-fifth of October finds Admiral Ozawa with his decoy force[M] eastward of Cape Engano (fortuitous name: Engano is Spanish for "lure" or "hoax"), prepared to die for the Emperor. At 0712, when the first American planes appear from the southeast, Ozawa knows he has at last succeeded in his luring mission. The day before he has at times despaired; some seventy to eighty of his carrier planes—all he has save for a small combat air patrol—have joined Japanese land-based planes in attacks upon Halsey's northern task group. But his planes have not come back; many have been lost, others have flown on to Philippine bases. This day twenty aircraft—token remnants of Japan's once great flying fleets—are all that Ozawa commands. A few are in the air—to die quickly beneath American guns, as the first heavy attacks from Halsey's carriers come in.

The American carrier pilots have a field day; the air is full of the jabberwock of the fliers.

"Pick one out, boys, and let 'em have it."

The Jap formation throws up a beautiful carpet of antiaircraft fire; the colored bursts and tracers frame the sky-sea battle. The Japanese ships twist and turn, maneuver violently in eccentric patterns to avoid the bombs and torpedoes—but their time has come. Before 8:30, with the day still young, some 150 U.S. carrier planes have wrought havoc. Carrier *Chiyoda* is hit; carrier *Chitose,* billowing clouds of smoke and fatally hurt, is stopped and listing heavily; the light cruiser *Tama,* torpedoed, is limping astern; destroyer *Akitsuki* has blown up; light carrier *Zuiho* is hit, and Ozawa's flagship, the *Zuikaku,* has taken a torpedo aft, which has wrecked the steering engine; she is steered by hand.

A second strike at 10 cripples *Chiyoda,* which dies a slow death, to be finished off later by U.S. surface ships. In early afternoon a third strike sinks carrier *Zuikaku,* the last survivor of the Japanese attack upon Pearl Harbor. She rolls over slowly and sinks, "flying a battle flag of tremendous size." At 1527 carrier *Zuiho* "follows her down." The hermaphrodite battleships, with flight decks aft—*Hyuga* and *Ise,* "fattest of the remaining targets"—are bombed repeatedly, their bulges are perforated, their decks inundated with tons of water from near misses; *Ise's* port catapult is hit—but they bear charmed lives. Admiral Ozawa, his flag transferred to cruiser *Oyodo,* his work of "luring" done, straggles northward with his cripples from the battle off Cape Engano. Throughout the day he is subject to incessant air attack, and in late afternoon and in the dark of the night of the twenty-fifth U.S. cruisers and destroyers, detached from the Third Fleet, finish off the cripples.

The price of success for Admiral Ozawa's decoy force is high; all four carriers, one of his three cruisers, and two of his eight destroyers are gone. But he has accomplished his mission; Halsey has been lured, San Bernardino Strait is unguarded, and the hawk Kurita is down among the chickens.

Off Samar that morning of the twenty-fifth, the sea is calm at sunup, the wind gentle, the sky overcast with spotted cumulus; occasional rain squalls dapple the surface. Aboard the sixteen escort carriers of Seventh Fleet and their escorting "small boys" (destroyers and destroyer escorts) the dawn alert has ended. The early missions have taken off (though not the search planes for the northern sectors). Many of the carriers' planes are already over Leyte, supporting the ground troops—the combat air patrol and ASW patrols are launched, and on the bridge of carrier *Fanshaw Bay,* Rear Admiral C. A. F. Sprague is having a second cup of coffee.

The coming day will be busy; the little escort carriers have support missions to fly for the troops ashore on Leyte, air defense and anti-submarine patrols, and a large strike scheduled to mop up the cripples and fleeing remnants of the Japanese force defeated in the night surface battle of Surigao Strait. The escort-carrier groups are spread out off the east coast of the Philippines from Mindanao to Samar; Sprague's northern group of six escort carriers, three destroyers, and four destroyer escorts is steaming northward at fourteen knots fifty miles off Samar and halfway up the island's coast.

The escort carriers, designated CVE's in naval abbreviation, are tin-clads-unarmored, converted from merchant ship or tanker hulls, slow, carrying eighteen to thirty-six planes. They are known by many uncomplimentary descriptives—"baby flat-tops," "tomato cans," "jeep carriers," and new recruits "coming aboard for the first time were told by the old hands that CVE stood for Combustible, Vulnerable, Expendable!" Their maximum of eighteen knots speed (made all-out) is too slow to give them safety in flight; their thin skins and "pop-guns"—five-inchers and under—do not fit them for surface slugging; they are ships of limited utility—intended for air support of ground operations ashore, anti-submarine and air defense missions —never for fleet action.

Yet they are to fight this morning a battle of jeeps against giants.

Admiral Sprague has scarcely finished his coffee when a contact report comes over the squawk-box. An ASW pilot reports enemy battleships, cruisers, destroyers twenty miles away and closing fast.

". . . check that identification," the admiral says, thinking some green pilot has mistaken Halsey's fast battleships for the enemy.

The answer is sharp and brief, the tension obvious: "Identification confirmed," the pilot's voice comes strained through the static. "Ships have pagoda masts."

Almost simultaneously radiomen hear Japanese chatter over the air; the northern CVE group sees antiaircraft bursts blossoming in the air to the northwest; blips of unidentified ships appear on the radar screens, and before 7 A.M. a signalman with a long glass has picked up the many-storied superstructures and the typical pagoda masts of Japanese ships.

Disbelief, amazement, and consternation struggle for supremacy; the escort carriers, Admiral Kinkaid himself—in fact, most of the Seventh Fleet—had been convinced the Japanese center force was still west of the Philippines[12] and that, in any case, Halsey's fast battleships—now far away to the north with the carriers in the battle for Cape Engano—were guarding San Bernardino Strait. But Kurita has arrived. . . . And about all that stands between him and the transports, supply ships, and amphibious craft in Leyte Gulf and Army headquarters and supply dumps on the beach are the "baby flat-tops" and their accompanying "small boys."

There's no time for planning; within five minutes of visual sighting Japanese heavy stuff—18-inch shells from *Yamato,* sister ship of the foundered *Musashi*—are whistling overhead. Sprague, giving his orders over the voice radio, turns his ships to the east into the wind, steps up speed to maximum, orders all planes scrambled. By 7:05 A.M. escort carrier *White Plains,* launching aircraft as fast as she can get them off, is straddled several times, with red, yellow, green, and blue spouts of water from the dye-marked shells foaming across her bridge, shaking the ship violently, damaging the starboard engine room, smashing electrical circuits, and throwing a fighter plane out of its chocks on the flight deck.

White Plains makes smoke and the Japs shift fire to the *St. Lo,* which takes near misses and casualties from fragments. The "small boys" make smoke—and the carriers, their boiler casings panting from maximum effort—pour out viscous clouds of oily black smoke from their stacks, which veils the sea. . . . There is a moment of surcease; the planes are launched, most of them armed with small-size or anti-personnel or general-purpose bombs or depth charges—no good against armored ships. But there has been no time to rearm. . . .

The air waves sound alarm. Sprague broadcasts danger in plain language; at 0724 Admiral Kinkaid, aboard his flagship *Wasatch* in Leyte Gulf, hears the worst has happened; the Jap fleet is three hours' steaming from the beachhead; the little escort carriers may be wiped out. Just five minutes before, Kinkaid has learned that his assumption that a Third Fleet cork was in the bottle of San Bernardino Strait was incorrect; in answer to a radioed query sent at 0412 Halsey informs him that Task Force 34—modern fast battleships—is with Third Fleet's carriers off Cape Engano far to the north.

Kinkaid in "urgent and priority" messages asks for the fast battleships, for carrier strikes, for immediate action. . . .

Even Admiral Nimitz, in far-off Hawaii, sends a message to Halsey: "All the world wants to know where is Task Force 34[13] [the fast battleships]?"[N]

But in Leyte Gulf and Surigao Strait the tocsin of alarm sounded via the radio waves puts Seventh Fleet—red-eyed[o] from days of shore bombardment and nights of battle—into frenetic action. Some of the old battleships and cruisers are recalled from Surigao Strait, formed into a task unit, and they prepare feverishly to ammunition and refuel. Seventh Fleet's heavy ships are in none too good shape for surface action; their ammunition is dangerously low from five days of shore bombardment, many of their armor-piercing projectiles were used in the night battle; destroyers are low on torpedoes, many ships short of fuel. . . .[P]

And in the battle off Samar, Sprague is fighting for his life.

Within twenty minutes, as the baby carriers steam to the east, launching planes, the range to the enemy has decreased to 25,000 yards—easy shooting for the big guns of the Japs, far beyond the effective reach of the American five-inchers. . . .

Destroyer *Johnston,* Commander Ernest E. Evans, commanding, sees her duty and does it. Without orders she dashes in at thirty knots to launch a spread of ten torpedoes against an enemy cruiser working up along a flank of the pounding carriers. She spouts smoke and fire as she charges—her five-inchers firing continuously as she closes the range. She escapes damage until she turns to retire; then a salvo of three 14-inchers, followed by three six-inch shells, hole her, wound her captain, wreck the steering engine, the after fire room and engine room, knock out her after guns and gyro compass, maim many of her crew, and leave her limping at sixteen knots.

Sprague and his carriers, veiled in part by smoke, find brief sanctuary in a heavy rain squall; the curtain of water saves temporarily wounded *Johnston*. But well before 8 A.M. Kurita has sent some of his faster ships seaward to head off and flank the escort carriers; gradually Sprague turns southward, the enemy coming hard on both his flanks and astern. . . .

"Small boys, launch torpedo attack," Sprague orders over the TBS circuit (talk-between-ships voice radio).

Destroyers *Heermann* and *Hoel* and wounded *Johnston,* her torpedoes already expended but her guns speaking in support, answer the command—three destroyers in a daylight attack against[14] the heaviest ships of the Japanese fleet, three tin-clads against four battleships, eight cruisers, and eleven destroyers.

"Buck," Commander Amos T. Hathaway, skipper of the *Heermann,* remarks coolly to his officer of the deck: "Buck, what we need is a bugler to sound the charge."

Hoel and *Heermann,* followed by limping *Johnston,* sally forth to their naval immortality.

In and out of rain squalls, wreathed in the black and oily smoke from the stacks and the white chemical smoke from the smoke generators on the fantails, the destroyers charge, backing violently to avoid collisions, closing the range. They hear the "express-train" roar of the 14-inchers going over; they fire spreads at a heavy cruiser, rake the superstructure of a battleship with their five-inchers, launch their last torpedoes at 4,400 yards range. Then Hathaway of the *Heermann* walks calmly into his pilothouse, calls Admiral Sprague on the TBS, and reports:

"Exercise completed."

But the destroyers are finished. *Hoel* has lost her port engine; she is steered manually; her decks are a holocaust of blood and wreckage; fire control and power are off; No. 3 gun, wreathed in white-hot steam venting from the burst steam pipes, is inoperable; No. 5 is frozen in train by a near miss; half the barrel of No. 4 is blown off—but Nos. 1 and 2 guns continue to fire.

By 8:30 P.M. power is lost on the starboard engine; all engineering spaces are flooding; the ship slows to dead in the water and, burning furiously, is raked by enemy guns. At 0840, with a twenty-degree list, the order is given to "abandon ship." Fifteen minutes later she rolls on her port side and sinks stern first—holed repeatedly by scores of major-caliber shells.

In *Heermann,* the crimson dye from enemy shell splashes mixes with the blood of men to daub bridge and superstructure reddish hues. A shell strikes a bean locker and spreads a brown paste across the decks. *Heermann* takes hits but, fishtailing and chasing salvos, she manages to live.

Not so, wounded *Johnston*. Spitting fire to the end, and virtually surrounded by the entire Jap fleet, she is overwhelmed under an avalanche of shells, to sink about an hour after *Hoel*.

The four smaller and slower destroyer escorts make the second torpedo attack. *Raymond* and *John C. Butler* live to tell about it; *Dennis* has her guns knocked out, but *Samuel B. Roberts,* deep in the smoke and framed by shell splashes, comes to her end in a mad melee. She is hit by many heavy-caliber projectiles, her speed reduced, and by 9 A.M. a salvo of 14-inch shells rips open her port side like a can opener, wrecks an engine room, starts raging fires. The *Roberts,* abaft her stack, looks like "an inert mass of battered metal"; she has no power; she is dead in the water.

But the crew of No. 2 gun load, ram, aim, and fire by hand. They know the chance they take; without compressed air to clear the bore of the burning bits of fragments from the previous charge, the silken powder bags may "cook off" and explode before the breach can be closed. But they fire six rounds, despite the risk. The seventh "cooks off" and kills instantly most of the gun crew; the breach is blown into a twisted inoperable mass of steel. But Gunner's Mate 3/c Paul Henry Carr, the gun captain—his body ripped open from neck to groin—still cradles the last 54-pound shell in his arms, and his last gasping words before he dies are pleas for aid to load the gun.

But smoke screens, rain squalls, and torpedo attacks have not saved the slow and lumbering baby flat-tops. Kurita has sent his cruisers curving seaward; slowly the fight swerves round from south to southwest; Sprague's carriers, strung out over miles of ocean, steam wounded toward Leyte Gulf, with the enemy destroyers coming hard on their landward flank, battleships astern and Jap cruisers to seaward.

The flat-tops dodge in and out of the 150-foot waterspouts from the major-caliber Japanese shells; they chase salvos and fire their five-inchers defiantly. *Fanshaw Bay* takes six hits from eight-inch shells, which wreck the catapult, knock holes in the hull, start fires. *Kalinin Bay* takes fifteen hits; *White Plains* is racked from stem to stern by straddles. But their thin skins save them; most of the huge armor-piercing projectiles pass clean through the unarmored carriers without exploding. *Gambier Bay,* trailing and on an exposed windward flank where the smoke screens do not shield her, takes a hit on the flight deck, a near miss close alongside, loses an engine, drops to eleven knots, then loses all power—and is doomed. For an hour, far behind the chase, she dies in agony, hit about once a minute by enemy fire. She sinks about 9 A.M., flaming brightly, gasoline exploding, a Jap cruiser still riddling her from only 2,000 yards away.

Well before 9:30 the chase which is drawing closer and closer to crowded Leyte Gulf, where frantic preparations are in progress, has enveloped the northern group of escort carriers; the central group is now under fire, and the sixteen jeep flat-tops have lost 105 planes.

". . . it seemed only a matter of time until the entire Northern Group would be wiped out and the Middle Group overtaken . . ."

Two destroyers, a destroyer escort, and a carrier are sunk or sinking; two carriers, a destroyer, and a destroyer escort are badly hurt.

Aboard *Kitkun Bay,* an officer quips:

"It won't be long now, boys; we're sucking 'em into 40-mm. range."

Suddenly at 0925, Vice-Admiral Kurita, with victory in his grasp, breaks off the action, turns his ships to the north, and ends the surface phase of the battle off Samar.

"Damn it," a sailor says. "They got away."

Kurita's action, inexplicable at the time, has some, though incomplete, justification. The charge of the American "small boys"—one of the most stirring episodes in the long history of naval war—and the desperate gallantry of the uncoordinated and improvised air strikes by the pilots of the escort carriers have had their effect. During the early action off Samar, U.S. carrier pilots—from the little CVE's—have harassed Kurita constantly, have shot down more than 100 enemy planes, dropped 191 tons of bombs and 83 torpedoes. The enemy ships have turned and maneuvered violently to avoid torpedoes. Effective smoke screens have confused the Japanese. The air attacks have been mounting in intensity and effectiveness as planes have been launched from the center and southern group of escort carriers and have been diverted from ground-support missions on

Leyte to the new emergency. Pilots have strafed the Japanese ships recklessly, have dropped depth charges and anti-personnel bombs, have zoomed above Japanese mastheads with no ammunition and no weapons to win time and to divert and to distract.

The torpedo attacks by surface ship and aircraft had damaged enemy ships, and Kurita's fleet—composed of units now capable of widely differing speeds—is strung out over miles of ocean. Cruiser *Kumano,* torpedoed, is down to sixteen knots; cruisers *Chikuma* and *Chokai* are crippled; superstructures, charthouses, and communication equipment in other ships are damaged by five-inch shell fire and aircraft strafing; the Japs are shaken. Kurita, who has lost close tactical control of his command,[15] does not comprehend his closeness to victory; he thinks he has engaged some of the big, fast carriers of Third Fleet instead of merely the escort carriers of Seventh Fleet. Intercepted U.S. radio traffic convinces him—erroneously—that Leyte airstrips are operational.[q] He believes the rest of Halsey's powerful forces are nearby; he knows that Nishimura's southern pincer has been defeated in Surigao Strait; he has never received messages from Ozawa, far to the north, reporting the success of his decoy mission. So Kurita recalls his ships and assembles his scattered forces—and his chance has gone.

Admiral Sprague notes his thankful bewilderment: ". . . the failure of the enemy . . . to completely wipe out all vessels of this Task Unit can be attributed to our successful smoke screen, our torpedo counterattack . . . and the definite partiality of Almighty God."

The rest was anticlimax.

Kurita's irresolution was reinforced by mounting American attacks. Only two hours from the soft-skinned amphibious shipping in Leyte Gulf—his original goal—Kurita wasted time assembling his scattered forces and aiding cripples, and his fleet milled around in much the same waters, steering varying courses. *Suzuya,* cruiser, was fatally damaged by air attack, and at 10:30 A.M., two to three hours' flying time to the eastward, Admiral "Slew" McCain's Task Group 38.1 (which had been sent to Ulithi for rest, hastily recalled, and was steaming hard to the rescue) launched a strike. The bell has tolled for Kurita, and Japan's rising sun has passed the zenith. And far to the north, "Bull" Halsey, striking at Ozawa's decoy force, was alarmed at length by Kinkaid's frantic appeals for help; his fleet reversed course when within forty miles of decisive surface action, and Halsey detached some of his fast battleships to steam southward at high speed— but too late to intervene.[16]

The rest of that day, the twenty-fifth, and all of the next—the twenty-sixth—was mop-up and fierce stab, as the Japanese survivors fled and Jap land-based aircraft struck hard in angry futility. Japanese Kamikaze planes, attacking after the crescendo of battle, hit the escort carriers—damaged three and broke the back of *St. Lo,* which had survived the 18-inch guns of *Yamato.* But Kurita, who reached so closely to the verge of fame, paid heavily for the luxury of indecision. Air attacks struck him again and again during the afternoon of the twenty-fifth. Three of his damaged cruisers, crippled and on fire, had to be sunk. *Tone,* one of his two remaining heavy cruisers, was hit aft and damaged, and during the night of the twenty-fifth, as Kurita took his battered survivors back through San Bernardino Strait, U.S. surface forces caught and sank destroyer *Nowake.* At midnight of the twenty-fifth only one of Kurita's ships, a destroyer, was wholly undamaged.

On the twenty-sixth there was more slow dying as Halsey's and Kinkaid's fliers, augmented by some Army Air Force land-based bombers, chivvied and attacked the retreating Japs; and the First Diversion Attack Force, "which had already undergone more air attacks than any other force in naval history, once again braced itself for the final ordeal." Destroyer *Noshiro* was sunk; *Yamato,* with its gigantic but futile 18-inchers, was hit twice and its superstructure sieved with splinters, and other cripples of the battle off Samar and the Battle of Surigao Strait, including cruiser *Abukuma* and destroyer *Hayashimo,* were finished off. And there still remained the gantlet of U.S. submarines. . . .

At 2130, October 28, "what remained of the Japanese Battle Fleet re-entered Brunei Bay."

The *Shō* plan—the great gamble—had failed completely. In the sprawling battle for Leyte Gulf, Japan had lost one large and three light aircraft carriers, three battleships, including one of the two largest warships in the world, six heavy cruisers, four light cruisers, and eleven destroyers; most of the rest of her engaged ships were damaged severely or lightly; hundreds of planes had been shot down, and between 7,475 and 10,000 Japanese seamen died. The Japanese Navy as a fighting fleet had ceased to exist; Leyte Gulf was a blow from which the enemy never recovered.

But for the United States it was, nevertheless, incomplete victory when we might have swept the boards. The penalty of divided command,[17] of failure to "fix definite areas of responsibility," and unwarranted assumptions by both Kinkaid and Halsey[R] led to the surprise of our jeep carriers and to the escape of Kurita with his battered survivors, including four battleships, and of Ozawa with ten of his original seventeen vessels. Admiral Halsey ran to the north, leaving behind a force (the Seventh Fleet) inadequate in strength and speed to insure Kurita's destruction, and then just at the time when he was about to destroy all of Ozawa's force, he turned about and ran to the south in answer to Kinkaid's urgent calls for help.[s] The Japanese "lure" worked, but the *Shō* plan, which depended fundamentally upon good communications, split-second co-ordination, and bold leadership, foundered in complete and fatal failure.

To the United States the cost of overwhelming victory was 2,803 lives, several hundred aircraft, one light carrier, two escort carriers, and the "small boys" who had helped turn the tide of battle—destroyers *Johnston* and *Hoel* and destroyer escort *Samuel B. Roberts,* fought by "well-trained crews in an inspired manner in accordance with the highest traditions of the Navy."

NOTES   The battle for Leyte Gulf will be, forever, a source of some controversy, comparable to—though in no way as bitter as—the Sampson-Schley controversy after the Spanish-American War, or the Jellicoe-Beatty differences after Jutland.[18] Admiral Halsey and Admiral Kinkaid to this day believe their judgments were justified; each feels the other could—and should—have covered San Bernardino Strait.[T]

Leyte Gulf is a case history of the importance of communications to victory. Grossly inadequate communications made the co-ordination essential to Japanese success impossible; Kurita, for instance, never received Ozawa's messages.[19] But in the U.S. forces too many messages—and some messages improperly phrased[20]—led to the assumptions which made possible Kurita's surprise of Sprague's jeep carriers.

On October 24, while Third Fleet was launching its air attacks against Kurita, who was then in the Sibuyan Sea, Halsey sent out "a preparatory dispatch"[v] to his principal Third Fleet commanders designating four of his six fast battleships, with supporting units, as Task Force 34.[8] This task group was to be detached from the main fleet and used as a surface battle line against the Japanese surface ships if developments warranted. Halsey did not actually form this task force; he merely informed his own commanders that this was a "battle plan" to be executed when directed. However, both Kinkaid, Nimitz and Vice-Admiral Marc A. Mitscher intercepted this message, though it was not directed to any of them, and later in the battle—and partly because of subsequent messages—all misconstrued it.

When Halsey made his decision late in the evening of the twenty-fourth to steam north with all his available fleet and attack Ozawa, he informed Kinkaid that he was "proceeding north with three groups." Kinkaid, having intercepted the earlier message about Task Force 34, thought Halsey was taking his three carrier groups to the north and was leaving four of his six fast battleships to guard San Bernardino Strait. But Kinkaid, busy with preparations for the night action of Surigao Strait, did not specifically ask Halsey whether or not Task Force 34 was guarding San Bernardino Strait until 0412 A.M., October 25, and he did not get a negative reply from Halsey until just about the time Kurita burst out of the morning mists upon the surprised Sprague.

If Kinkaid had tried to clarify the situation earlier; if he had *not* intercepted the Task Force 34 message, or if Halsey had reported to him that he was "proceeding north with all my available forces," instead of "proceeding north with three groups," the surprise would not have occurred.[v]

There was one other factor that contributed to surprise. Kinkaid *did* send one or two aircraft to scout southward of San Bernardino Strait along the coast of Samar on the night of the twenty-fourth –twenty-fifth and the morning of the twenty-fifth. There was no report from the night search plane—a lumbering PBY "Black Cat," and the dawn search did not start until about the time Kurita's top hamper appeared over the horizon.[21] Halsey's fleet also sent out night "snoopers" and one report was received by Third Fleet on the night of the twenty-fourth indicating Kurita had turned east again toward San Bernardino.

The fact remains, however, that there had been no clear understanding, prior to the event, between Seventh and Third Fleets about San Bernardino Strait; the "coordination" required by Admiral Halsey's orders was defective, and he himself has written (in the *U. S. Naval Institute Proceedings*)[22] that Leyte Gulf "illustrates the necessity for a single naval command in a combat area responsible for and in full control of all combat units involved.[w]

"Division of operational control in a combat area leads at the least to confusion, lack of coordination, and overloaded communications (a fault which was pronounced during the battle on the American side), and could result in disaster."

In Third Fleet's after-action report of January 25, 1945, Admiral Halsey's reasoning which led him to take all of his available forces to the north in answer to Ozawa's "lure" is phrased as follows:

"Admiral Kinkaid appeared to have every advantage of position and power with which to cope with the Southern (Japanese) force. The Center force might plod on through San Bernardino Strait toward Leyte, but good damage assessment reports, carefully evaluated, convinced Commander Third Fleet, that even if Center Force did sortie from San Bernardino Strait, its fighting efficiency had been too greatly impaired to be able to win a decision against the Leyte forces (Seventh Fleet). The Northern force (Ozawa) was powerful, dangerous, undamaged, and as yet unhampered. Commander Third Fleet decided to (a) strike the Northern force suddenly and in full force; (b) keep all his forces concentrated; and (c) trust to his judgment as to the fatally weakened condition of the Center force—judgment which happily was vindicated by the Japs' inability to deal with the CVE's and small fry which stood toe-to-toe with them and stopped them in their tracks."[23]

Admiral Kinkaid's position, as stated in *Battle Report,* obviously does not agree completely with these conclusions:

". . . one must keep in mind the *missions* of the forces," Admiral Kinkaid is quoted. "The key to the Battle for Leyte Gulf lies in the missions of the two fleets.

"The mission must be clearly understood. The mission of the Seventh Fleet was to land and support the invasion force. My title was Commander of the Central Philippines Attack Force. Our job was to land troops and keep them ashore. The ships were armed accordingly with a very low percentage of armor-piercing projectiles.[x] The CVE's carried anti-personnel bombs instead of torpedoes and heavy bombs. We were not prepared to fight a naval action. . . .

"The only thing I can think of that I would have done differently if I had known Kurita was definitely coming through San Bernardino unopposed is that I would have moved the northern CVE group more to the south and I would have had a striking group from the escort carriers up looking for him at dawn.

"What mistakes were made during the battle were *not* due to lack of plans. Any errors made were errors of judgment, not errors of organization. The two areas coming together—the Central Pacific and the Southwest Pacific—posed a difficult problem of command, but one head would not have altered things."[24] [y]

Despite errors of omission and commission and initially exaggerated reports of damage by our fliers, Leyte Gulf was indubitably a major American victory. But the Japanese, who had a gambling chance—never of all-out victory—but at the best of causing the United States sufficient losses to extend the war, contributed to their own decisive defeat—by their communications failure,[z] their lack of air cover, the unco-ordinated nature of their air and surface operations, amazing deficiencies in timing, and the irresolution or blundering ineptitude of three of their four principal commanders. Only Admiral Ozawa, the "bait," really carried out his mission.

Luck, as well as judgment, obviously played a major part in the battle. But luck lay, in the final analysis, with the larger fleet and the more skilled commanders. The Japanese took their "eye off the ball," abandoned their fundamental objective—the thin-skinned amphibious shipping in Leyte Gulf—in the midst of battle, and thereby violated a cardinal military principle.

And the Americans—Third and Seventh Fleets—as Admiral Halsey radioed to Hawaii and Washington, broke "the back" of the Japanese Fleet "in the course of protecting our Leyte landings."

ACKNOWLEDGMENTS   After-action reports of the Third Fleet and of the U.S.S. *Hoel, Heermann, Johnston,* and other ships have been consulted for this account.

Two of the best published sources—which have served as reference "Bibles" for this account of the world's greatest naval battle—are *The Japanese at Leyte Gulf,* by James A. Field, Jr., Princeton University Press, 1947, and *The Battle for Leyte Gulf,* by C. Vann Woodward, the Macmillan Company, 1947. Another major source, particularly for some of the "human-interest" side lights of the battle, is *Battle Report—The End of an Empire,* by Captain Walter Karig, USNR, Lt. Comdr. Russell L. Harris, USNR, and Lt. Comdr. Frank A. Monson, USN, Rinehart and Company, Inc., 1948. I am primarily indebted to these three books for source data and occasional quotation.

The Campaigns of the Pacific War—U. S. Strategic Bombing Survey (Pacific) Naval Analysis Division, U. S. Government Printing Office, 1946—is a basic, though terse source. Other references consulted include: *The Army Air Force in World War II—Volume V,* edited by W. F. Craven and J. L. Cate, the University of Chicago Press, 1953; *Combat Command,* by Admiral Frederick C. Sherman, USN, retired, E. P. Dutton and Company, 1950; *Admiral Halsey's Story,* by Fleet Admiral William F. Halsey, USN, and Lt. Comdr. J. Bryan III, USNR, Whittlesey House, 1947; *MacArthur, 1941–1951,* by Major Gen. Charles A. Willoughby and John Chamberlain, McGraw-Hill Book Company, 1954; *The Great Pacific Victory,* Gilbert Cant, The John Day Company, 1945; *The Story of the Second World War,* edited by Henry Steele Commager, Little, Brown and Company, 1945, and *U. S. Navy at War—1941–1945,* Official Reports by Fleet Admiral Ernest J. King, USN, U. S. Navy Department, 1946.

A brief account of the battle, giving succinct reasons for the decision made by Admiral Halsey, will be found in *The Battle for Leyte Gulf,* by Admiral Halsey, *U. S. Naval Institute Proceedings,* May, 1952. Additional comments by Admiral Halsey, under the Special Notes, were written specifically for this chapter.

Admiral Kinkaid, the other principal U.S. naval commander, has not yet published his memoirs, but his reasoning will be found in *Battle Report* and in the Special Notes to this chapter. I am indebted to him for permission to quote him in his own words.

The surviving Japanese commanders' after-the-war explanations are itemized in Field's *The Japanese at Leyte Gulf.*

Samuel Eliot Morison's semi-official operational naval history of World War II had not yet published a volume dealing with the Leyte Gulf battle when this book was published.

The most authoritative and detailed study of the battle—still unfinished in late 1954—is being completed by Rear Admiral Richard W. Bates, USN, retired, and his staff at the Naval War College in Newport, R.I. These accounts, however, are primarily for naval use and as yet are restricted to official circulation.

SPECIAL NOTES BY
ADMIRAL THOMAS C. KINKAID, USN (RET.)

The notes are keyed to numerals or letters in text.
Explanatory material in brackets inserted by author.

1. The invasion armada was "MacArthur's armada" in the sense that it came from his area, S.W.P.A. [Southwest Pacific Area], and might well be called the "great armada from Down Under" [or from MacArthur's area, or S.W.P.A.]. MacArthur derived his authority from the Combined Chiefs of Staff. He was designated "Supreme Commander" in S.W.P.A. and was specifically prohibited from taking personal command of any of his forces. He was required to exercise command through his three major commanders for land, sea, and air, Blamey [General Sir George Blamey, Australian Army general commanding land forces]; Kinkaid, and Kenney [General George C. Kenney, U. S. Army Air Forces, commanding air forces].

From the time we departed from ports in the Admiralties and New

Guinea to invade the Philippines, I had direct command of the "armada," including the Army forces embarked, until I turned over command of the Army forces ashore in Leyte to Krueger [Lt. Gen. Walter Krueger, commanding Sixth Army]. MacArthur was present as a passenger in his capacity as Supreme Commander, Southwest Pacific Area. I exercised direct command, as witness the fact that I decided to go ahead with the operation without referring to Mac-Arthur when Halsey sent a despatch, received when we were a few hours out from Hollandia, stating that he was concentrating his forces to attack the Japanese Fleet and would not be able to give the planned support to our landing at Leyte. When MacArthur joined our convoy, I sent him a bridge signal: "Welcome to our city." He replied with a gracious message referring to the fact that this was the first time he had sailed under my command and ending with: "Believe it or not we are on our way."

2. Nishimura was due in Leyte one hour before Kurita. He was ahead of schedule without reason—a serious error in a coordinated effort. Kurita was late for good and sufficient reasons.

3. The Seventh Fleet had eighteen CVE's. Two had been sent to Halmahera for replacement planes and only sixteen were present during the action. The Seventh Fleet had a few PBY's, tender-based. Counting eighteen CVE's, the total number of [U.S.] carriers was thirty-four.

4. It is interesting that the *Darter* and *Dace* paced Kurita through the night in Palawan Passage and attacked at dawn—a good job. An extremely important fact, from the operations point of view, is that Kurita was separated from most of his communication personnel in the transfer from *Atago* to *Kishanani* to *Yamato*. Any naval commander will sympathize with him in that situation.

5. Only one strike was made on Nishimura and that only by small search-attack scouting groups. Davison [Rear Admiral Ralph E. Davison, commanding Task Group 38.4 of the Third Fleet] reported that the move to concentrate was taking him out of range of the enemy

southern force, but Halsey continued the concentration. In the Seventh Fleet we felt well able to take care of the [enemy] southern force and had all day to make plans for its reception. I was not informed directly by Halsey that he was leaving Nishimura to me.

6. Halsey had ordered a morning search to northward by the northern group, but Jap attacks prevented it from getting off until the afternoon.

7. In the Seventh Fleet we had counted noses carefully and had come to the conclusion that only two BB's [battleships]—*Ise* and *Hyuga*—could be with Ozawa in the [enemy] northern force.

8. Halsey had four groups of carriers and had given preparatory orders to form TF [Task Force] 34. ". . . proceeding north with three groups" is phraseology which failed to give information of vital import not only to me and to Nimitz but to many others. Mitscher [Vice-Admiral Marc A. Mitscher, commanding Task Force 38—the four carrier task groups and their supporting combat ships of the Third Fleet] actually sent instructions for the employment of the two BB's which were to stay with him, believing that TF 34 would be left behind to guard San Bernardino. It was impossible to believe anything else. The proposed composition of TF 34 was exactly correct in the circumstances.

Even though Halsey banked "too heavily" on the exaggerated claims of his pilots, he knew from the *Independence* night search planes that Kurita was headed for San Bernardino and he should have realized:

a. That the composition of the Seventh Fleet was designed to provide support for the amphibious landing and the troops ashore— not for major combat. Slow speed of the old battleships and a high proportion of high-capacity projectiles in their magazines made them an inadequate adversary for the Japanese central force, even if they had been available and were filled with fuel and ammunition.

b. That the Seventh Fleet would be engaged through the night with surface forces in Surigao Strait and, in any case, could not leave Leyte Gulf unguarded and take station off San Bernardino.

c. That the three CVE groups of the Seventh Fleet would be on station at daylight 25 Oct. carrying out their mission and would need cover.

d. That my destroyers would have expended their torpedoes in Surigao Strait and that the battleships would be low in AP ammunition and even in HC ammunition, having rendered gunfire support to forces ashore for several days.

9. Rarely has a commander had all day to stay quietly (except for the antics of Jap planes) in port and prepare without serious interruption for a night action. The tactical dispositions and plans of the Seventh Fleet were checked and counterchecked by all concerned.

10. I believe contact was made about 2215 [10:15 P.M.] a few miles south of Bohol Island. All three PT's of that group were damaged by gunfire and unable to report the contact, but one of them (using his head) managed to make contact with the next PT group to eastward which sent through a message, which was received by Oldendorf [Rear Admiral J. B. Oldendorf, who was in tactical or direct command at Surigao Strait] about twenty-six minutes after midnight.

11. Fired by *PT 137*. The PT fired at a destroyer, missed, but hit and badly damaged the cruiser [*Abukuma*].

12. No, we did not think that the Jap central force was west of the Philippines, but we did think that TF 34 was guarding San Bernardino. Also, it is of interest that in Leyte Gulf the temporary headquarters of the Army commanders were only a few yards from the water's edge and the beaches were piled high with food and supplies and ammunition for immediate use. Destruction of those supply dumps would have left our forces ashore without food and ammunition. Halsey has said that Kurita could only have "harassed" our forces in Leyte Gulf.

13. I think it should be pointed out that the first six words of Nimitz's despatch was "padding" [inserted by the communications officer for code security]. The despatch was first brought to me without padding, as it should have been. Later I was told of the "padding."

[Halsey originally took this phrase, "All the world wants to know . . ." as tacit criticism of him and was irritated.]

14. The attack of the DD's [destroyers] and DE's [destroyer escorts] against the Jap heavy ships was the most courageous and also the most effective incident brought to my attention during the war.

15. Kurita committed a grave error in losing tactical control of his force. He had lost most of his communication personnel. He had been seriously damaged by torpedo hits from Seventh Fleet planes and surface ships and by bomb hits from Seventh Fleet planes, and the upper works of his ships, charthouse, radio, etc., suffered from five-inch shellfire and from strafing. His ships sheered out of formation to dodge torpedo attacks, real or dummy, made by planes and escort vessels. Soon his individual units became widely separated, which he should not have permitted, and he could not see his forces, or the enemy's, because of the heavy smoke laid by the CVE's and their escorts. He was confused and his subordinates did not help him by reporting the nature of the enemy they were attacking. Ozawa had failed to inform him of his success in drawing Halsey away. Also, I have no doubt that Kurita was physically exhausted after three grueling days.

16. McCain sensed what was going on long before Halsey did and he launched his strike beyond range for a return flight—340 miles.

The following paragraphs constitute my analysis of what occurred: *Halsey had done exactly what the Japs wanted him to do.* He had left San Bernardino unguarded, permitting Kurita to pass through the strait unopposed. Having taken all six of his BB's 300 miles to the north, when two would have been adequate and four were needed at San Bernardino, he belatedly at 11:15 turned south in response to my appeals and to the despatch from Nimitz, again taking all six BB's with him and leaving Mitscher without any. Mitscher urgently needed two BB's. By that time, 11:15, Mitscher's planes had developed Ozawa's force and the *Ise* and *Hyuga* were known to be with him, but Halsey took all six BB's south. Later Mitscher sent DuBose [Rear Admiral Laurence T. DuBose] to mop up the cripples (with four cruisers and twelve destroyers). Ozawa was informed of the actions of DuBose, and sent the *Ise* and *Hyuga* south to look for him. Fortunately the Jap BB's passed to eastward of our cruisers on their way south and again on their return course to northward.

Halsey informed me that he would arrive off San Bernardino at 0800 26 Oct. Too late! Later, at 1600 [4 P.M.], after fueling, he decided to speed up and took two of his fastest BB's, *Iowa* and *New Jersey,* with three cruisers and eight DD's, south at 28 knots. He missed Kurita entering the strait by two hours. Suppose he had intercepted him? Were two BB's enough?

Suppose Halsey had turned south at top speed immediately upon receipt of my first urgent message at 0825. He would have been about five hours closer to San Bernardino. Actually he steamed north for two and three quarters hours at 25 knots—69 miles—whereas if he had steamed south at 28 knots—77 miles—there would have been a total of 146 miles difference in his 11:15 position.

The net result of all of this was that the six strongest battleships in the world—except the *Yamato* and *Musashi*—steamed about 300 miles north and 300 miles south during the "greatest naval battle of the Second World War and the largest engagement ever fought upon the high seas"—and they did not fire a single shot. I can well imagine the feelings of my classmate, Lee [Rear Admiral Willis A. Lee, commanding the battleships of Third Fleet].

Even today Halsey believes it was not a mistake to take the whole Third Fleet north and he apparently overlooks the fact that the absence of TF 34 from San Bernardino Strait precluded the total destruction of Kurita's force on the spot, to say nothing of the loss of American lives and ships of the CVE force. The threat to our invasion of the Philippines seems not to have come to his mind. Halsey has stated that I should have sent CVE planes to scout the Sibuyan Sea and San Bernardino Strait during the night of 24–25 Oct. As is evident, I believed that TF 34 was guarding San Bernardino and that Lee was being kept informed by the night-flying planes from the *Independence.* Actually, I did order a search to the northward during the night by PBY's and a search toward San Bernardino at daylight by CVE planes, mostly out of curiosity to find out what was going on.

Even if I had known that San Bernardino was wide open, I did not have the force to meet Kurita. You have quoted me correctly from

Battle Report. I would not have denuded Leyte Gulf of a defense force. I would have moved the CVE's clear of direct contact with Kurita's surface forces. And, of course, I would have sent planes from the CVE's to keep track of Kurita, although none were equipped or trained for night search.

In that case would Kurita have reached Leyte? It is interesting to speculate. It is very possible. His direct contact with the northern group of CVE's, though painful to us, delayed his progress, seriously damaged his forces, and so confused him that he turned back within two hours of his goal.

17. "Divided command" is, of course, not sound procedure. The hard, cold fact is, however, that despite the divided command both Halsey and I had what appeared to me to be clear-cut definite missions. Had Halsey been mindful of his covering mission when Ozawa beckoned him to come north, he never would have left San Bernardino wide open. Also, he would have told me in a clearly worded despatch just what he was going to do about it.

The "unwarranted assumption" which you attribute to me probably refers to my assumption that TF 34 was guarding San Bernardino. Perhaps that was unwarranted, but, to my not unprejudiced mind, all logic seems to point the other way. Halsey's mission included covering our amphibious operation from interruption by the Japanese Fleet. His preparatory order to form TF 34, which I intercepted, set up a plan to guard San Bernardino against the passage of Kurita's forces which was perfect in concept and perfect in composition of the forces assigned to TF 34. I did not intercept further modifying messages regarding TF 34. Had I done so, I most certainly would not have remained silent.

It was inconceivable that Halsey could have scrapped a perfect plan. His message, "going north with three groups," meant to me that TF 34 plus a carrier group was being left behind—entirely sound. Not only did I and my staff believe it, and Nimitz and, presumably, his staff believe it, but Mitscher and his staff believed it also. As I have already pointed out, Mitscher actually gave orders for utilization of the two battleships which were to accompany him on the northern trek [four of the Third Fleet's six battleships were to have been left behind in TF 34 to guard San Bernardino; two were to have gone north with Mitscher's carriers after Ozawa]. When Mitscher and his staff found out that TF 34 was not being left to guard the strait, his chief of staff—[Captain] Arleigh Burke, tried to get Mitscher to send a message to Halsey on the subject, but Mitscher declined on the ground that Halsey probably had information not known to him.

Later in your notes you point out that I did not specifically ask Halsey whether or not TF 34 was guarding San Bernardino until 0412 25 Oct. That is correct. In the absence of information to the contrary from Halsey, anything else was unthinkable. Early in the morning of 25 Oct. a meeting of the staff was held in my cabin to check for errors of commission or of omission. It broke up about 0400 and my operations officer, Dick Cruzen [Captain Richard H. Cruzen], came back into the cabin and said, "Admiral, I can think of only one other thing. We have never directly asked Halsey if TF 34 is guarding San Bernardino." I told him to send the message.

18. The controversy has not been bitter for the simple and sole reason that I refused to take part in it. I have not publicly stated my side of the case but have kept quiet for ten years—not so Halsey. He has published several articles or interviews in addition to his book endeavoring to justify his actions at Leyte, sometimes at my expense.

19. I believe that the radio on Ozawa's flagship went out with the the first bomb hit, but other ships could have sent a message to Kurita for him.

20. Only Halsey's strangely phrased message led to Kurita's surprise of Sprague's carriers.

In the early morning some important messages from me to Halsey were delayed in transmission and that should not have been.

21. Actually one or two PBY's took off from a tender in Surigao Strait to make the northern night search. They were ill equipped for that sort of mission. They had quite a hell of a time because every U.S. ship they came near fired at them. I imagine that their greatest concern was to avoid U.S. ships rather than to find Jap ships.

The dawn search ordered from the CVE's should have gotten off much earlier.

22. Halsey's writings in the *Naval Institute Proceedings* were subjective. If he had been mindful of his covering mission, and had no other distractions, the question of "a single naval command" would be purely academic.

23. Halsey's reasoning regarding the [enemy] center force falls short of the mark. His "careful evaluation" of the damage reports was not shared by everyone. Kurita's movements seemed to belie any such evaluation. We knew from our plot that Kurita was approaching San Bernardino at 22 knots. Some plodding! Halsey had a later report from the *Independence* plane which was not forwarded to me. Did he not plot Kurita's progress?

A count of noses by my staff showed that Ozawa's force could not have been as "powerful and dangerous" as Halsey seems to have thought. He took 119 ships north to deal with 19 ships in the [enemy] northern force. An intelligent *division* of his forces was in order. In setting up TF 34, he had actually made that intelligent division of forces but he failed to implement it.

Halsey's decisions (a) and (b) would have been sound if he had had no other obligations. His decision (c) can be described only as erroneous. I doubt if anyone will disagree with the statement that the only reason why Kurita did not reach Leyte Gulf, destroying the CVE's en route, was that he turned back when victory was within his grasp. His [Halsey's] judgment as to the "fatally weakened condition of the [enemy] center force" was definitely shown to be in error. Did his "judgment which was happily vindicated" include a forecast that Kurita would break off the action? If so, his crystal ball was certainly in fine working order. Does anyone believe in the "Japs' *inability* to deal with the CVE's and small fry"? They did not deal with them as they could have, but is that "inability"?

24. I am quoted correctly, but I did not have an opportunity to edit my remarks. In the last line "one head would not have altered things" might have been reworded because it meant that "one head

would not have produced a better end result if both Halsey and I had carried out our specific missions."

SPECIAL NOTES BY
FLEET ADMIRAL WILLIAM F. HALSEY, USN (RET.)

A. I do not remember what Radio Manila was playing. They were usually sending out lying propaganda from "Tokyo Rose" or some other renegade Japanese Nisei. We used Radio Manila as an alarm clock. As soon as we heard the air-raid alarm, we knew our pilots had been sighted.

The change in the American strategy was the direct result of a recommendation sent by me. I recommended that the taking of Yap and Palau be eliminated and that a landing be made in the central Philippines instead of Mindanao. I had once previously recommended that the seizure of Palau be dropped. Admiral Nimitz approved my recommendation, except that about Palau, and immediately forwarded it to the Combined Chiefs of Staff, then sitting in Quebec. General Sutherland, in Hollandia, General MacArthur's chief of staff, in MacArthur's temporary absence, approved the landing in the central Philippines instead of Mindanao. The Combined Chiefs of Staff approved, and it received almost immediate approval from President Roosevelt and Prime Minister Churchill. It was fortunate that the Quebec Conference was on at that time.

The 1st Marine Division had heavy losses on Peleliu (in the Palau group), in many ways comparable to Tarawa. One combat team from the Army 81st (Wildcat) Division also received many losses in the fighting on Peleliu, where they so ably assisted. We constructed airfields on Anguar, captured by the 81st Army Division, and on Peleliu Island, and a partial naval base in Kossol Roads. Kossol Roads was not occupied by the Japanese and we merely had to make arrangement for its defense from the Japanese on Babelthuap Island, the largest island of the Palau archipelago. I mention these actions and this timing to show that this was not a "Monday quarterback" estimate of the situation on my part. Ulithi was not recommended to be dropped, as I always considered this a necessity as a fleet anchorage.

It was occupied without opposition. Peleliu, Anguar, and Kossol Roads were a great convenience, but I thought then, and I think now, not a necessity for the further campaign in the Pacific.

The beginning of the end of the war in the Pacific was evident before the Battle of Leyte Gulf. When our fleet obtained freedom of movement, practically anywhere in the Pacific, the Japanese were doomed to defeat.

The *Shō* plan was just another of the many plans the Japs devised. They all failed.

Toyoda had carriers, but with few planes and half-trained pilots. Now that it is the Monday after the Saturday game, everyone seemed to know this excepting my staff and me. We bore the responsibility. If the rest of the Navy did not then know it, we, in the Third Fleet, were thoroughly cognizant that the carrier had replaced the battleship, and was potentially the strongest and most dangerous naval weapon our opponents possessed. We had been fighting the Japs for several years. We did not know how many planes the Japs had, but we could not take a chance. We knew the *Princeton* had been attacked and it was reported they were carrier planes. As we stood northward on the morning of the twenty-sixth, we had a large "bogie" on our screen. We naturally thought they were carrier planes heading toward the Japanese carriers. They finally went off our screen heading toward Luzon. We had been "shuttle-bombed" many times by the Nips, and only once off Guadalcanal had succeeded in reversing this process.

My decision to go north was not based on pilots' reports solely. A possible battle with the Japanese Fleet had long been a matter of discussion and study by us. We had played it frequently on a game board constructed on the deck of the flag quarters. We had long since decided the carriers were potentially the most dangerous ships the Japs had, not only to ourselves, but to MacArthur and the Pacific campaign. We named them our primary targets. We knew Kurita's ships had suffered damage from our attacks, particularly to their upper works and probably to their fire-control instruments. This was borne out by their poor shooting against the baby carriers.

B. The "Turkey Shoot" in the Marianas (the Battle of the Philippine Sea) was a magnificent show. That it alone broke the back of Japanese naval aviation, despite its great success, I seriously doubt.

I cannot and will not forget the wonderful American pilots in the South Pacific and Southwest Pacific who had knocked out so many Japanese naval air groups and squadrons based on Rabaul. This statement is based on Japanese answers to American interrogations after the war. The fliers who accomplished this were from the U. S. Army Air Force, U. S. Naval and Marine Aviation, the R.N.Z.A.F. and the R.A.A.F. The Japs made their usual mistake of feeding in these groups piecemeal and were thoroughly knocked out.

c. The Japanese Navy had a number of carriers nearing completion in the Inland Sea. I have a fairly good-sized circular plaque, presented to me after the war. In the middle is a U.S. ensign—around the U.S. ensign and near the periphery are the silhouettes of various Japanese ships representing carriers, battleships, a heavy cruiser, light cruisers, and submarines. On the periphery it bears the inscription: "Plaque made of metal obtained from these vessels sunk by U.S. Carrier planes, July 1945 at Kure Naval Base, Kure, Japan." The names and numbers are interesting. CV-ASO, CV-AMAGI, CVE-RYUHO, BB-ISE, BB-HYUGA, BB-HARUNA, CA-SETTSU, CL-TONE, CL-OYADA (fleet flagship), CL-AOBA, CL-IZUMA, CL-AWATE and 5 SS. (CV large carrier, CVE small or jeep carrier, BB battleship, CA heavy cruiser, CL light cruiser, and SS submarines.)

We had orders to get rid of the Japanese Navy so that they could not interfere with the Russians if they decided to invade Japan. I sometimes wonder, in view of present-day events! Of course these ships were sitting ducks, and even high-altitude bombing, with some luck, might have hit them.

There is one Japanese cruiser that I would have felt sorry for, if I could have felt sorry for a Japanese man-of-war in those days. She had escaped from the Battle of Leyte Gulf, sorely wounded. The Japs had brought her into a bay or cove on the west side of Luzon, and heavily camouflaged her and made her almost invisible. They were working night and day to make her seaworthy to return her to the home land. In the meantime, our fliers were combing every nook and corner, looking for Jap ships. As one of our last flights was about to return, a lucky photograph was taken of this hideout. Our photographic interpreters made out this cruiser. A heavy strike was made on her the first thing next morning, and that was curtains for this cruiser.

D. A "Betty" tried to land among our parked planes on the *Enterprise* during our attack on the Marshall and Gilbert Islands on 1 Feb. 1942 (Eastern Time). Thanks to the masterly ship handling by then Captain, now Admiral (Retired), George D. Murray, U. S. Navy, the "Betty" was forced into a slip while coming up "the groove" and did only minor damage. The "Betty" hit the edge of the flight deck, broke her back, and went over the side. She was undoubtedly on fire when she hit us. She cut off a gasoline riser aft and set it on fire. She cut off another gasoline riser forward, but no fire resulted, and cut off the tail of one of our SBD planes. The fire from the gasoline riser was soon under control, and I remember no further damage, except some slight and easily repairable damage to the flight deck. This was my first encounter with a Kamikaze plane; I saw many later. I doubt if this Japanese even knew he was a Kamikaze. She had dropped all her bombs and fortunately, for us, missed the *Enterprise*. His intentions were very clear. He knew his plane was doomed, and determined to do us as much damage as possible. He tried to land among some thirty-five or forty of our planes, lately returned from a strike, refueling and awaiting the return of all planes for respotting. The quick thinking of the ship's captain prevented what might have been a catastrophe. I do not mean to detract from Rear Admiral Masabumi Arima's very brave, but very foolhardy, suicide dive. Apparently we fought to live, the Japanese to die.

E. My orders went further than the quoted "to cover and support forces in the Southwest Pacific, in order to assist in the seizure and occupation of objectives in the Central Philippines." This is being written from memory without the advantage of notes, so my overriding orders can only be vaguely quoted. They were that, other conditions notwithstanding, the destruction of the Japanese Fleet was my paramount objective.

F. "Necessary measures for detailed coordination of operations between the [Third Fleet] and the [Seventh Fleet] will be arranged by their commanders." These are just so many words and nothing more. They were impossible of accomplishment. Kinkaid and I had not seen each other since we met in Hollandia, just after the plans for the invasion of the Philippines had been changed. Some key members of my staff and I had flown from Saipan to Hollandia to discuss preliminary arrangements with Kinkaid and his staff and MacArthur's staff. Both Kinkaid and I had been too busily occupied to confer during the Philippine invasion. This illustrates, as nothing else can, the importance of a unified command in the combat zone. Had Kinkaid or I been in Supreme Command at the time of the Battle of Leyte Gulf, I am sure it would have been fought differently. Whether for better or for worse can never be answered.

G. In addition to PBY's, I believe the Seventh Fleet had some PBM's under their control at that time.

H. Night snoopers not only scouted the northern force but also the Sibuyan Sea and made reports of Kurita turning once again to the eastward—heading toward San Bernardino Strait. A report of this was directed sent to Kinkaid around 2100 or 2130 that night.

I. I had no operational control of submarines, except those specifically assigned to us for some operation. I had no submarines assigned to me at that time.

J. I never thought Kurita's force had been stopped by the day's air attacks. I had received and directed transmittal of a report that his force was again heading toward San Bernardino Strait. I did not bank too heavily on so-called exaggerated claims from pilots. We had rather good evaluation of pilots' reports at this time. I did think Kurita had been rather badly mauled by our pilots, particularly in their upper works and that their fire control would be poor. Their poor shooting against the CVE's, destroyers, and destroyer escorts the next day tendered to corroborate this. I did not expect them to be opposed by CVE's, destroyers, and destroyer escorts. Their thin skins probably saved them somewhat. After the Battle of Guadalcanal, in which Rear Admiral Callaghan and Rear Admiral Scott lost their lives, there were some thin-skinned ships that were holed by heavy-armor piercing shells with little damage. I remember one destroyer, I have forgotten her name, that I inspected later. As I remember it, she had fourteen 14-inch hits from a Jap battleship. Her commanding officer was Commander Coward. Never did a man have a name so inappropriate to fit with his actions in battle.

K. I object to the statement "that on such misunderstandings rest the course of history and the fate of nations." I had no misunderstandings, with the possible exception (if true) that the Jap carriers had no planes. I knew what I was doing at all times, and deliberately took the risks, in order to get rid of the Jap carriers. My estimate that the Seventh Fleet could take care of Kurita's battered forces was amply justified even against the CVE's and small fry during the action of Oct. 26. These brave American ships put up a fight that will be an epic for all time. My hat is off to them.

L. The battle of Surigao Strait, with Admiral Oldendorf in tactical command, was beautifully conceived and executed. Never has a T been so efficiently capped, and never has a force been so completely defeated and demoralized as was the Jap Surigao force.

M. I am still far from sure that Ozawa's force was intended solely as a lure. The Japs had continuously lied during the war, even to each other. Why believe them implicitly as soon as the war ends? They had plenty of time, before reciting them, to make their stories fit their needs. Despite their "banzai" charges, their "Kamikaze" planes, their "foolish bombs" (men-driven), their one- and two-man submarines, built for the purpose of sacrificing their crew, and the many other foolish things they did, it is still difficult for me to believe that they would deliberately use their potentially most dangerous ships as deliberate sacrifices. This is partially borne out by reports from Americans who interviewed Admiral Kurita after the war. When asked why he turned away from Leyte Gulf, he stated that he intended to join forces with Ozawa and attack the Third Fleet.

N. Admiral Nimitz's despatch to me was "Where is Task Force 34?" The despatch as quoted is a gross violation of security regulations. [This despatch has been quoted in its entirety in numerous previous publications.]

O. I note the Seventh Fleet is described as red-eyed from days of shore bombardment and nights of battle. My fleet had been fighting almost continually since early September. When we finally reached Ulithi in late September, for rest and replenishment, we were chased out by a typhoon after a one-night stand. We were almost continually in combat, until some time after the Battle of Leyte Gulf. I wonder what color my splendid pilots' eyes were? I do not know, but I do know they were approaching a stage of exhaustion that kept me on edge. I dared not let up on the Japs when we were running them ragged. This goes for all my officers and men, manning battle stations, above and below decks. It was an almost unendurable strain. We fought no battle for Cape Engano—we fought to do away with the Jap carriers.

P. I knew what force Kinkaid had and believed them capable of taking on Kurita's damaged force. I did not know of Kinkaid's ammunition situation in his old battleships. I have since been told that one of these battleships in the Surigao Strait action did not fire a single shot from her main battery.

In moving north, I took a calculated risk. I figured then, and still believe, that if Kurita had arrived at Leyte Gulf he could make nothing but a "hit-and-run bombardment." While in command of the South Pacific, my forces in Guadalcanal had many times been bombarded by Japanese battleships, cruisers, and destroyers. The forces ashore caught unmerciful hell, but these bombardments served to delay us no more than a short time. Shipping put to sea, usually only partly unloaded, and moved away from the bombardment area. The troops ashore had to take it in such dugouts as they had. On most occasions I had no heavy fighting ships to oppose them, and they bombarded at their leisure. On one occasion PT boats drove them away. On another, Dan Callaghan and Norm Scott (both rear admirals) made the supreme sacrifice, but with their few ships, cruisers, antiaircraft vessels and destroyers, they routed the Japanese forces consisting of battleships, cruisers, and destroyers. Their supreme sacrifice was not in vain. As a result of this action, the Japanese lost the Battleship *Hiyei*—left a derelict and sunk by our planes the next day. During one of their last bombardments, we had been able to fool them and got two of our new battleships near Savo Island, the *South Dakota* and the *Washington,* under command of Rear Admiral, later Vice-Admiral, W. A. Lee, Jr., USN. As a result of the night action that followed, the Japs lost various destroyers and one battleship. She was sunk that night.

Q. A statement is made that Kurita's intercepted radio traffic convinced him, erroneously, that Leyte airstrips were operational. This was not entirely erroneous. Admiral McCain flew his planes off at such a distance that it was impossible for them to return to their mother carriers. They were directed to land on Leyte airstrips. They did, and for a few days thereafter they operated from these fields until I was directed to return them to Ulithi. This was done, via Palau to Ulithi. Incidentally, I do not remember seeing a report of the damage McCain's fliers inflicted on Kurita's force. It must have been not inconsiderable.

R. I do not fully understand what the author means by unwarranted assumptions by me. Possibly that I placed too much credence in the pilots' reports; I do not believe that I did. These reports were carefully evaluated, and after due consideration a calculated risk was taken. My estimate that the Seventh Fleet could take care of Kurita's battered forces was amply justified. "The proof of the pudding is in the eating." Remember this estimate was "Saturday quarterbacking" and not "Monday quarterbacking."

S. I am in agreement that I made a mistake in bowing to pressure and turning south. I consider this the gravest error I committed during the Battle of Leyte Gulf.

T. I have never stated, to my knowledge and remembrance, that Kinkaid could and should have covered San Bernardino Strait. I have stated that I felt that Kinkaid's force could have taken care of Kurita's battered force, and furthermore, that Kurita was only capable of a hit-and-run attack if he entered Leyte Gulf. Such an attack, by my experience in the South Pacific, would have little effect on the troops ashore and could cause only a slight delay in the over-all picture.

U. I did not send a preparatory despatch, but instead a "Battle Plan" addressed only to the Third Fleet. To insure that the Third Fleet did not misunderstand, I sent a further message saying this plan would not be executed until directed by me. As Commander Task Force 38, Vice-Admiral Mitscher should have received both messages.

V. The statement that, had I sent a despatch to Kinkaid that I was "proceeding north with all my available forces" instead of "proceeding north with three groups," the surprise would not have occurred is purely academic. I did not know that he had intercepted my battle plan and believed it had been executed. A carrier task group was well defined, and every naval commander in the area knew its composition. My despatch was a correct one. I had notified all interested parties when Admiral McCain's Carrier Task Group started for Ulithi. I am sure no one misconstrued that message.

w. I have explained before that orders requiring "coordination" were mere words and meant nothing. I still stand by what I have written about Leyte Gulf, that "it illustrates the necessity for a single naval command in a combat area, responsible for, and in full control of, all combat units involved."

x. I knew nothing of how the Seventh Fleet was armed. At that time I believe we were rearming the Third Fleet under way. I gave no thought to the Seventh Fleet's armament of shells.

y. I am in agreement with Admiral Kinkaid when he says any errors made were errors of judgment. I am in complete disagreement when he states, "The two areas coming together—the Central Pacific and the Southwest Pacific—posed a difficult problem of command, but one head would not have altered things." As I have previously stated, "had either Admiral Kinkaid or I been in supreme command, the battle would have been fought quite differently."

z. There is only one word to describe the communications on the American side during this battle, and that word is rotten. We sent in a long report describing the deficiencies and interference we encountered, also a recommendation for drastic changes. As I remember, our combat circuit was filled with long and relatively unimportant intelligence summaries that could and should have been deferred. Most of these were not Navy reports. As a consequence, there were long and intolerable delays in getting urgent messages through. This should never be permitted again.

These comments have been written almost entirely from memory and without the advantage of any notes or reports. I hope I am not trusting my memory too far; ten and a half years is a long time.

1842

Mutiny
on the Brig *Somers*

With the sea chuckling beneath her forefoot, and royals, skysails, and stunsails bellying taut in the soft breath of the northeast trades, the United States brig *Somers* bowled gently over a tropic sea toward Charlotte Amalie, Danish West Indies.

It was the second dog watch, Friday, November 25, 1842; the sudden twilight of the tropics had faded swiftly into night. Overside the bow wave curled quietly aft in a fine feather of white, and phosphorescence gleamed briefly in the dark waters.

On deck the running rigging had been neatly coiled, the boat falls flemished down, the spit kids stowed beneath the spar deck guns, and the ship was settling down into the restless sleep of night upon the ocean.

Aft by the wheel were the officer of the deck and the helmsman, their sun-tanned faces sharp in the faint glow from the binnacle. Forward near the bitts J. W. Wales, the purser's steward, was lolling, taking the air after supper and smoking a bedtime pipe. There were few others on the spar deck except the watch.

Wales puffed out a strong mouthful of smoke and turned to find Midshipman Philip Spencer at his side. Spencer made some remark about the weather; Wales answered in an offhand manner, for Spencer, though he was the son of John Canfield Spencer, Secretary of War in the cabinet of President John Tyler, was not popular with his shipmates: "He was a constant offender in a matter in which a self-respecting officer may never offend; he was always trying to bridge an unbridgeable distance in rank between man and officer."

"Come up on the booms with me; I've something to say to you."

Spencer's eyes gleamed, and Wales, startled and curious, knocked the ashes from his pipe and accompanied the midshipman aft, clambering up on the clutter of boats and spare gear stowed in the booms.

It was black dark on the booms; only the faint pinprick of the stars in the sky. Spencer's sudden strained voice broke through the gentle creak of cordage and the slap of waves:

"Do you fear death? Do you fear a dead man? Are you afraid to kill a man?"

Wales, frightened, edged away.

"I don't doubt your courage at all; I know it. But can you keep a secret and will you keep one? If so, take an oath."

Word for word and phrase for phrase, to satisfy Spencer, the steward repeated a solemn oath not to reveal the conversation which was about to take place between the two. Then, with the soft winds sloughing through the shrouds, Spencer told the horrified Wales of a plot to murder the captain and officers, to seize the brig, and to hoist the Jolly Roger to her main-truck.

"Feel of my neck handkerchief," he commanded.

Wales did so. There was "a rumpling, which showed that there was a paper in the back part of it."

Spencer told him this was "a secret writing"—the plan and stations of the mutineers. There were about twenty of them, he said. They were to start a fight on the forecastle; Spencer would bring the men to the mast and get the officer of the deck to come and settle the difficulty; and as soon as the officer got to the gangway he would be seized and thrown overboard. The scuttles to the spar deck from the cabin and steerage, the only exits to the main deck from the officers' country, would be guarded, the arms chest opened, and all officers and others who did not fit in with Spencer's plans would be murdered.

There was much more of it; for half an hour an excited torrent of words poured from the lips of the nineteen-year-old midshipman—the Isle of Pines, the skull and crossbones, piracy, captured ships scuttled without trace, blood and gold, beautiful women. "It was his object . . . to select such of the female passengers [of captured ships] as were suitable, and after they had used them sufficiently to dispose of them." Spencer's eyes flashed, and Wales, scared but dissembling, cringed back against the cutter strakes.

Spencer gave him no chance to reply; toward the end of his monologue—it was almost eight bells and the watch was stirring about the deck—he called out to a seaman, Elisha Small, who was passing beneath the booms and told him to come up. Speaking first in Spanish, Spencer then switched to English to say,

"Oh, you need not be under any apprehension on *his* account, as I have sounded him pretty well, and find he is one of us."

Small nodded and went away, and the strange interview ended with tentative arrangements for another on the morrow—and with threats by Spencer of violent and immediate death if the steward repeated a syllable of their conversation.

Wales was left a shaken and terrified man, obsessed with the necessity, despite his oath, of getting the news to the captain—Commander Alexander Slidell Mackenzie. As soon as Spencer had turned in in his hammock, Wales came up on the quarterdeck and hung about the cabin entrance; but he saw Seaman Small watching him and, frightened, slunk away. Next he tried to get into the wardroom to report to the first lieutenant, Guert Gansevoort; but Spencer saw him coming into the steerage and questioned him.

"Why in the devil are you cruising around this place at this time of night? Why don't you turn in?"

And so the night dragged on. Wales lay trembling until dawn while the brig *Somers,* running her westing down, sailed quietly on toward Charlotte Amalie, seventeen hundred miles away.

Saturday, November 26, 1842 In the early morning Wales got into the wardroom on some pretext and told Purser H. M. Heiskell of the incipient mutiny. The purser informed Lieutenant Gansevoort, the second-in-command; and Gansevoort, thoroughly alarmed, hurried to inform Commander Mackenzie.

Mackenzie was thirty-nine years old, an officer with a record of unusual ability in his profession, and author of several books of biography and travel. He was highly esteemed and well fitted by character, ability, and temperament to command the *Somers* with his

crew of thirteen officers and one hundred and eighty "men"—some
eighty of them apprentice boys. At first he refused to take the mutiny
seriously. He listened attentively to all Gansevoort said: asked a number of rather impatient questions; smoothed his thin auburn hair; and
then declared that the vessel was in good discipline and that he found
it difficult to credit Wales' report. He directed Gansevoort, however,
to watch Spencer without seeming to do so, and also to watch the
crew.

The lieutenant carried out his instructions. There was little to report
at first. Spencer spent the day "rather sullenly in one corner of the
steerage, as was his custom, engaged in examining a small piece of
paper and writing on it with his pencil, and occasionally finding relax-
ation in working with his penknife at the tail of a devil fish, one of
the joints of which he had formed into a sliding ring for his cravat."
He was seen in the wardroom looking at a chart of the West Indies
and making inquiries about the Isle of Pines. He went to the foretop,
where an apprentice, Benjamin F. Green, tattooed "some love devices"
on his arm. That was all; but Gansevoort learned other things—that
Spencer had been trying for some time to ascertain "the rate of the
chronometer"; that he had been seen "in secret and nightly confer-
ences with Boatswain's Mate Samuel Cromwell and Seaman Elisha
Small"; that he had been intimate with the crew, though reserved with
the officers; that he had given money to Small, and money and tobacco
to others; that he had caused the wardroom steward to steal brandy
from the mess, and had been drunk; that "he had the habit of amusing
the crew by making music with his jaw," and that he had been dismissed in disgrace from the Navy's Brazilian squadron.

These things, to Gansevoort, were cumulative evidence; and when
he detected the midshipman looking at him "with the most infernal
expression I have ever seen upon a human face," the uneasy lieutenant was satisfied of Spencer's guilt. He reported to the captain and
communicated some of his alarm to him.

As the day wore on and the sun sank toward a mass of cumulus
clouds in the western sky Commander Mackenzie, wearied with much
thinking and disturbed by the tension of an uncertain danger, became
more and more apprehensive. He was not an easy man to frighten
when faced with the actuality of danger; but he possessed the sensi-

tive imagination of the writer, and the bare suggestion of mutiny, dropped into the eager workings of his mind, had been churned into a froth of suspicion. . . . *This thing could not be; it was beyond reason; his was a well-ordered ship; yet was it not safer to be wise before the fact? Yes, the safety of ship and crew demanded action, and he was the master.*

At evening quarters he ordered all officers aft on the quarterdeck; then, approaching Spencer, he said:

"I learn, Mr. Spencer, that you aspire to command of the *Somers?*"

With a bland but deferential smile the midshipman shook his head.

"Did you not tell Mr. Wales, sir, that you had a project to kill the commander, the officers, and a considerable portion of the crew of this vessel and convert her into a pirate?"

"I may have told him so, sir, but it was in joke."

"This, sir, is joking on a forbidden subject; this joke may cost you your life. Be pleased to remove your neck handkerchief."

But there was no longer any "rumpling"; the paper had gone.

Spencer was arrested, his sword taken from him, and he was placed on the port arms chest on the quarterdeck, double-ironed and handcuffed. He was warned that if he communicated with the crew in any way he would be put "to instant death," and Lieutenant Gansevoort was directed to see that these orders were carried out. The officer of the deck was armed with cutlass and pistol, while the amazed crew, dismissed from quarters, slunk forward, eying each other warily and talking in groups in guarded whispers. Gansevoort and Midshipman Henry Rodgers went below to the steerage to search Spencer's locker. Two papers with Greek characters were found. Rodgers translated them and presented the result to the captain as follows:

CERTAIN

P. Spencer	*D. McKinley*
E. Andrews	*Wales*

DOUBTFUL

Wilson	*x*	*Van Veltzor*
McKee	*x*	*Sullivan*

Warner	*Godfrey*
Green	*Gallia* x
Gedney	*Howard* x

Those doubtful marked x will probably be induced to join before the project is carried into execution. The remainder of the doubtful will probably join when the thing is done, if not, they must be forced. If any not marked down wish to join after the thing is done we will pick out the best and dispose of the rest.

NOLENS VOLENS

Sibley	*Strummond*	*Scott*
Van Brunt	*Witmore*	*Crawley*
Blackwell	*Waltham*	*Rodman*
Clarke	*Nevilles*	*Selsor*
Corney	*Dickinson*	*The Doctor*
Garratrantz	*Riley*	

Wheel: McKee
Cabin: Spencer, Small, Wilson
Wardroom: Spencer
Steerage: Spencer, Small, Wilson
Arm Chest: McKinley

Mackenzie, face strained and eyes bloodshot from sleeplessness, pored hour after hour over the names, as dancing shadows from the swinging lamp flickered about his cabin. Along the darkened decks, beneath the canvas faintly creaking in the boltropes, the officer of the deck—armed and uneasy, trusting no one, jumpy from suspense— made the rounds of the ship. Spencer slept peacefully on the arms chest, his chains clanking as the ship rolled. Mackenzie still sat wakefully below, worrying, seeing his kingdom of the sea, all he knew and loved and had built up, wavering like the crazy shadows in his cabin.

Sunday, November 27   It was a glorious Sunday; the flood of blinding tropic sunlight should have washed clean all the terrors of the dark. Fair winds still bellied the bleached canvas and ruffled the shining sea.

The wind freshened in the early morning, and after sail was shortened the crew stood to quarters ready for inspection. Commander Mackenzie eyed his men closely—men he once could trust—as they lined up with their battle-axes. Forward was Samuel Cromwell, boatswain's mate: ready with tongue and marlinespike, the tallest man in the crew, a bushy-bearded mustachioed sailor, cruel, violent, profane, and able, seamed with the scars of his slaving days. "He had a determined and dangerous air." Elisha Small was a weazened, shriveled little man with a timorous face. He shifted his battle-axe from hand to hand, stood on one foot and then the other, and avoided the captain's glance.

After quarters divine services were held. Again the captain, while he read the Psalms and led the men—they were once *his* men—in the singing of the hymns, watched the crew closely. His searching eyes flickered from face to face, looking, looking; but there was nothing.

However, there was no longer any peace aboard the brig *Somers,* running her westing down from Liberia to Charlotte Amalie. Tension and fear; the fear of a stab in the back, or a skull split from behind by a battle-axe, hung like a pall over the wardroom and the midshipmen's steerage; the officers glowered at Spencer chained on the arms chest, walked uneasily about their duties, or stood apart, wrapped in their thoughts, convinced of the imminence of disaster. The crew too —even the apprentice boys—was infected with unrest; gone were the idle, carefree Sundays when they would lie out on the bowsprit and watch the dolphin striker stabbing at the spray, when the captain sat at ease within his cabin and composed mellifluous essays on men and nations, when the officers lazed about the tiny wardroom and the midshipmen plaited white-line belts in the steerage. The *Somers* was an uneasy ship.

In the afternoon, the wind having moderated, skysails and royal stunsails were set. An apprentice was on the main royal yard, and Small and another seaman were pulling at the brace when, with a crash of splintering wood, snapped stays, and flapping canvas, the topgallant mast carried away in the sheave hole, taking with it the main royal mast, with the skysail, studding sail, t'gallant staysail, and part of the gaff topsail. "Occurring at this time, this incident immediately took on a sinister appearance both to Commander Mackenzie and his first lieutenant, whose minds at once rushed to the conclusion that it was intentional." Lieutenant Gansevoort hurried to the deck and took charge of clearing the wreckage; he noted that all those most conspicuously named in Spencer's Greek papers had mustered at the main topmast head—— "The coincidence confirmed the existence of a dangerous conspiracy."

Later, when the wreckage was cleared away and the new t'gallant mast was about to be swayed up from the deck, a group of men started running aft in each gangway toward the quarterdeck. Gansevoort, excited, leaped onto the trunk, drew and cocked his pistol, rushed forward to meet them, and screamed to the commander:

"God, I believe they're coming!" and to the men, "Stay for'd . . . stay for'd! I'll blow out the brains of the first man who puts his foot on the quarterdeck!"

Frightened, amazed, the men halted, huddled in groups; then, from forward, Midshipman Rodgers relieved the tension when he sang out that he had sent the men aft to the mast rope.

The wreckage was cleared without trouble, new canvas was sent up, and by late afternoon the *Somers* was bowling along under full sail with a whispering wind astern; but nerves were twitching and throats dry, for night, "the season of danger," was at hand.

The harassed captain consulted his first lieutenant; and together they agreed that Cromwell, the hard-case boatswain's mate, should be arrested. All the officers were armed and stationed about the spar deck; it was almost dusk. Cromwell, a huge bearded figure of a man, was climbing slowly down the rigging. As he set foot on deck he was met by Gansevoort with a cocked pistol, and, surrounded by officers, he was led aft to the quarterdeck where he was questioned by Mackenzie as to the "secret conversation he had held the night before with Mr. Spencer."

"It was not me, sir—it was Small."

Small was brought aft and charged with having listened to Spencer's mutinous plots. He answered meekly.

"Yes, sir."

Both men were clapped in double irons. Cromwell was put on the starboard arms chest directly across from Spencer, and Small on the starboard quarterdeck near the after gun. They were told they would be taken home for trial. Cromwell protested his innocence.

"I don't know anything about it," he repeated again and again.

Wales, the steward, was armed and set as guard on the prisoners. "Increased vigilance was now enjoined upon all the officers; all were perpetually armed"; either Commander Mackenzie or Lieutenant Gansevoort was always on deck, and generally both of them were.

Monday, November 28 The officers came red-eyed upon deck to greet the sun. It had been a sleepless night, with cutlasses and pistols as bedfellows. Mackenzie's thoughts were feverish. *This waiting—this eternal waiting; if only they would come! He was ready for them. But would they come? Was there a widespread plot? How extensive had Spencer's efforts been; how many—— How many?* His tortured mind raced on. *There must be many: Spencer's evil genius had infected the crew. Small and Cromwell, with their hangdog looks; that falling spar, and those damned papers—conclusive evidence. This must be stopped—violence must be met with violence.*

Monday was another soft and sunlit day, but the terrors of the night did not die with the dawn. Hysteria strode the quarterdeck, was master, mate, and crew.

After a breakfast of salt horse and hardtack with a pannikin of "jamoke," all hands were called to witness punishment. There were two to be flogged. One of them was Charles Lambert, boy, who had stolen some sennit for a hat from the apprentice, Gagely. The lad was stripped to the waist, his wrists and ankles spread-eagled to a grating, and the crew paraded at quarters, the armed officers looking on. A petty officer wielded the cat. The nine-tails whistled through the air and cracked across the boy's naked back. He shuddered, gasped. Red welts, crisscrossed, faintly oozing purple blood, ridged the skin of his back, curved beneath his armpits and reached out onto his chest. The cat cracked again; the boy strained at his bonds. Six lashes—fifty-four welts—a curving pattern of scarified skin.

Henry Waltham, the wardroom steward, was next. He had stolen the brandy for Spencer. He did not "wince nor cry aloud"; when his punishment was ended and his bonds released, he sullenly drew a shirt over his bleeding shoulders and hurried below.

The flogging finished, Commander Mackenzie mounted the trunk and addressed the crew. He told them for the first time in general terms of Spencer's plot; he emphasized that many of them had been "marked for murder" by Spencer; he "exhorted them to think of their homes and kindred and to rejoice at the prospect of being with their families again in about three weeks." Some of the boys shuddered; some wept at his words. The tears impressed the captain; he "now considered the crew tranquillized and the vessel safe."

But not for long.

Tuesday, November 29 The creeping shadows of the night had done their work once more. Fear and suspicion were the messmates of the crew of the *Somers*. Man looked upon man askance. Even the slatting of canvas, the creak of the booms, the whisper of the waves were ominous—not the pleasant murmur they once had been. Dark circles curved beneath the captain's eyes. Apprehensions beset his mind. The brig *Somers*—the United States Ship *Somers*—mutiny. Mutiny on his ship. *They ought to be hanged at the yardarm. . . .*

Again that day the pipe shrilled: "All hands witness punishment." Waltham again. This time he had told a boy of three bottles of wine that could conveniently be pilfered, "his object being no doubt to furnish the means of excitement to the conspirators." Another speech, "but the whole crew was far from being tranquillized."

That afternoon Commander Mackenzie became convinced the conspirators were planning a sudden rush to rescue the three prisoners chained upon the quarterdeck. Indeed, Wales, the steward, detected Charles A. Wilson, sailmaker's mate, attempting to draw a handspike from beneath the launch. He leveled his pistol at Wilson's head, and the man dropped the spike and ran. It was a disquieting incident.

Commander Mackenzie, more anxious than he yet had been, remained constantly on deck. Mad images thronged his tired brain as he paced the quarterdeck between the arms chests. Spencer to port; Cromwell to starboard; the frightened Small abaft the gun; others—how many others?—still at liberty, slinking about the spar deck, watching the wardroom, waiting for night and its shifting shadows.

Wednesday, November 30 Another fair morning, and Charlotte Amalie five days to the westward. The sea, gold and blue in the sunlight, danced in little waves to the far horizon. The muzzles of the smoothbores glared from port and starboard out upon an empty ocean. The captain paced restlessly on the quarterdeck. The rising sun found him where the moon had left him—on deck, sleepless, red-eyed, haggard, cutlass by his side, a brace of pistols in his belt. Landsman McKinley and Apprentice Green had missed their muster when the watch was called at midnight; most suspicious; where was this thing to end?

At nine o'clock quarters, four more arrests were made; Wilson, the sailmaker's mate; McKinley, on Spencer's list as "certain"; Green, and Alexander McKie, friend of Cromwell. In double irons the new prisoners were placed beside Spencer, Cromwell, and Small on the quarterdeck, "in the way of everybody and interfering seriously with the working of the ship." In Wilson's sail bag was found "an African knife of an extraordinary shape . . . it was of no use for any honest purpose; it was fit only to kill."

Commander Mackenzie kept the deck still, pacing between the ironed prisoners, his thoughts racing with his steps. *With fine weather and bright nights there was already a disposition to make an attack and rescue the prisoners. When bad weather should interfere with the attention of the officers. . . .*

But Spencer, Cromwell, and Small were the only suspects capable of navigating the ship. Article 13 of the Laws for the Government of the Navy (Article 13, Article 24, Article 14—the captain knew each syllable and comma now; nor would he ever forget) provided that "if any person in the Navy shall make or attempt to make any mutinous assembly, he shall, on conviction thereof by a court-martial, suffer death. . . ." *He shall, on conviction thereof by a court-martial, suffer death.*

Immediately after quarters the captain addressed a letter to the *Somers'* four wardroom officers and the three oldest midshipmen, asking their opinion as to the best course to be pursued "in view of the disaffection among a crew which has so long and so systematically and assiduously been tampered with by an officer."

The seven officers at once convened in the wardroom and began to examine "witnesses." They did not constitute in any sense a court-martial but merely an unofficial body, functioning in an unofficial way. There followed, hour after hour, all the day long as Mackenzie kept the deck with the younger midshipmen, a long parade of frightened seamen and apprentices, most of whom "thought," "believed," "felt," or "were sure" that Spencer, Cromwell, and Small were the leaders in a mutinous plot. The testimony was mostly opinion, little fact.

George Warner, ordinary seaman: "The damned son of a bitch [Cromwell] ought to be hung. If I had my way of it, I would hang him."

M. H. Garty, sergeant of marines: "The vessel would be safer if Cromwell, Spencer, and Small were put to death."

O. B. Browning: "To tell you God Almighty's truth, I believe that some of the cooks around the galley, I think they are the main backers."

Thomas Dickinson: "I think if Cromwell, Small, and Spencer were made way with, it would put a stop to, and I think by that means the vessel will be safe——"

Without a halt for meals, through the long hot day until the sun was reddening the western sky, the apprehensive officers, their fears mounting as they felt the growing hysteria of the crew, sat in the tiny wardroom, Purser Heiskill scribbling notes on sheets of paper. At dusk the captain adjourned the proceedings and made his dispositions for the night. Gansevoort took the larboard watch and he the starboard; it was another night of heavy-lidded sleeplessness, of starts, alarums, and fears. Shadows of the bellied sails traced ominous patterns across the brig's white deck; a line's loose end swayed—like a noose—from the main t'gallant yard.

Thursday, December 1 The council, ragged from sleeplessness, ended its sittings before quarters, and at nine o'clock in the morning its verdict was handed to Captain Mackenzie:

U. S. Brig Somers
December 1, 1842

Sir:

In answer to your letter of yesterday, requesting our counsel as to the best course to be pursued with the prisoners, Acting Midshipman

*Philip Spencer, Boatswain's Mate Samuel Cromwell, and Seaman
Elisha Small, we would state, that the evidence which has come to our
knowledge is of such a nature as, after as dispassionate and deliberate
a consideration of the case as the exigencies of the time would admit,
we have come to a cool, decided, and unanimous opinion that they
have been guilty of a full and determined intention to commit a mutiny
on board of this vessel of a most atrocious nature; and that the revelation of circumstances having made it necessary to confine others with
them, the uncertainty as to what extent they are leagued with others
still at large, the impossibility of guarding against the contingencies
which "a day or an hour may bring forth," we are convinced that it
would be impossible to carry them to the United States, and that the
safety of the public property, the lives of ourselves, and of those committed to our charge, require that (giving them sufficient time to prepare) they should be put to death, in a manner best calculated as an
example to make a beneficial impression upon the disaffected. This
opinion we give, bearing in mind our duty to our God, our country,
and to the service.*

We are, sir, very respectfully, your obedient servants.

Guert Gansevoort, Lieutenant
R. W. Leecock, Past Assistant Surgeon
H. M. Heiskill, Purser
M. C. Perry, Acting Master
Henry Rodgers, Midshipman
Egbert Thompson, Midshipman
Chas. W. Hayes, Midshipman

Mackenzie did not hesitate. He gave orders "to make immediate
preparations for hanging the three principal criminals at the main
yardarms."

The day was fair, with scalloped clouds tracing a pattern across a
deep blue sky. The gentle rollers easily lifted the brig's two hundred
and sixty-six tons; the main yardarm swayed slightly.

"All hands witness punishment." Again the shrill bo's'n's pipe.

*The afterguard and idlers of both watches were mustered on the
quarterdeck at the whip intended for Mr. Spencer; the forecastle men
and foretop men at that of Cromwell, to whose corruption they had*

been chiefly exposed; the maintop men of both watches at that in-
tended for Small, who for a month or more had held the situation of
captain of the maintop.

The officers and trusted petty officers, cutlasses in hands and pistols
tucked in their belts, were stationed about the spar deck with "orders
to cut down whoever should let go the whip with even one hand, or
fail to haul on it when ordered." The ensign and pennant were bent
on and ready for hoisting; Captain Mackenzie left the deck for the
first time in many hours, went to his cabin and donned his full-dress
uniform, and "proceeded to execute the most painful duty that has
developed upon an American commander—that of announcing to the
criminals their fate."

Mackenzie first confronted Spencer, the still bland and almost deb-
onair midshipman, the son of a Cabinet officer.

"Mr. Spencer, sir, when you were about to take my life, to dishonor
me as an officer when in the execution of my rightful duty, to take my
life without cause or offense to you, it was your intention, sir, to re-
move me suddenly from the world in the darkness of the night, in my
sleep, without a moment to utter one word of affection to my wife and
children or one prayer for their welfare. Your life, sir, is now forfeited
to your country; the dire necessities of the case growing out of your
corruption of the crew, compel me to take it. I shall not, however,
imitate your intended example, and send you to your Maker without
preparation. If there yet remains to you one feeling true to nature, it
shall be gratified; if you have any word to send to your parents it shall
be noted and faithfully delivered. You will have ten minutes for this
purpose."

The midshipman's composure entirely vanished. "He sank, with
tears, upon his knees and said that he was not fit to die." Urged to die
like an officer and to set an example to the men he had seduced, he
shudderingly regained his self-control and began, quietly, to pray.

Cromwell, the hard-case boatswain, was even more unnerved; he
protested his innocence, falling upon his knees, his chains clanking on
the deck, and begging for mercy for his wife's sake. Only Elisha
Small, the scared-looking conspirator who had been set down "as the

poltroon of the three" received the announcement calmly; he had, he said, no preparations to make.

"I have nobody to care for me but my poor old mother, and I would rather that she should not know how I have died."

Spencer, praying, suddenly looked up, his eyes swimming in tears, as Mackenzie passed:

"As these are my last words, I trust that they will be believed. Cromwell is innocent."

The captain was staggered. He consulted Lieutenant Gansevoort, who said, "there was not a shadow of doubt." The first lieutenant consulted the ship's petty officers, and Cromwell, the ex-slaver, was "condemned by acclamation."

The fair trade winds still held. They pulled gently at the taut canvas as the minutes passed. Spencer objected to the shortness of time for preparation, and asked for an hour; no answer was made to this request, but he was not hurried, and more than the hour for which he asked was allowed to elapse.

"He requested that his face might be covered; this was readily granted, and he was asked with what it should be covered; he did not care; a handkerchief was sought in his locker; none but a black one found and this brought for the purpose."

"Tell them," Spencer breathed, "tell my family I die wishing them every blessing and happiness; I deserve death for this and many other crimes. There are few crimes that I have not committed; I feel sincerely penitent, and my only fear of death is that my repentance may be too late."

The little waves slapped briskly against the weed-grown strakes.

"This will kill my poor mother," he sobbed, and then: "But haven't you formed an exaggerated estimate of the extent of this conspiracy? Aren't you going too far—too fast? Does the law entirely justify you?"

"All your brother officers, your messmates included, believe you guilty," Mackenzie replied, "and your death justified."

"They are right . . . they are right," the prisoner muttered. "Oh, God, how am I to die?"

The captain explained the manner of his death.

"Oh, let me be shot!"

The sun-tanned boys and bearded seamen, barefooted, tattooed, brawny, stood in silent uneasy ranks with fearful eyes strained aft.

A Bible and a prayer book were brought for the midshipman; "frocks" to cover the heads of Small and Cromwell. The three walked slowly aft, their chains clanking, a sad procession.

Spencer to Mackenzie: "I beg your forgiveness for what I have meditated against you."

Spencer to Wales: "Mr. Wales, I earnestly hope you will forgive me for tampering with your fidelity."

The steward broke into tears and sobbed: "I do forgive you from the bottom of my heart, and I hope that God may forgive you also."

Spencer to Small: "Small, forgive me for leading you into this trouble."

Small to Spencer: "No, by God! Mr. Spencer, I can't forgive you."

Spencer to Small: "Small, forgive me . . . you must forgive me."

Small to Spencer: "Ah, Mr. Spencer, that is a hard thing for you to ask me. We shall soon be before the face of God, and there we shall know all about it."

The captain intervened, pleaded with Small; immediately the weazened little seaman held out his hand: "I do forgive you, Mr. Spencer; may God Almighty forgive you also."

Small to the captain: "You are doing your duty, and I honor you for it. God bless the flag and prosper it."

The prisoners were placed by the gangway on the hammock nettings fore and aft. The nooses were adjusted and Spencer asked permission to give the signal of execution. Small asked for a last word with the crew and, "his face being uncovered," said:

"Shipmates and topmates, take warning by my example: I never was a pirate, I never killed a man—it's for saying that I would do it that I am about to depart this life . . . see what a word will do. It was going in a Guineaman [a slaver] that brought me to this; beware of a Guineaman—I am now ready to die, Mr. Spencer; are you?"

Cromwell's muffled voice through the frock that hid his face: "Tell my wife I die an innocent man; tell Lieutenant Morris I die an innocent man."

Silent the prisoners stood upon the hammock nettings, hands bound behind their backs, chains looped about their feet, faces muffled in the hanging shrouds. The sweet winds whispered in their ears; the warmth—a tender warmth—of the southern sun beat down upon their bodies; the pulse of life flowed strongly in their veins; temples throbbed to the terrible rhythm of racing hearts; a sob racked Spencer's body.

The crew of the brig *Somers* stood and waited in silent ranks, their hands upon the whips, ready to heave their shipmates into eternity. Cold-eyed, wary, hands upon cutlasses, the officers and trusted petty officers stood near them, while aft on the quarter-deck, the other prisoners lay in chains, watching with frightened fascination.

Captain Mackenzie, his gold epaulets glinting in the sun, mounted the trunk and "waited for some time but no word was given." The slow minutes passed. There was no sound but the soft chuckle of the little waves; no sight, for the hooded men, but the red glare of sunlight through the coarse warp of cloth.

The glowing coal by the signal gun grew dull; a boy fetched a live one from the galley.

The hooded head of the son of the Secretary of War moved dumbly; a hoarse unnatural voice whispered to a boatswain's mate named Browning that he could not give the word——

Immediately the captain spoke: "Fire!"

The glowing coal dropped upon live powder; the muzzle-loader spoke, roaring across an empty ocean.

"Whip," shouted Gansevoort.

Cutlass blades gleamed in the sunlight—but there was no need. Nervous hands clutched at the trailing lines; the nooses tightened; beneath the hoods breath stopped and praying lips grew blue; heels were snatched from hammock nettings; the ensign sprang to the gaff— and, as if to keep the colors company, the bodies of Spencer, Small, and Cromwell were run up in jig time to the main yardarms.

The thing was done.

The brig *Somers* sailed on beneath a mackerel sky toward Charlotte Amalie, where once in days gone by pirates had fought and died.

The bodies swung like gruesome pendulums all the day; Spencer, the officer, alone at the port yardarm. An hour after the crew's dinner, the watch was set and the bodies were lowered to be laid out for burial. For the midshipman a crude coffin was made of two mess chests; he was dressed in complete uniform, "except the sword, which he had forfeited the right to wear." The two seamen, tended by their messmates, were dressed decently and sewed up in their hammocks by the sailmaker. In accordance with the age-old tradition of the sea, the last stitches pierced the noses of the deceased. Round shot went at their heads and feet—and all was ready.

It was almost twilight, and the sky was no longer fair, but dark and lowering, with great masses of heavy clouds. A squall sprang up; tarpaulins were hastily thrown over the corpses while the watch shortened sail. The decks streamed water; the black guns dripped damp and ugly; fierce rain beat upon the canvas covering the bodies.

It was dark when the rain had ended and final preparations were complete.

"All hands bury the dead!"

On the damp spar deck, with the wet sails drawing to the wind, the crew of the *Somers*—chastened, solemn, subdued—gathered by the light of battle lanterns to read the last offices for the dead. They were on the booms and in the gangways and in the quarter boat. Gnarled hands of seamen turned the flimsy pages of prayer books, and the responses of the young apprentices sounded high and thin. The prisoners in their chains whispered the service. The lanterns, flickering and faint, lit up a group of drawn faces, a bit of deck, a triangle of wet canvas; while overhead, above the tracery of rigging and dark sails, pale stars struggled through a rack of clouds.

The captain's voice read on: "We therefore commend the souls of our brothers departed unto Almighty God, and we commit their bodies to the deep."

Three dull splashes, louder than the slap of waves against the strakes, louder than the creak of cordage or the flap of canvas; and the brig *Somers* sailed on toward Charlotte Amalie.

NOTES   The *Somers* arrived at Charlotte Amalie December 4, and stood into New York December 14, ending the fateful cruise which had taken her to Madeira, Tenerife, Porto Praia, and Liberia. She was isolated from shore; no visitors were allowed; eight more of the crew were arrested immediately upon arrival; Midshipman Perry proceeded at once to Washington with a report to the Secretary of the Navy, and Captain Mackenzie led the whole ship's company ashore to the nearest church, "where he gave public thanks to Almighty God for the recent miraculous preservation of his ship and her company from the horrors of capture and murder by mutineers." It was not long before the story was out, and the "mutiny" on the brig *Somers* had become a *cause célèbre*. James Fenimore Cooper wrote scathing castigations of Commander Mackenzie's conduct; Richard Henry Dana and Charles Sumner took up the cudgels in his behalf. Because of the prominence of Spencer's father, then Secretary of War, the case became something of a political issue; because of Mackenzie's excellent reputation as an officer and author, his actions found many supporters. There was a court of inquiry, followed by a court-martial of Commander Mackenzie, on which some of the highest ranking officers in the Navy sat in judgment. After a lengthy trial Mackenzie was acquitted, but not unanimously, and the twelve of his crew he had arrested were released without the filing of charges. Cromwell's wife tried vainly to get retribution through the civil courts; Mackenzie, shaken by the blasts of criticism which followed him through life, died less than six years later, after distinguishing himself "in the land attack on Vera Cruz in the war with Mexico"; and the brig *Somers,* scene of the most famous "mutiny" in the American Navy, was wrecked, drowning three midshipmen and thirty-seven of her crew. To posterity Mackenzie left his defense: "In the necessities of my position I found my law, and in them also I must trust to find my justification."

But Commander Mackenzie did not find his "justification" in life, nor in the literary posterity which the "mutiny" on the brig *Somers* fathered. Lieutenant Guert Gansevoort, second in command of the *Somers,* was a cousin of Herman Melville, and Melville—in the words of Richard T. Stavig—"drew heavily on the *Somers* incident" for his famous novel, *Billy Budd, Foretopman.* Mr. Stavig, of Washington and Jefferson College, Washington, Pa., is the author of a Ph.D. dissertation, "Melville's *Billy Budd*—A New Approach to the Problem of Interpretation," which was submitted to Princeton University in November, 1953. He writes in a letter to the author, dated March

30, 1954, "I believe I have established that Melville used the historical incident (i.e., the *Somers* 'mutiny') very extensively in the writing of this novel."

Furthermore, the way in which Melville used the Somers *material and his attitude toward Mackenzie's action (he called it "murder" at one time) suggest the general trend of the book, an interpretation which internal evidence supports. Although many critics would disagree with me, I believe Melville was making a bitter protest against blind and complete obedience—in this case to naval law, rather than to a superior officer. Man must never sacrifice his humanity, Melville is saying. . . .*

In his dissertation, Mr. Stavig condemns Mackenzie bitterly. Mr. Stavig emphasizes Mackenzie's paternalistic relationships with some of the midshipmen aboard the *Somers*, a relationship which in his view strongly influenced the judgment of the "drum-head court-martial" that advised death for Spencer and his mates. Two midshipmen in the *Somers* were related to Mackenzie by "blood," two by "alliance," and seven officers were between sixteen and twenty-one years old.

Moreover, Mackenzie, as Stavig points out, was a brother-in-law of Commodore Matthew Calbraith Perry, who was personally interested in the experiment the *Somers* was carrying out—the apprentice training of enlisted men. Mr. Stavig believes that Mackenzie's mind was already made up before he convened the council of officers to advise him, and that the "evidence" produced by this council was so flimsy that twice Lt. Gansevoort reported "the council's unreadiness to recommend the executions. . . .

"Each time he was sent back to the Council meeting with instructions that the deliberations should be continued; the officers had apparently not examined the evidence carefully enough."

The evidence upon which this contention is based is to be found chiefly in the *Autobiography of Thurlow Weed,* admittedly a second-hand source. Weed states he was told about the *Somers* case by "Hunn" Gansevoort, a cousin of Guert. Mr. Stavig also tends to accept the "brilliant" review of the case by James Fenimore Cooper, a landsman who knew little of the sea and who excoriated Mackenzie, while discounting the defense of Mackenzie by Richard Henry Dana, who knew the hard facts of life before the mast in those days from personal experience. Mr. Stavig emphasizes that Mackenzie based the necessity for the executions on one major premise—his alleged inability to bring the ship into port safely with so large a number of prisoners in irons. They interfered, he held, with the working of the ship. His arrest of additional prisoners—after the prior ironing of Spencer, Small and Cromwell—necessitated, therefore, the execution of the first three. In other words Mackenzie's own deliberate actions —rather than the findings of the Council—doomed Spencer and his mates. As Stavig puts it, "in a very real sense, he created the necessity for the executions."

Mr. Stavig's interesting and well-documented discussion makes a brilliant case of parallels between Melville's *Billy Budd, Foretopman* and the *Somers* incident. But this author feels that in his justifiable condemnation of Mackenzie he has relied too much upon Weed and other second-hand evidence and has weighted too heavily Cooper and other writers of the day, some of whom were passionately (in the vernacular of the modern generation) "anti-Brass" (biased against officers). However, there can be little disagreement from anyone who has studied the case, with the following judgment of Mr. Stavig:

Captain Mackenzie, in deciding to execute Spencer, evidently did not, or could not because of personal inadequacies, give sufficient consideration to the modifying circumstances, consideration necessary for any sound interpretation of the factual evidence in the case. Spencer was a romantic, unbalanced youth and the "mutiny" had to be judged in terms of his character. [Stavig points out, "Spencer lived in a dream fantasy peopled by pirates and exotic maidens . . . he had made mutinous plans to take over almost every ship on which he had served."] *. . . According to his own* [Spencer's] *testimony he did make overtures to Wales regarding mutiny and piracy, and apparently was not merely joking. There is considerable evidence to show that he wanted to commit an act of mutiny aboard the* Somers. *This does not mean, however, that he seriously believed that he could, or even would do so, or that he was a serious threat to the ship. Mackenzie, because he failed to interpret the so-called mutiny in terms of the human personalities involved, vastly exaggerated the possible danger.*

According to the laws of the Navy, Spencer's "trial"—if it can be called such—was not only unfair, but extralegal, though according to the laws of the sea Mackenzie might have been justified in such extreme measures if the safety of his ship were actually imperiled. But it seems to be the verdict of posterity that Mackenzie acted too hastily and without certain and sure evidence to justify the death penalty.

The *Somers* case served a very useful purpose. Public attention was drawn by the investigation to the haphazard, politically influenced system of appointing midshipmen then in effect, and to the lack of training and educational facilities for midshipmen. The *Somers* "mutiny" was, therefore, a powerful factor in the establishment of the Naval Academy three years later under the regime of Secretary of the Navy George Bancroft.

Of the four men marked "certain" on Spencer's list, there was "no person on board of the name of E. Andrews," as James Fenimore Cooper later pointed out in his discussion of the famous case. After the arrival of the *Somers* in the United States the name of "E. Andrews" was "presumed to be an alias for Samuel Cromwell," Cooper further states. It is interesting that the name of Wales, the informer, appears on the "certain" list, while neither the name of Cromwell nor of Small is included either under "certain" or "doubtful."

It is also interesting to note that to many members of Chi Psi, Spencer's college fraternity, Spencer is a romanticized martyr; though judging from one or two letters the author has received not all Chi Psi men are now firmly convinced that he deserves to be. Spencer was one of the five original members and founders of the fraternity at Union College, Schenectady, N.Y., and ever since his death fraternity tradition has it that the Greek papers found in Spencer's locker hid Chi Psi secrets, "for the preservation of which Spencer forfeited his life." There are no substantiating facts for this belief, but nevertheless, the fraternity's song still proclaims that Spencer——

> *When sinking down beneath the wave,*
> *Loud shouted out "Chi Psi!"*

A letter from the late Dr. Carl E. McCombs, a trustee of the Chi Psi fraternity at Union College, who made a special study of the Spencer case, points out that in May, 1941, the Chi Psi fraternity presented to

Union College, in connection with the centennial of the fraternity's founding, a portrait of Philip Spencer. This portrait, together with a portrait of Spencer's father—John C. Spencer—hang in a special Chi Psi alcove of the Union College Library which has been dedicated to the use of the college for special works on American history and culture.

"Your fine story of the so-called conspiracy and the execution of Spencer and his mates is in accordance with the evidence," Dr. McCombs declares. "My own construction is, however, that Mackenzie was an incompetent, to put it mildly, and that his incompetence was all the more disastrous in this case because he was supposed to be a properly trained naval officer. My good friend, Kenneth Roberts (the author) of Kennebunkport, Maine, also of Chi Psi, with whom I have discussed this subject many times, declares, 'Spencer got what he deserved.' If he did, he was the only person involved in this so-called conspiracy who was so successful."

That Spencer was considerable of a scamp and a scalawag prior to the *Somers* affair seems to be apparent. Letters in the possession of the Judge Advocate General in the Navy Department indicate that he had at least talked about mutiny on another ship (the *Potomac*) on which he had previously served, and that his family had warned and reprimanded him. He undoubtedly owed to political influence his reinstatement in the Navy, after his previous dismissal from the Brazilian squadron.

Some of the descendants of the unfortunate midshipman's family are not as ardent in his defense as some Chi Psi men still are, judging from one letter the author has received which describes Philip Spencer as a *bête noire* to the preceding generation.

"It is rather sad," Mrs. Mabel W. Francis writes, "that we know so little of Philip's life, but he was never mentioned if it were possible to avoid it. His father was a most unpleasant man who had no feeling for anyone save himself and his own political future. He possessed undoubted talents, but could never make a friend. . . . That he [Philip Spencer] was foolish is certain, but he was very young and had a most unfair trial. Captain Mackenzie evidently lost his nerve and there may have been some political undercurrent. John Canfield Spencer had most bitter enemies."

ACKNOWLEDGMENTS   The quotations in the chapter are from
Mackenzie's report to the Secretary of the Navy. I have also drawn,
though to a lesser degree, from an article in the November, 1925,
United States Naval Institute Proceedings, by Rear Admiral Liv-
ingston Hunt. Records of the proceedings of the court of inquiry into
the "mutiny" and the court-martial of Commander Mackenzie also
have been consulted, as have the writings of James Fenimore Cooper
and of other authors who have dealt with the case.

An interesting and well-documented recent discussion of the case
is Richard T. Stavig's unpublished thesis, "Melville's *Billy Budd,*"
referred to in the Notes on this chapter. Another recent discussion
of this famous "mutiny"—in book-length form—will be found in
Frederic F. Van de Water's *The Captain Called It Mutiny,* Ives
Washburn, 1954.

1939

Sea Raider

THE LIFE AND DEATH
OF THE *ADMIRAL GRAF SPEE*

> *Her upper works seemed to be but a shambles of torn and
> twisted iron and steel, and through the holes in her side . . .
> could be seen dull red glows as the flames gradually gained the
> mastery between decks. She seemed to many to be entirely
> beaten, but she renewed her fire almost as briskly as ever in
> spite of the condition she was in. . . . Only one of the
> Scharnhorst's four funnels remained upright; she had a heavy
> and increasing list to port; and her stern was ablaze. At 4:40
> she fired a last shot from her fore turret and then turned very
> gently over, her flag still flying . . . and finally vanished bows
> foremost. . . . From Admiral von Spee's flagship not a soul
> escaped.*
>
> From the official account of the
> Battle of the Falkland Islands, December 8, 1914.

A forest of tapering masts and rakish funnels rose above Southampton
Water and the Solent on May 20, 1937. The power and glory of
Britain and men-of-war of seventeen other nations rode at anchor
upon the misty waters to do homage to a new-crowned king.

It was the Coronation Naval Review, and in a place of prominence
lay the "Panzerschiff" *Admiral Graf Spee,* launched at Wilhelms-

haven in 1934, named for a sailor who fought his ship till she sank, and now the pride of a new Germany and representative of a renascent sea power. She was a sight then to stir a seaman's heart—the lean strength of her, with her fine flowing lines and her unbroken main deck sweeping to abaft the after turret. Below decks her young sailors seemed different from those who mutinied in 1918; they were the smartest of all the seamen, picturesquely resplendent in their short brass-buttoned jackets and long trailing cap ribbons. The Prussianistic spirit of the Kaiser's navy was absent; the men sat at their mess tables drinking beer, and on bulkheads and door panels they had painted scenes of the Fatherland.

The *Admiral Graf Spee* was the newest of Germany's three "pocket battleships," a type that startled the naval world and was one of the direct causes of the naval race that gradually gathered headway between 1930 and 1939 and added fuel to the seething fires of a continent.

The *Deutschland,* first of the class, was laid down in 1929, well before Hitler assumed power, and all three of the type—*Deutschland, Admiral Scheer,* and *Admiral Graf Spee* (completed in 1936)—were designed and begun by a pre-Nazi Germany, a Germany bowed by the World War, but intent upon establishing German supremacy.

Limited by the Versailles treaty to warships of no more than 10,000 tons displacement, German technicians evolved the *Graf Spee* type, and by the extensive use of welding instead of riveting and by employing weight-saving Diesel engines they produced what were actually armored cruisers of an exceptionally powerful type, more heavily gunned than any other cruiser in the world; faster, with their twenty-six knot speed, than any other ship that could outgun them, except three then afloat, the British battle cruisers *Hood, Repulse, Renown.*

Mounting six eleven-inch guns (in only two turrets) and with enough oil capacity for long cruises, the three ships were conceived, designed and built for just two reasons: (1) commerce raiding and the creation of a strategical diversion far from the main theater of naval action; (2) the satisfaction of German pride in the building of a man-of-war that for her size was unmatched in power.

The "pocket battleships" became at once not only formidable instruments of naval strategy, but symbols of the new Germany. And

as such they elicited immediate answers in the chancelleries and shipyards of the world. At Brest and Penhoet welding torches hissed and
steel clanged on steel as France built the thirteen-inch-gunned,
26,500-ton thirty-knot *Dunkerque* and *Strasbourg*—direct response
in an international argument that grew—with Hitler—into the tragedy
of war.

The *Admiral Graf Spee,* Captain Hans Langsdorff commanding,
and with a crew of 1,107 aboard, was already bowing to the long
swell of the Western Ocean when war started on September 1, 1939.
She steamed south from the theater of war at high speed, and for three
and a half months she roved the southern seas preying upon British
commerce.

The *Graf Spee* almost met her fate early in her cruise. On September 11, the pocket battleship's reconnaissance plane sighted a British
cruiser about thirty miles from the *Spee*. The plane escaped undetected
and the raider stood away into the wastes of the South Atlantic.

For the first four weeks of roving, the *Graf Spee's* fangs were
drawn. Adolph Hitler's political blindness, which led him alternately,
during the Great War, from mad optimism to contemptuous conde-
scension, persuaded him that with the conquest of Poland a *fait
accompli,* Britain and France might make peace. Accordingly the
Spee—and her sister-ship, the *Deutschland,* which was lurking in the
North Atlantic—were not permitted to start their attacks on British
shipping until September 26, and on French ships until mid-October.

The British S.S. *Clement,* sunk off the coast of Brazil on September
30, was the *Graf Spee's* first victim. In October she sank five British
merchantmen on the trade routes to the Cape of Good Hope. The
raider refueled at a mid-Atlantic rendezvous from her supply ship—
the *Altmark*—transferred some of her prisoners to the merchantmen,
and disappeared into the blue, rounding the Cape of Good Hope into
the Indian Ocean to wait for the wool freighters from Australia. She
got a small tanker in the Mozambique Channel, but the freighters
were late, the pickings were scarce, and by now the hunt was on, the
pack was closing in, and the *Graf Spee* doubled back into the Atlantic,
refueling once again from *Altmark* in late November in the far seas off
Tristan da Cunha.

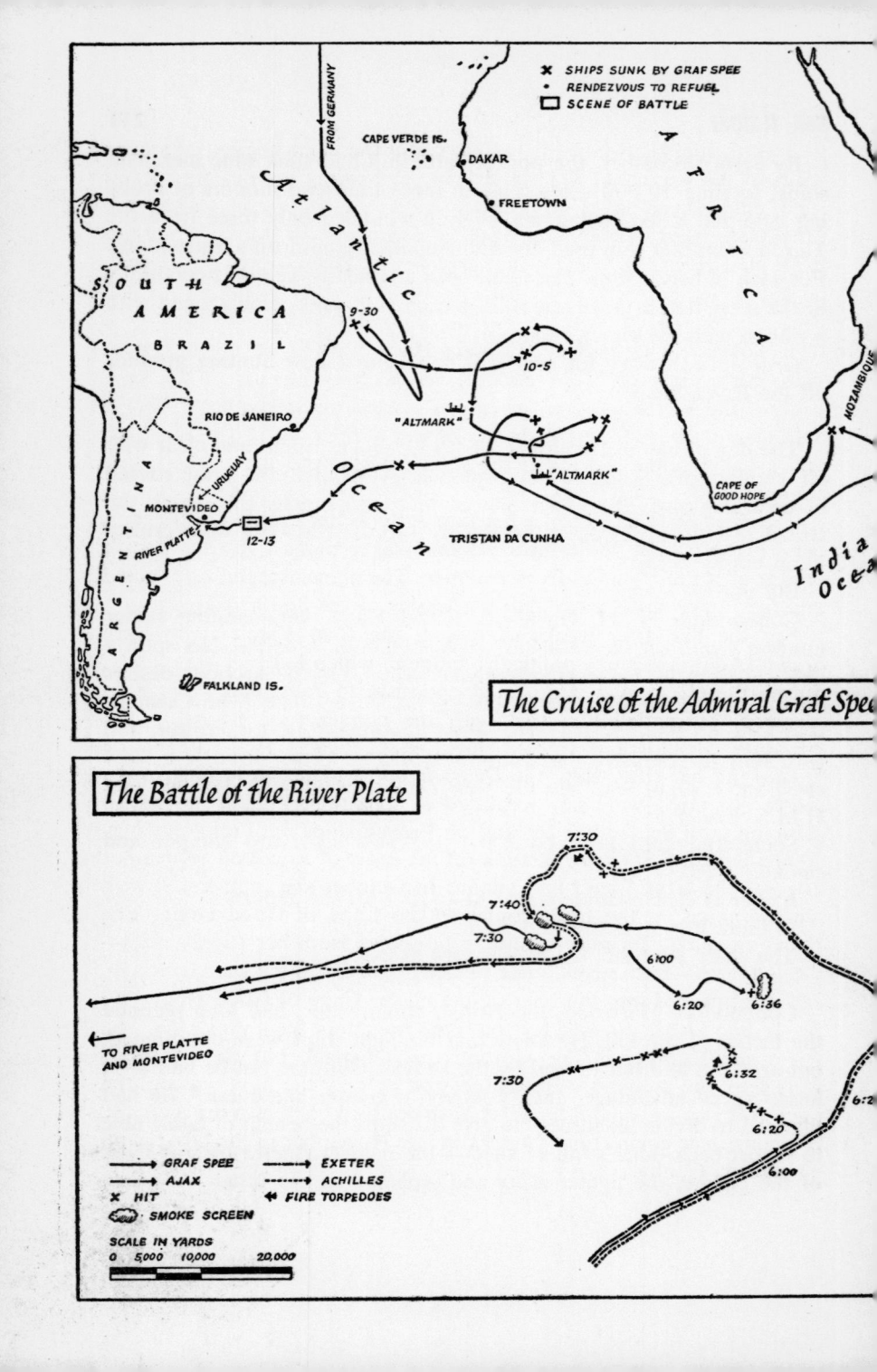

SHIPS SUNK BY GRAF SPEE ✗
RENDEZVOUS TO REFUEL •
SCENE OF BATTLE ▢

FROM GERMANY

CAPE VERDE IS.

DAKAR

FREETOWN

Atlantic

SOUTH AMERICA

BRAZIL

9-30

RIO DE JANEIRO

10-5

"ALTMARK"

"ALTMARK"

Ocean

URUGUAY

MONTEVIDEO

RIVER PLATTE

12-13

TRISTAN DA CUNHA

CAPE OF GOOD HOPE

MOZAMBIQUE

AFRICA

India Ocea

ARGENTINA

FALKLAND IS.

The Cruise of the Admiral Graf Spee

The Battle of the River Plate

7:30

7:40

7:30

7:30

6:00

6:20

6:36

TO RIVER PLATTE AND MONTEVIDEO

7:30

6:32

6:20

6:2

6:00

→ GRAF SPEE   → EXETER
-→ AJAX   ----→ ACHILLES
✗ HIT   ← FIRE TORPEDOES
〰 SMOKE SCREEN

SCALE IN YARDS
0   5,000   10,000   20,000

By early December, the pocket-battleship had sunk nine merchant ships, totaling 50,000 gross tons, in more than two months of cruising. She had killed no seamen, slightly wounded only three from the *Tairoa* when that ship used her radio against Langsdorff's instructions. For each of her victims, there had been a typically Teutonic ceremony in the mess flat; a green wreath for each ship sunk, emblazoned with a ribbon with the victim's name.

Graf Spee, hungry for rich pickings, sought new hunting grounds off the River Plate.

The day of battle, December 13, 1939, dawns bright and clear with all the glory of a South Atlantic summer. At daylight the white stretch of creaming surf, the green line of hills and forests that mark the Brazilian-Uruguayan coast, lies far to starboard as *Graf Spee* cruises in an empty ocean.

But not for long.

Commodore H. H. Harwood, Royal Navy, commanding raider hunting group off the southeast coast of South America, has spun a nautical web; he has correctly divined *Graf Spee's* lascivious desires on the plump shipping routes out of the River Plate. The Commodore's Broad Pendant flies from H.M.S. *Ajax,* 7,000-ton cruiser, and with him in company—steaming at fourteen knots through a "low swell and a slight sea," are the New Zealander, H.M.S. *Achilles,* and H.M.S. *Exeter.*

Soon after four bells (6 A.M.) lookouts sight top hamper and smoke.

Exeter is sent to investigate. At 6:16 A.M. she reports:

"I think it is a pocket-battleship."

The chase is ended; the wolf is now at bay.

Commodore Harwood, the British commander, had long planned the tactics of the kill. He knew that his light ships were out-gunned, out-armored and out-ranged by the heavier German, but he had a six knots' speed advantage, and "possibly, a greater handiness." He had planned to divide his forces "to give his ships the benefit of being able to report each other's fall of shot"—the heavier *Exeter* on one flank of the enemy, the lighter *Ajax* and *Achilles* on the other—harrying

and chivvying. Such a disposition would force the *Spee* to divide the
fire of her two eleven-inch turrets, or to concentrate on one target
while leaving the other uncovered. Like Nelson before him Harwood
had discussed the battle with his captains before the event.

Alarm gongs sound and the crews run to battle stations as *Graf
Spee* and *Exeter* steam toward each other, closing the range, while
away on the horizon to the eastward *Ajax* and *Achilles*—working up
to speed—seek out the enemy's other flank. Battle colors—His Majesty's White Ensign—are hoisted above H.M.S. *Exeter*—Captain
F. S. Bell commanding—six eight-inch guns in three turrets, and Par-
sons turbines to give her a speed of thirty-two knots. And above *Graf
Spee* flies the swastika; the long days of lurking the sea lanes are over;
Der Tag has come.

The blowers whine to a high crescendo aboard *Exeter* and the
boiler casings pant as the cruiser speeds up to the full power of her
80,000 horse in twenty minutes. She kicks up her heels and is away
toward the sea's rim, her turrets training toward *Graf Spee,* and young
Ronald Hill of Plymouth, seventeen-year-old bugler, soon to die,
standing ready for orders, bugle to lips, on the forebridge.

The range finder operators on all ships pick up the enemy, twirl
knobs, read the ranges.

"Two o o double o (20,000 yards). . . . One nine eight double
o. . . ."

Graf Spee's great eleven-inchers open fire at 19,400 yards. She has
split her targets; shell splashes leap near *Exeter* and others are
bunched around *Ajax,* Captain C. H. L. Woodhouse commanding,
handy little 7,000-ton light cruiser, with a fast pair of heels and eight
six-inch guns in four turrets. The day is still young; it is only four
minutes since the tell-tale streamer of smoke was first sighted against
the dawn sky.

At 6:20 *Exeter* opens with her two forward turrets; the range is
9½ sea miles. *Achilles,* New Zealand sister of *Ajax*—Captain W. E.
Parry commanding—opens at 6:21 with her light six-inchers; *Ajax*
follows two minutes later, and soon above all the speeding ships
powder smoke billows in wind-whipped and funereal wreaths.

Exeter sees the ocean open up about her as *Graf Spee's* salvos fall close. The first is short; the second bunches up close astern with the ocean spouting upward in great geysers. The *Spee* has concentrated all her eleven-inchers now on *Exeter;* she duels with her secondary battery of eight 5.9-inch guns with the lighter British cruisers. The third eleven-inch salvo is a straddle; the German has the range!

At 6:23 a shell from the *Graf Spee's* fifth salvo falls close aboard *Exeter;* splinters kill some of the torpedo tube crews, riddle funnels and searchlights, damage communications. Engine Room Artificer (2d. Class) James McGarry, stunned by the concussion, floods the gasoline tanks, prevents conflagration. But *Exeter's* guns still shoot; the quadruple screws still flail the sea. The sixth German salvo misses, but at least one shell from the seventh hits her square and she shudders, as the red mushrooming flame of the shell-burst blossoms into twisted steel and billowing smoke. B turret is out—its men mangled and slain. In the wrecked turret Sergeant Wilde of the Royal Marines —most of his crew dead around him—puts a rope tourniquet around the stump of a severed arm, organizes a bucket brigade to put out a blazing cordite charge lying in the turret rammer. Splinters sweep the bridge; young Ronald Hill of Plymouth lies dead with his bugle near him; the wheel-house communications are wrecked; all the conn— except the captain and two beside him—are dead or injured.

But *Exeter* still closes the range, her own guns speaking; at 6:32 she fires torpedoes, and *Ajax* and *Achilles* work around to the north, away to the open sea to head off the enemy and turn her again toward the land. And she turns; about 6:36 as the *Ajax,* pounding hard at twenty-eight knots, catapults her plane for spotting the fall of shot, *Graf Spee* pours out a cloud of viscous oily smoke and under its cover, sheers away toward the west.

The day draws on and the southern sun grows hot as the guns pound and the engines throb. *Spee* is hit; her waterline is scarred with shell splinters; below in the sickbay the surgeon works in a bloody welter; the carpenter and his mates repair damages, shore up bulkheads, put out fires.

Before 7 A.M. *Achilles* and *Ajax* have worked up to thirty-one knots and below in the steaming boiler rooms the flames from the furnaces leap—with the concussion of each gun blast—about a foot from the boiler casings. "Yet the stokers, many of them youngsters, never pause[d] in their work or move[d] back from the boilers."

Before the battle is an hour old, *Exeter* takes fearful punishment. *Exeter* is hit again and again, but she takes it and keeps on firing. The fight runs on westward towards the Uruguayan coast as men die and others moan.

By seven o'clock, or soon thereafter, *Exeter* is a shambles. Shots riddle the ship's side; fires flare all over the ship. *Graf Spee's* 670-pound eleven-inchers are doing fearful havoc; even the Germans' 5.9-inch battery is bearing now, so close is the range, but in turn *Exeter's* 256-pound eight-inchers and the 100-pound six-inchers of *Achilles* and *Ajax* are searching out the German ship.

The British smaller guns are firing faster; together His Majesty's three cruisers, outclassed in weight of single broadside (the German has about 4,800 pounds to the combined British 3,136), are delivering more salvos per minute.

Down below decks, locked in *Graf Spee's* brig, some sixty British mariners, captives taken from the nine merchant ships sunk by the *Spee* in her weeks of commerce raiding, hear the great forward turret above them thump and the ship shudder as it fires; know that a British victory may mean their death, but cheer and sing and cheer again as British shells strike *Graf Spee.*

Through rivet holes in their prison, they smell the powder smoke, they see the glare of flames as *Graf Spee's* sea plane burns on its catapult. A British shell strikes near them; the concussion and splinters stun; one man is slightly wounded.

Still in the early morning before the sun is high *Exeter* is a wreck. Captain Bell shifts from the wrecked forward station to the after control. He steers the ship for forty-five minutes through a chain of ten sailors, who pass his commands by word of mouth to the after steering wheel and the engine room. Only her after turret is still firing and that is served by hand. The power leads to the electric powder hoists, to the snakelike rammer, to the shell hoists are long since severed. The turret is trained and the gun is loaded by man power. The raging fires grow brighter; gradually *Exeter* slows.

She has taken fearful punishment; "all her compass repeaters had been smashed, and the captain was conning the ship with the help of a small boat's compass." She is flooded and on fire, has a seven-degree list and is down by the bow, her speed drops, and at 7:30 A.M.—less than an hour after the first shots were fired—flooding immobilizes her after turret, and her guns fall silent. She turns southeastward, "no longer serviceable as a fighting unit," out of action, her decks littered with sixty-one dead and twenty-three wounded, but the White Ensign is still flying.

The *Ajax,* too, is sore hurt; with the *Exeter* crippled, *Graf Spee* turns all her eleven-inchers on the light cruisers. *Ajax's* twin after turrets are both "dead"; one gun forward is out of action, her topmast is down, and *Achilles* bridge has been raked by splinters which kill four ratings, stun the gunnery officer and slightly wound the skipper and the chief yeoman of signals. *Ajax* fires torpedoes at a range of four and a half miles; *Graf Spee* turns sharply to port and lays smoke.

By 7:40 A.M., as stricken *Exeter* laden with her dead sheers seaward to limp to dockyard haven in the Falkland Islands, 1,000 miles away, Harwood has had enough. The range is down to four miles, and the fast-firing six-inchers have taken their toll of *Graf Spee;* the great ship, worried and hurt, has not been able to shake off her harrying pursuers. But *Ajax* is hurt, *Achilles* damaged; both when sound are no match for the heavier German—and more important, "Guns" reports to the Commodore that ammunition expenditures have been so high there is danger of a shortage if the action is prolonged.

The signal flags flutter; Harwood turns away to the eastward under cover of smoke, lengthening the range.

The rest is largely a pursuit.

For a time the battle sobs and dies, with the British in a long stern chase shadowing their quarry. The guns are quiet; the men gulp food, but the racing cruisers pound along the coast. The sun drops lower in the west; *Graf Spee,* her hull vibrating to the power of her Diesels, is heading for the broad estuary of the River Plate, but off Cape Jose Ignacio and Lobos Island *Ajax* is shoreword of the German, her course converging with that of *Graf Spee,* while *Achilles* speeds off *Graf Spee's* port quarter.

The guns speak again; the handy British cruisers wheel and turn, in and out of their own smoke screens—to sting and be gone before *Graf Spee's* great guns can find them.

Between Cape Jose Ignacio and Punta del Este, from five o'clock to nine, when the sun sets and night closes down, again the guns are fired as *Graf Spee* barks at her pursuers. As the day dies *Graf Spee* lays down a heavy smoke screen to assist the night, swings seaward, but turns again and charges at high speed up the estuary channel. The sixteen-hour running fight is broken off near 10 P.M. when she arrives off Montevideo with thirty-six dead, sixty wounded.

Off the River Plate *Ajax* (seven dead, five wounded, two of her four turrets out of action, her upper works shredded with shell splinters) and *Achilles* (four dead, three wounded) patrolled, waited, their crews sleeping at their guns.

In Montevideo harbor the tedious processes of diplomacy dragged on, while Captain Hans Langsdorff and his crew hastily took aboard foodstuffs, supplies, and oil from the supply ship *Tacoma,* stopped up shell holes, welded plates, buried their dead, succored their wounded. *Graf Spee* had entered port at high speed, guns still blazing; she was not vitally damaged, although her water line forward was scarred and bitten; there was a large hole in the bow and a shell had gone through the control tower and damaged the main battery fire control; her planes were wrecked. She was short of ammunition—perhaps her greatest weakness. She was battered, no doubt of it, but her turrets were intact and the after control showed no damage; she still could run and fight.

But Captain Langsdorff asked for at least fifteen days to repair damages to seaworthiness; Britain and Germany brought pressure upon Uruguay. The decision: *Graf Spee* must leave by evening of the seventeenth or be interned.

Ajax—the flag no longer of Commodore Harwood, but, by His Majesty's pleasure, Rear Admiral Sir Henry Harwood, K.C.B.—and *Achilles,* her sister ship, still waited off the Plate, while broken *Exeter,* with forty to fifty shell hits, steamed slowly toward the Falkland Island base, her place taken by the eight-inch-gunned *Cumberland.* Battle cruiser *Renown,* aircraft carrier *Ark Royal* pounded hard from Rio a thousand miles away. Would the *Graf Spee* steam out?

An order came direct from Hitler in Berlin. Sunday afternoon, December 17, the pocket battleship, symbol of German might, headed seaward down the Plate, while the world watched. In the fading day battle flags flew from her mastheads. Langsdorff was going to fight her till she sank! She anchored; her crew left her. As the daylight died Captain Langsdorff, standing in a launch alongside, pressed a button, scuttled his ship.

Three days later, on December 20, 1939, with the Second World War still young, Captain Hans Langsdorff, veteran of Jutland, interned with his crew in Buenos Aires, wrote several notes, put a pistol to his head, and died.

NOTES   Winston Churchill, in his World War II history, called Captain Langsdorff of *Graf Spee,* a "high-class person," and the British official naval history notes, "it must stand to [Langsdorff's] credit that not one British life was lost through his ship's action against defenseless merchantmen."

When the *Graf Spee* entered Montevideo harbor after the battle, Langsdorff immediately released the British prisoners taken from the merchant ships she had sunk. Captain Patrick G. Dove, master of the sunken *Africa Shell,* was called to the bridge and told by Langsdorff that the British "cruisers made a gallant fight. When people fight like that, personal enmity is lost—these British are hard."

Langsdorff, though a decent man, did not fight a brilliant action, and his end was ignominious and prophetic of the Wagnerian immolation of the Third Reich of Adolf Hitler. With her superior range, heavy broadside, and thicker armor, *Graf Spee* should have tried to lengthen the range; as a commerce raider her only hope was to avoid serious damage or being brought to bay in a neutral harbor. Because of the British cruisers' superior speed, it is unlikely that the *Spee* could have avoided action altogether, but she made no such attempt until too late. On the other hand, once the action had been joined and the *Exeter* severely punished, Langsdorff should have pushed his advantage. The heavy cruiser was at his mercy; Hitler (among many others) said later that the *Exeter* could, and should, have been sunk. Langsdorff's tactics, however, were undoubtedly inhibited by the cautious policies that dictated the movements of Germany's sea raiders; "enemy naval forces, even if inferior, were only to be engaged if such action would further the chief task" of commerce destruction. The British Official naval history comments that this policy "led not only to irresolution in action on the part of German senior officers but to the engagement of the enemy—even if superior in strength—with enhanced confidence by our own ships." Divine declares, though much too strongly, that "Captain Hans Langsdorff, captain of the *Graf Spee,* was never from the start, captain of himself. He fought, trammelled, bound and hampered."

Langsdorff's "irresolution" contributed to the strategic victory of the British over the *Graf Spee,* even though the British cruisers were far more badly mauled than the German.

German gunnery in the initial morning action was superior to the British (as it was, indeed, at Jutland in World War I), perhaps partially because *Graf Spee,* unlike the British ships, had a radar—though it was not for gun-laying. During the battle the *Exeter* fired some six torpedoes; the *Ajax* four, and the *Graf Spee* four. None hit, in part because of the long torpedo ranges, in part due to the violent turns and maneuverings during the battle, in part due to the smoke screens used extensively by both sides.

The final ignominious ending of the *Graf Spee* and the suicide of Langsdorff were, in part, the responsibility of clever British propaganda and, in part, attributable to Hitler and his admirals. The *Graf Spee,* despite many splinter holes above her armor belt, a wrecked galley, and several large shell holes in her upper forecastle and control tower, was not badly damaged. Two Uruguayan naval officers estimated that provisional repairs could be carried out in three days. Her chief weakness was her shortage of ammunition, which could not be supplied in Montevideo. But Britain was mobilizing as rapidly as possible all available naval forces to reinforce the blockade off the estuary of the Plate, and as the ships were steaming hard to Harwood's aid, British representatives in Montevideo used psychological warfare to strengthen the British hand. The cruiser *Cumberland,* with two more eight-inch guns than the crippled *Exeter,* arrived on the patrol station off the mouth of the river on December 14 after a full-speed run from the Falkland Islands. But the battle cruiser *Renown,* with 15-inch guns, and the aircraft carrier, *Ark Royal,* and the cruiser, *Neptune,* were still 1,000 miles away, when *Graf Spee* stood down river on the seventeenth. Three destroyers were still further away, and *Dorsetshire* and *Shropshire* were at Capetown. *Cumberland, Ajax* and *Achilles* were the only British men-of-war off the estuary when *Graf Spee* left Montevideo on the seventeenth.

But Langsdorff believed an overwhelming force had been concentrated against him—due in part to reports deliberately released in Montevideo by the British, in part to the power of suggestion. One of the *Spee's* own officers reported to Langsdorff as early as the fifteenth that he had seen the top hamper of the *Renown* patrolling off the estuary. The rumors prevalent in Montevideo of major British reinforcements also mentioned the French battleships *Strasbourg* and *Dunkerque,* which were thousands of miles away. These reports and the German defeat in the diplomatic battle of Montevideo, which raged around Langsdorff's head, led to the deliberate blowing up of the ship.

Langsdorff reported to the German Admiralty on December 16:

1. Strategic position off Montevideo: Besides the cruisers and destroyers, Ark Royal *and* Renown. *Close blockade at night. Escape into open sea and break-through to home waters hopeless.*

2. Propose putting out as far as neutral boundary [in the Plate]. *If it possible to fight our way through to Buenos Aires* [Argentina was believed to be more friendly to Germany than was Uruguay], *using remaining ammunition, this will be attempted.*

3. If a break-through would result in certain destruction of Graf Spee *without opportunity of damaging enemy, request decision on whether the ship should be scuttled in spite of insufficient depth in the estuary of the La Plata, or whether internment is to be preferred.*

4. Decision requested by radiogram.

Commander, Graf Spee.

Churchill reports that "at a conference presided over by the Fuehrer (Hitler), at which Raeder and Jodl were present," the decision against internment was made.

The response from the German Admiralty sent on the sixteenth, and confirmed again on the seventeenth, after Uruguay refused to extend *Graf Spee's* permissible time in port was:

1. Attempt by all means to extend the time in neutral waters in order to guarantee freedom of action as long as possible.

2. With reference to No. 2: Approved.

3. With reference to No. 3: No *internment in Uruguay. Attempt effective destruction if ship is scuttled.*

Raeder.

After the destruction of the *Graf Spee,* her crew and her skipper were transferred to internment in Buenos Aires, where Langsdorff ended his life.

Langsdorff, though limited and advised by Hitler, bore like any captain the responsibility for his ship. He accepted it. In a letter he wrote on December 19, quoted by Martienssen in *Hitler and His Admirals,* he declared:

After a long struggle, I reached the grave decision to scuttle the pocket battleship Admiral Graf Spee, *in order to prevent her from falling into enemy hands. I am still convinced that under the circumstances, this decision was the only one left, once I had taken my ship into the trap of Montevideo. For with the ammunition remaining any attempt to fight my way back to open and deep water was bound to fail. And yet only in deep water could I have scuttled the ship, after having used the remaining ammunition, thus avoiding her falling to the enemy.*

Sooner than expose my ship to the danger that after a brave fight she would fall partly or completely into enemy hands, I decided not to fight but to destroy the equipment and then scuttle the ship. It was clear to me that this decision might be consciously or unwittingly misconstrued by persons ignorant of my motives, as being attributable entirely or partly to personal considerations. Therefore, I decided from the beginning to bear the consequences involved in this decision. For a Captain with a sense of honour, it goes without saying that his personal fate cannot be separated from that of his ship. . . .

. . . I alone bear the responsibility for scuttling the pocket battleship Admiral Graf Spee. *I am happy to pay with my life for any pos-*

sible reflection on the honour of the flag. I shall face my fate with firm faith in the cause and the future of the nation and of my Fuehrer. . . .

ACKNOWLEDGMENTS   The principal sources for this narrative are: *The War at Sea (History of the Second World War), Volume I, The Defensive,* by Captain S. W. Roskill, R.N., United Kingdom Military Series, Her Majesty's Stationery Office, London, 1954; *The Battle of the River Plate,* a White Paper published by His Majesty's Stationery Office, London, 1940 (reprinted, 1943); *The Gathering Storm,* by Winston S. Churchill, Houghton Mifflin Company, 1948; *The Battle of the River Plate,* by Lord Strabolgi, R.N., Hutchinson and Co., London; *The Wake of the Raider,* by Arthur D. Divine, London, 1940; *I Was an Altmark Prisoner,* by Thomas Foley, London, 1940; and *Hitler and His Admirals,* by Anthony Martienssen, New York, E. P. Dutton and Company. The quotations are largely from the White Paper.

The author visited the *Graf Spee* during the Coronation Naval Review in 1937, and wrote what was probably the first account of the *Spee* battle for the New York *Times* on December 24, 1939, from details furnished in part by John W. White, then South American correspondent of the *Times*. This original account has been largely rewritten on the basis of later post-war information.

The British official naval history, *The War At Sea,* gives only a sketchy and somewhat partial account of the battle, and neither this book, nor Winston Churchill's *The Gathering Storm* mentions Langsdorff's claim of ammunition shortage, which was a determining factor in the captain's decision to destroy his ship.

The quotation at the start of the chapter, dealing with the Battle of the Falkland Islands in World War I, is from *Naval Operations, Volume I, Official History of the War,* by Sir Julian S. Corbett, Longmans, Green and Company.

1915

The Torpedoing
of the *Lusitania*

In West Street barrooms, and around the London docks,
cheap lithographs proclaimed her greatness: her beam five
feet more than the famous *Great Eastern,* her length almost equal
to the combined heights of New York's skyscrapers—the Park Row,
the Flatiron, and the St. Paul buildings. She was the first four-
propeller turbine-drive steamship; her four great funnels and her
fine lines gave promise of her speed; she was a floating palace, a ten-
million-dollar ship with a capacity for three thousand souls; she was
the Queen of the Seas.

Ten thousand lusty British throats roared out the old song of triumph at her launching:

> *"Rule Britannia, Britannia rules the waves;*
> *Britons never, never will be slaves."*

On her first run to sea in 1907 she steamed the nine hundred miles
around Ireland handsomely, with the white wake of her bow wave
curling back gracefully from her forefoot: her stokers shoveling,
slicing, hoeing the great beds of white glowing coals to give her
strength. She skirted the Old Head of Kinsale beyond the forty-fathom
curve, leaving behind her a trail of troubled water over a spot she
was to know again. . . .

She broke the crossing record on her maiden trip, and once in 1908
she turned up an average of twenty-six and a third knots for the

twenty-four hours, her best speed. But Friday, September 13, 1907, was her real triumph, when she took the speed laurels of the Western Ocean. And the superstition of Friday the thirteenth pursued her to her grave; Hoboken and the Clydeside, the Liverpool wharf rats and the Water Street bums muttered of no good end for that ship named *Lusitania*.

An old-fashioned autocrat of the sea, Captain William Thomas Turner, a "little man, ruddy-cheeked and with sharp blue eyes," was on the *Lusitania's* bridge when tugs warped her away from her pier at 12:20 on the afternoon of May 1, 1915. Her departure had in it more than the customary excitement of a Cunard sailing; it was wartime and there had been ominous rumors before the bights of her lines were cast off from the dock bollards. Later the world was to talk of spies and *saboteurs,* of a plot hatched in a limousine speeding through the dark of Central Park, of a coded wireless message dispatched from Sayville, of warning letters sent to several passengers, signed *Morte.* But that May morning, with the stewards panting up the gangways, with the passengers clustered on A deck waving to friends on the pier, there was but one topic of conversation. Inserted in the morning's New York *Times,* as a paid advertisement, was the following:

NOTICE

Travellers intending to embark on the Atlantic voyage are reminded that a state of war exists between Germany and her allies and Great Britain and her allies, that the zone of war includes the waters adjacent to the British Isles; that in accordance with final notice given by the Imperial German Government vessels flying the flag of Great Britain, or of any of her allies, are liable to destruction in those waters and that travellers sailing in the war zone on ships of Great Britain or her allies do so at their own risk.
IMPERIAL GERMAN EMBASSY

Washington, D. C.
April 22, 1915

Alfred Gwynne Vanderbilt, that young man who at thirty-seven owned some sixteen million dollars, showed it to a fellow passenger.

"How ridiculous this thing is," he commented. "The Germans would not dare to make an attempt to sink this ship."

Sir Hugh Lane, who was sailing for London after disposing of the Holbein portrait of Thomas Cromwell to Henry C. Frick, thought the advertisement too absurd for discussion; and Elbert Hubbard, the fifty-nine-year-old Sage of East Aurora, told a ship-news reporter laughingly:

"If the *Lucy* is torpedoed I will get even with the Kaiser in *The Philistine* when I return."

There were no cancellations among the passengers.

The whistle blew. Charles Frohman, the great dramatic producer, limped along deck with the aid of his cane and waved good-bye to his sisters on the pier. Forward, deck hands were driving the wedges tight over the battens of the cargo hatches, above well-stowed holds loaded with a $736,000 miscellany of goods mostly for war consumption: sheet brass, copper, beef, furs, 189 packages of military goods; 5,468 cases of cartridges and ammunition (stowed forward on the orlop or lower decks), bronze shell cases, and fuses.

Justus Miles Forman, novelist; Lindon Bates, Jr., en route to Europe to assist Herbert Hoover in Belgian relief; genealogist Lothrop Withington; Dr. Fred Stark Pearson, who had just lost ten million dollars and was out to recoup his fortune; Miss Theodate Pope, on her way to England to pursue psychic research; Mrs. Margaret Beattie and her husband, a missionary; "Dave Samuels, song-and-dance artist and Hebrew impersonator and monologist"—these were a few of the cross section of humanity gathered in the *Lusitania's* decks and lounges that May day. Below, in the red hell of the fireroom, pot-bellied broad-shouldered Owen Connelly, with a sweat-rag about his neck and the glare of the furnaces in his eyes, was anticipating his last trip as a stoker: he had made arrangements to quit the sea and take employment with a building contractor. And passenger Alexander Campbell was looking forward with joy to that beauty he loved, Scotland in Maytime.

On the dock as the great liner straightened out for the sea and the fluttering handkerchiefs grew dim, Charles P. Sumner, general agent in New York of the Cunard Line, was telling a reporter that he didn't consider that the German warning placed the *Lusitania* in any peril, and that he had no fear whatsoever of submarines.

How could he know that the day before, April 30, the German submarine U-20, Lieutenant Commander Walther Schwieger commanding, had cleared Borkum Roads bound for the Irish Sea?

It was a smiling voyage—calm seas and fair weather until the liner neared the Irish coast. There had been, for a time, considerable nervousness among some passengers; a few women slept together in the same berths; others kept life preservers by their sides and scanned the sea anxiously. There were rumors; two men who kept to themselves were generally alluded to as Germans—the war thrust its tentacles across the thoughts and speech of all aboard. But there was the usual seasickness and the usual ship's routine; a daily pool on the vessel's run, and rest and recreation for all who wanted it. The ship's officers and crew did not seem to be concerned about the submarine peril; there were boat drills—but not for the passengers, and the lifeboats were not uncovered, lifted out of the chocks, and swung overside until Thursday, May 6, the day before the *Lusitania* was scheduled to make her landfall on the Irish coast. Anxiety waned; no one took seriously the possibility of death at sea.

In the early morning of the sixth, when the crew were still scrubbing decks and the sun was yet a glowing red ball, Anderson, the staff captain, reported to Captain Turner that all lifeboats had been swung out and the falls flemished down ready for lowering. Later many of the bulkhead doors were closed; the Chief Steward reported that all side ports up to B deck had been dogged down; Turner and Anderson inspected the boats; lookouts were doubled—two men in the crow's nest and two in the "eyes"—and two officers and two quartermasters were always on the bridge.

It was a quiet day and not until eight bells in the evening watch was there a hint of danger.

By that time U-20, cruising in the fairway of St. George's Channel and on the steamer lanes hugging Ireland, had already bagged three ships.

Then, from the Admiral commanding Queenstown to *Lusitania:*
"Submarines active off the south coast of Ireland."

At 8:30, with the passengers gathering their wraps about them for a stroll on the dark decks, there was another general warning:

"Take Liverpool pilot at bar and avoid headlands. Pass harbors at full speed. Steer mid-channel course. Submarines off Fastnet."

The *Lusitania* acknowledged at 8:32 P.M., May 6.

Friday, May 7, dawned fair, and the wet earthy smell of the green hills of Ireland was in the air. The drone of the engines lulled at eight o'clock as the ship dropped to eighteen knots; Captain Turner slowed to make the Mersey Lightship and the Liverpool bar with the Saturday morning tide. Shortly after the watch was set the liner ran into a patch of fog; first-class passenger Charles Lauriat heard the foghorn and turned over for another nap; the speed dropped to fifteen knots.

At eleven that morning the ship ran out of the fog patch; the engine room annunciator tinkled; the speed was increased again and on the port bow rose the low smudge that was Ireland. It was a beautiful sunny day, with the haze of the fog bank still astern and the sea the faint rippled smoothness of fine glass.

There were other radioed warnings of submarine activity during the morning, but the speed stayed at eighteen; the Old Head of Kinsale rose out of the ocean; there was journey's end and safety looming on the horizon, and the passengers went below to their roast beef and Yorkshire pudding.

"One does get such an appetite at sea."

The dining saloon on D deck, a "massive and gorgeous apartment," with its great dome of cathedral glass towering up through two decks, was crowded. Some people had finished lunch and were strolling the deck; Elbert Hubbard, leaning with his wife on the rail of the promenade deck, was telling Mr. Lauriat that he didn't believe he would ever be a welcome visitor in Germany because of his recent essay, "Who Lifted the Lid Off Hell?"

There was no warning.

Oliver P. Barnard, scenic artist of the Covent Garden Opera, saw a white feather of foam and then a long streaking stream of bubbles lick out toward the ship on the starboard side. He was fascinated by it, so stunned he found no answer when a woman asked him casually: "This isn't a torpedo, is it?"

But on the forecastle head young Able Seaman Leslie N. Morton, who had just taken his station on the two-to-four lookout watch, knew what that ruffled path of ocean meant.

Through a megaphone his excited young voice boomed upward to the bridge:

"Torpedo coming on starboard side!"

It was about eight minutes past two.

To some it was a "terrible explosion," to Lauriat and the Hubbards only a "muffled heavy sound." Another who lived to tell of it thought it sounded "like the banging of a door on a windy day." But it was death, and the ship trembled.

Sudden death for some in Nos. 1 and 2 boiler rooms, where the torpedo struck. Those on deck saw a geyser of sea and coal dust and debris and "thick black smoke" and splinters of a lifeboat spout up between the third and fourth funnels on the starboard side; some standing there leaped to the shelter of the saloon doorway as gallons of water roared down upon the awning, rending canvas, breaking strongbacks. Of those in the boiler rooms few had time to sense catastrophe. Life was present; then it was not. The ocean bore in upon them, and they died. The *Lusitania* took a sudden sharp list to starboard, drooped by the head as though tired, but plowed on swiftly across the tranquil sea with the Old Head of Kinsale in the distance. She plowed on, for her four screws turned as the turbines spinned, as the steam dropped slowly, as the ocean roared in; there was no answering tinkle from the engine room to the annunciator signals from the bridge. Her way could not be checked. And she was not long to live.

The explosion—followed quickly, many thought, by a second blast of sound—burst close to the dining saloon; the force of it smashed in many of the great ports that were not already open; the startled passengers dropped half-raised forks and fled. There was a crowd in the companionway, but no screaming, no panic, and a man standing there was saying over and over again:

"Keep calm, keep calm."

The stewards, serving sweets and fruit or clearing away the debris of a midday meal, dropped their crockery and turned forward to their glory hole for life preservers. They groped in darkness, for the rushing water had lapped quickly above the generators—375 kilowatts, the wonders of their day—and the lights had gone.

On deck Charles Lauriat tapped the Sage of East Aurora on the shoulder and told the Hubbards to wait where they were until he returned with life preservers. They seemed stunned and did not move; like many in that first frozen moment they were numbed with a strange paralysis—not fear, but that mental and sensory narcosis which so often precedes the first sharp stab of pain or realization. Lauriat left them, but when he returned they were gone and he never saw them again. Someone else saw them step into a cabin on one of the upper decks and close the door quietly behind them. . . .

There was a rush of people to the upper decks, a freshet of men and women and children, pouring up the companionways, spilling out along the port and starboard sides, women holding tightly to the hands of little children, questioning.

The *Lusitania* dragged on more slowly, her propellers beating the sea, her great bulk listing, mortally wounded. Frantic passengers started trying to lower the port side boats.

"Do not lower the boats! Do not lower the boats!"

The stentorian orders came from the bridge where the grim figures of Captains Turner and Anderson were silhouetted against disaster.

"Captain," a woman passenger called in a "clear calm voice"— "what do you want us to do?"

"Stay where you are, madam; she's all right."

"Where do you get your information?"

"From the engine room, madam."

It was, perhaps, eleven minutes after two.

Some measure of assurance rippled through the ship; after all, that growing smudge on the horizon was land; the *Lusitania* was a good stout ship. Many passengers went below for their life preservers; others retied the hastily looped tapes and waited.

They had not long to wait. Leith, the Marconi operator, was tapping out an SOS. The dynamo died beneath his fist; hastily he switched to the emergency set; again the sparks began:

"SOS. Come at once—big list—ten miles south Head Old Kinsale —SOS—"

Just a short time before in Buckingham Palace in London, the King of England had asked Colonel House a hypothetical question: "Suppose they [the Germans] should sink the Lusitania *with American passengers on board?"*

Now the starboard lifeboats are lowered to the rail. The helm is thrown hard over to head the ship toward land; but the *Lusitania* responds sluggishly, canting heavily—further and further.

"Women and children first."

The age-old cry of the sea. Faces pale; convulsive sobbing.

Two forward boats on the portside are filled, apparently without orders or direction, and are lowered, scraping crazily against the ship's side with their precious freight. A passenger on the forward falls takes off a turn too many from the deck bitts; the fall whistles through its sheaves; the boat tilts down by the head; women and children pitch into the sea. The second boat also meets disaster. Cries, and white faces in the massed crowds on deck.

Captain Anderson moves among the throngs; takes charge of the boats. Scores are searching for relatives, for friends:

"Have you seen my husband?"

"Margaret—Margaret."

A great hum and frantic scurrying pervade the ship.

Rugged old John Davies, the boatswain, young Leslie Morton, and other crew members are at their stations; the ship is slowing, and the boats are being lowered. It is time, for those still below decks seeking life preservers or rummaging for valuables in their rooms scramble back to the decks only by walking in the angle irons of the corridors, clinging to handrails. The heavy starboard list hampers the rescue efforts; the starboard boats, dangling from the davits, swing so far outboard that passengers must clamber in by falls or leap across swaying space. Few of the port side boats can be lowered at all; they are glued to the ship's side by gravity, and sweating men work in vain, fending and straining with oars and arms; they succeed only in staving in the strakes on the ship's steel sides. Of all the port side boats only two are floated—leaking. The chance of rescue is reduced.

The decks are black with people, clinging to rails and stanchions, braced against the list; working, waiting, searching. There is no panic as the ship's motion slows and the great leviathan dies, no panic though now the massed thousands know that sinking is a matter of minutes.

It is still "women and children first"; only one or two men try to shove their way into well-loaded boats; a sailor threatens one with an axe. The women are stoic, dry-eyed for the most part. A few of the steerage passengers mill and jostle; an old Italian grandmother with her brood, bewildered, appeals for her *bambini;* cannot understand those who answer her. In a first-class lounge a Catholic priest is praying mutely.

Outside the palm saloon on the starboard side Alfred Gwynne Vanderbilt, that rich young man, is calling to his valet:

"Come along, boy! Get all the women and children you can into these boats."

Steward Smith helps lower No. 21; Mrs. Henry Adams, bride of a few weeks, sits on a collapsible boat stowed in chocks on the boat deck, quietly holding the hand of her husband.

It is perhaps a quarter after two.

There is "no more suggestion of panic than picnickers will exhibit when they are embarking on an excursion steamer with the knowledge that the scheduled time of sailing has already passed." No panic, but much confusion and little order. Boats are lowered haphazardly. Lindon Bates, Jr., goes below to look for the children of a friend; he is never seen again. People leap into the sea; the surface commences to be speckled with dark heads, with life jackets, with all the debris of disaster.

In the wireless shack two cool young men are still tapping out in the terse terminology of Morse code the news of the disaster. There is doubt that the weak voice of the emergency set is heard, but Leith finally gets an acknowledgment; the marine observer at the wireless station on the Old Head of Kinsale has seen the *Lusitania* list and stop; he gets her last message:

"Send help quickly; am listing badly."

The message reaches Queenstown at 2:15; the admiral commanding drives his fleet to sea; tugs *Stormcock* and *Warrior* throw their lines off the dock bollards and steam out in great bursting billows of smoke; the trawlers *Brock* and *Bradford* cast off from a coal lighter, and, with their decks and men all grimy, hurry out with *Flying Fox*

and *Golden Effort;* three torpedo boats, plunging madly, steam at
forced draft toward that spot off Old Head of Kinsale; the Queenstown wireless flashes the alarm to the *Indian Empire* fifty miles away,
and to a ship off Fastnet, and even the examination steamer *Julia,*
on station off Queenstown Harbor, turns her prow to the southwest.

But it is already too late.

The great ship *Lusitania,* Queen of the Seas, leans to her death.
The grimly waiting passengers, clinging with locked arms to handrails
and bulkheads on the canted deck, can step from the boat deck into
lifeboats alongside, floating even now with the starboard scuppers.
The sea climbs upward; a few sob and some women weep hysterically.
Aft in the steerage men and women from a dozen nations stumble
about and shriek.

Young Vanderbilt, who loved coaching but will coach no more in
London's fashionable West End, offers his lifebelt to a motherly-look-
ing gray-haired stewardess—though he cannot swim a stroke. She
points to a woman passenger nearby:

"Give it to her."

He does so.

There are scores now in the water; others slip from the flooded
starboard decks into the closely lapping sea; a few slither down
lines, with rope-burned hands, from the high-tilted portside or the
uprearing stern; some collapsible boats are man-hauled overside. In
the wireless shack the radio is dead; the time draws on toward half-
past two. The junior radio operator cheerfully grins at Oliver P.
Barnard, a passenger, drags a chair out of the deck house and asks
Barnard facetiously to "take a seat and make yourself comfortable";
the chair skitters down the steep deck into the water. The radio
operator crouches in the scuppers and takes snapshots of the stricken
ship. A dying stoker floats in the sea, his arm hanging by a shred.
Barnard throws his pocketbook into a nearby boat and steps into the
water from the boat deck.

Lifeboats still ride alongside, loaded to the gunwales; others steering away from the wreck fill slowly with water, their strakes leaking
or their plugs not in. The great overreaching funnels lower above the
waiting boats; the davits press down on the bow and stern thwarts;
the boats are trapped—they will go down with the ship.

First-class passenger Lauriat climbs into the stern of a boat along-side, still bound by its falls to the davits a foot or so above. He clears it aft, but forward a steward hacks vainly at the stout lines with a pocket knife. The boat lifts on a slight swell; Lauriat is fetched a hard blow in the back from the davit pressing ever downward as the *Lusitania* turns upon her starboard side. The bow of the trapped boat is dragged under; Lauriat, calling upon others to follow him, jumps into the sea.

The end is near. It has been at most only twenty-two minutes (some think less) since the even tenor of two thousand persons' lives has been blasted. It is hard to remember so far back. Then the problem had been the selection of a tasty dessert; now it is survival. But the decks are still black with people, those who, like passenger Barnard, cannot swim and find the prospects of a leap into the sea hopeless. But the sea too is black; men leap and swim; boats move outward from the dying giant—those that can; men and women trapped alongside raise eyes of terror to the funnels crunching down from above. The waters lap up toward the center line; on the upper decks long lines of people cling to the high-raised port rail; they are locked in queues, arm into arm; some lose their grip and slither down-ward, caroming off bulkheads and stanchions to splash into the reaching ocean. The stern lifts; the screws, still feebly flailing, kill swimmers in the water, lop deeply into the leg of a man hanging onto a rope. A shrieking wail rises from the steerage aft.

A little stunted deck steward with a funny waxed mustache chops a trapped boat clear; another with vacant eyes and a blank face regrets courteously to a passenger that he has no life jacket and continues his aimless work of brushing up broken crockery from the floor of a deck pantry near the veranda cafe.

"Oh, come along, my darling, I will be all right." A man forces his wife into the last boat. In the water, in the boats, confused shriek-ings:

"The funnels, the funnels."

"My God! . . . The *'Lucy's'* going!"

On the promenade deck "C.F."—Charles Frohman—stands locked hand in hand with William Scott, George Vernon, and Rita Jolivet.

"Why fear death?" he asks, a calm smile on his lips. "It is the most beautiful adventure in life."

The stern rears high and higher; the ship suddenly lurches back toward an even keel; a lone figure slides swiftly, hands burning to the bone, down a hundred and fifty feet of rope into the troubled sea. From forward aft a great rolling surge of water, wreckage and human beings roars along the steep-pitched decks, licking men to death. The *Lusitania* plunges bow first, stern towering, toward the bottom.

It was 2:30 when she foundered, with rescue vessels miles away, and the dead and struggling living gushed up from the depths in the maelstrom of her passing. Swimmers were caught by wireless antennae and dragged fathoms deep; a woman was sucked by an inrush of water into one of the funnels, then spewed out in a great bubble of air and coal dust and soot and steam, black as a Negro. Of the eight boats that got clear, most dragged in capacity cargoes and headed for shore or for a fishing trawler miles away; some slowly filled and capsized. The collapsible boats, which floated clear from the upper deck, were the salvation of many: men climbed upon them, clung to them—they were islands of life in a sea of death.

The center of the white broken water above the spot where the *Lusitania* had gone was for a time pocked with debris and wreckage—in some places jammed so tightly together as to form an undulating horrible mattress of deck chairs, oars, boxes, and human heads. Men were broken and crushed by the wreckage; to others it was salvation. In places swimmers were dragged down by the despairing hands of the drowning. Many died quickly in this brief battle for existence; scores perished who performed heroic acts that no man will ever know; some lived and will carry the shame of their living to the grave.

Many hundreds might have been saved had a ship or fishing boats been nearby, but the *Bluebell* and *Stormcock* and *Flying Fox* were still coming hard miles away, and only one small fishing smack was in the distance—becalmed by lack of wind. It was some hours before the first ship arrived. But then the low, inarticulate sound, the cries and coughings and groans, had largely died out. Dr. Daniel V. Moore, who kept a steward called Freeman afloat, saw them go. "Some appeared to be sleepy and worn out just before they went down; others grew gradually blue, and an air of hunger gave their features a sardonic smile. . . ."

Captain Turner, who was carried down from his bridge into the vortex of disaster, was one of those spewed up by the sea; he grasped an oar, then a deck chair, and was finally picked up after more than three hours in the water. But Staff Captain Anderson was lost; Vanderbilt was never seen again after his last gallant gesture; Charles Frohman sampled his great adventure; and with them died 1,198 people of that company of 1,959 passengers and crew, who had sailed so bravely from the North River docks just six days before. For the most part the Lusitania's company died or lived gallantly. Young Frank Hook, ten years old, with a fractured thigh, suffered patiently aboard the Brock and asked only if there were any funny papers aboard: Lauriat, desperately trying to shore up the sides of a collapsible boat and to pick people out of the water, spoke impatiently to a man lying in his way in the boat's bottom and was answered apologetically: "I'm sorry, old chap, but I can't move very fast; my leg is broken."

Fishermen and rescue vessels swept the sea late in the afternoon and all that night and brought to Queenstown the living and the dead. The corpses, with wet matted hair and foam upon their lips, lay in an old hall at Queenstown—men and women, babies and children, crew and passenger, rich and poor.

But many were never found. Scores went down with the ship; scores of others slept and moved with the moving waves, their only grave the restless waters of the Western Ocean. On May 9, the American liner St. Paul passed through a mass of wreckage near the Lusitania's grave, and her officers and crew saw the bodies of a number of victims. One close alongside was that of a mother, her right arm still firmly gripping the side of a life raft, her left clasping a baby close to her breast. The waves cradled them and the face of the baby rose and fell with the sea.

NOTES   In any chronicle of disaster one is struck by
the close similarity between many of the circumstances in the *Lusitania* and the *Titanic* sinkings. There were differences; one sank
quickly, the other slowly; in one there were more bravery and confusion than panic and inefficiency, while in the *Titanic* great courage,
great cowardice, and gross carelessness were strangely mixed. One
was an act of God, the other an act of man. Yet in both we find one
of the greatest liners of its day sinking with some of the most prominent people of the time. The greater courage shown by the greater
number in the *Lusitania* sinking may perhaps be due to the greater
speed of disaster; numbed minds had little time to accommodate
themselves to acceptance of death before death was upon them. In
the case of the *Titanic* the slow suspense of awful hours snapped
human nerves.

There is one other curious and awful coincidence. Survivors of
the *Titanic* and of the *Lusitania* spoke in almost identical phrases
of that terrible sound which rose above the sea when the ships
foundered and struggling thousands fought for life. To both, it seemed
a "long, lingering moan."

There was much talk of the baneful hand of Boy-Ed, troublesome
German naval attaché in Washington, of plottings and connivings,
of a prearranged rendezvous at which the U-20 was to await the
Lusitania, and of various other unexplained happenings *after* the
sinking of the great liner. The rumors persist to this day; but despite
the "evidence" supposed to have been adduced by various investigators, this writer is not satisfied that any such plot ever existed. On
the contrary, there is evidence that Schwieger himself did not know
what ship he had torpedoed until after the deed was done, *teste*
his diary of May 7: "Right ahead appear four funnels and two masts
of a steamer. . . . Clean bow shot from 700 meters range. . . .
Shot hits starboard side right behind bridge. An unusually heavy
detonation follows with a very strong explosion cloud. . . . She has
the appearance of being about to capsize. Great confusion on board.
. . . In the bow appears the name *Lusitania*. . . ." Later, when the
Germans realized the consequences of their act, rumors were launched
(not finally refuted until after the war when the Collector of the Port
made public his report) that the *Lusitania* had been armed, had car-

ried a great load of ammunition, etc. These were all disproved (though she did carry the small arms ammunition listed in the text), and a man named Gustav Stahl, who swore he had seen 15 cm. guns on the decks of the *Lusitania* prior to her sailing, subsequently admitted he had perjured himself and was sent to Atlanta Penitentiary.

The *Lusitania* was equipped with twenty-five cylindrical coal-burning boilers, and had a normal speed of 24½ to 25 knots. However, with the outbreak of the war the Cunard Company had decided that the transatlantic traffic would not justify the operation of the *Lusitania* at this high speed, so six boilers were closed off and the ship commenced a monthly round-trip schedule at a speed of 21 knots. Twenty-one knots, therefore, was her maximum off the Irish coast, but even this had been reduced to 18 knots (although the captain knew he was in dangerous waters) in order to prevent the *Lusitania* from arriving off the Mersey before daybreak the following day.

Several of the passengers and crew saw the torpedo momentarily before it struck; some of the passengers later claimed to have seen the submarine's conning tower or periscope briefly a few seconds before. Many passengers were certain that two torpedoes struck the ship, and some thought three had been fired at her. Even the British *Official History of the World War* and the British Board of Trade investigation made this mistake. It seems certain, however, in the light of after-knowledge, that only one torpedo was fired by the U-20, and that found its mark. The second explosion was undoubtedly an internal one caused by the torpedo; it was probably a steam explosion (the boilers), or possibly (though improbably) the ammunition carried on the orlop and lower decks.

Both Captain Turner and his crew appear to have acted, on the whole, bravely and to the best of their ability. But there is irrefutable evidence as to the limited speed of the ship in a danger zone; there is also evidence that some of the ports were open, and after the ship was struck, though there was no panic, there was little order. The crew was mostly composed of green men and boys, since the bulk of the *Lusitania's* regular crew had entered the Royal Naval Reserve for war service at the outbreak of hostilities.

Frohman's last remark is variously quoted; the substance of it seems to be as I have written it.

The dead included 124 Americans, among them the Hubbards; Charles Klein, the playwright; Justus Miles Forman; Albert Lloyd Hopkins, president of the Newport News Shipbuilding and Dry Dock Company; Herbert S. Stone, and many others prominent on two continents. Of the 125 children and babies aboard the great liner only thirty-five were saved. Miss Pope, who sought to find the meaning of the other world, was lost; a mother and four of her children died— two were saved; the Rev. Mr. Beattie, the missionary, was lost and his wife saved; and "Dave Samuels" (whose real name was David Samoilescu), the "song-and-dance artist" also died.

After the news of the sinking was flashed over the world there were anti-German riots in Liverpool; the column rules were turned in American papers, and mourning was worn in hundreds of homes. Germany struck a medal; Wilson wrote a note; the consequences of the thing went on forever. More than any other single incident the sinking of the *Lusitania* helped to drag America into the war; two years later recruiting posters in a hundred towns urged "Remember the *Lusitania!*" The claims of victims or relatives of victims were still dragging through the protracted processes of the Mixed Claims Commission in the late 20's. Some who were rescued never recovered from the shock or injuries received; young Mrs. Roland Anderson and the son she was bearing when the *Lusitania* sank both died in later years as direct results of that single torpedo from the U-20. Lieutenant-Commander Schwieger was a marked man thereafter to the British Secret Service, but not until 1917 was the *Lusitania* avenged. Schwieger had gone from command of the U-20 to the U-88, and on September 7, 1917, he tried to dive his ship under the mine field near Horn's Reef. Fathoms deep in darkness he and his crew met their end much as did those stokers and engineers of the *Lusitania* who died when the sea burst in upon them: the U-88 pushed her blunt bow into a mined net and was never seen again. One month later, in October, 1917, the U-20 ran aground in a pea-soup fog on the Danish coast and had to be blown up. And in another year the convoy system and the depth charge, the mine fields and the listening devices, and American shipyards working overtime had broken the back of the German submarine campaign. Yankee destroyers were charging in a white smother of foam over that grave where a dead ship lay; the

Kaiser fled to Holland and so it was all in vain. But the *Lusitania* will not be forgotten.

ACKNOWLEDGMENTS   The principal and primary sources for this tale of the *Lusitania* are the investigation of the British Court, with Lord Mersey as Wreck Commissioner; the investigation of the District Court of New York, Southern District, on the petition of the Cunard Steamship Line for a limitation of its liability; the British *Official Naval History of the Great War:* Volume I—Hurd, Chapter X; Volume II—Corbett, page 391 ff.

Secondary but important sources are Walter Millis' *The Road to War,* from which the incident about Colonel House and the King is quoted; Charles E. Lauriat's *The Lusitania's Last Voyage; Danger Zone,* by E. Keble Chatterton; *Their Secret Purposes,* by Hector Bywater; Administrative Decisions (in the Lusitania case) of the Mixed Proceedings, and the *Journal of the American Society of Naval Engineers; Germany and the Lusitania Medal,* The Rosemary Press; the files of the New York *Times,* the New York *World,* and various miscellaneous pamphlets and publications. Quotations in the article are mainly from passengers' eyewitness accounts of the sinking or from one or the other of the publications credited above.

1872

The Strange Case
of the *Mary Celeste*

Gibraltar, by cable

FOUND FOURTH AND BROUGHT HERE MARY CELESTE, ABAN-
DONED SEAWORTHY. ADMIRALTY IMPOSITION. NOTIFY ALL PAR-
TIES. TELEGRAPH OFFER OF SALVAGE.

MOREHOUSE

Footing along handily over a rough but moderating sea with brisk
northerly winds filling her fore-and-afters and swelling the square sails
on her foremast, the British brigantine *Dei Gratia* stood toward
Gibraltar that fourth of December,[1] 1872.

It was sometime after two bells in the afternoon watch, and her
master—Captain David Reed Morehouse—had checked his ship's
position as about 38-20′ North, 17.37′ West,[2] about 600 miles off the
coast of Portugal, to the north of the direct route between the Azores
and Gibraltar. The *Dei Gratia* was on the port tack when her lookout
reported a sail—at first nothing but a dark smudge, hull down on the
horizon—later a brigantine, jib trimmed to port but plainly on the
starboard tack and yawing and falling off in a curious manner as if
there were no man at the wheel.

Morehouse ran down closer to have a look at the stranger . . .
and thus wrote the first chapter in a classic mystery of the sea—the
strange case of the *Mary Celeste*.

She was out of the Parrsboro district in Nova Scotia, and already she had been sailing the seas (whenever she could find a cargo) those past eleven years when she cleared New York November 4, 1872, on her fatal voyage.

Joshua Dewis was her master builder and he laid her down out of mixed wood—some of it soft—at Spencer's Island in 1861. She had changed names and hands several times before she came into history in that year 1872. Originally christened the *Amazon*,[3] she was renamed the *Mary Celeste;* originally under British registry, she was rebuilt and changed to American registry on December 31, 1868, some time after stranding in a gale at Cape Breton in 1867. She had changed owners too—and skippers; hers were the usual vicissitudes of the sailing tramp. She had been knocked about a good bit in the trade, but she was still a good ship, paying her way and a little more in that year 1872.

She was a brigantine then[4] (square sails on her fore, fore-and-aft on her mainmast). She was a double deck 282-ton brigantine then, and her topsails drew full and sweetly and her deck houses were comfortable in most weathers. She was about 100 feet long, with 25½ foot beam, and she needed at least 11.7 feet of clear salt water beneath her plimsoll mark. She was not new, not as ships go—but she'd had a thorough overhaul that October of 1872, with new timbers, new transoms, a remodeled cabin, part-new knightheads and stem, and other repairs and alterations, and her underwriters—the Atlantic Mutual Insurance Company—gave her carte blanche, and their surveyors noted even then—"appears well built."

The brigantine, or "half-brig" as she was sometimes described, was owned in part by her master, Captain Benjamin S. Briggs, and in part by Captain James H. Winchester of New York, who had sailed as master of some of his own ships in the past. Since 1866 Captain Winchester had operated a small and variable fleet of brigs, brigantines, and schooners (such as the *Wandering Jew*) and he was to build up a vigorous steamship agency and ship brokerage business which was to be passed down to his grandson, Winchester Noyes, under the name of J. H. Winchester and Company.[5] There were other part owners,[6] but J. H. Winchester and Company were the operating agents, and Captain Winchester and Captain Briggs the chiefly interested parties.

Such was the brigantine *Celeste* before she sailed out of New York into history.

There wasn't much notice taken of her departure, though those were the days when the waterfront was covered and news of the seven seas was the *Herald's* specialty. But the *Celeste* was too little, and the papers were too full of Grant's re-election battle, and of a strange disease (the reporters had a lot of fun; they called it—variously— "Epizoatic," "Hipporhinorrhea," etc.) that was attacking the horses of the Atlantic Seaboard and thus tying up the horse-car traffic in New York.

The *Celeste* had as skipper at her sailing Captain Benjamin S. Briggs,[7] thirty-eight-year-old Wareham (Massachusetts) man, who "bore the highest character for seamanship and correctness." Briggs was a "typical sailing master of what is termed the old school," a disciplinarian though not a martinet, and a man who loved his ship, his family, and his God.[8]

With Briggs sailed his wife, Sarah (Elizabeth) Everson Cobb Briggs, and their two-year-old daughter, Sophia M. Briggs. Behind in New Bedford, Mass., in care of his grandmother, Mrs. Nathan Briggs, remained Arthur S. Briggs, seven years old, son of the master, and Arthur's fourteen-year-old cousin, Oliver W. Cobb, later a respected physician and *Mary Celeste* enthusiast of Easthampton, Mass.[9] With the little family went the usual clothes, toys, paraphernalia, and baggage incidental to women and children aboard ship, a melodeon, a sewing machine, etc. Briggs had been sailing the seas too long to be a great hand for souvenirs, but he had the common liking for the odd and rare, and somewhere in his cabin he had stowed away an old sword "of Italian make," with the "cross of Savoy [described by others as a cross of Navarre] on the hilt," which he had picked up on a previous voyage while visiting an old battlefield near the head of the Adriatic sea.

Albert G. Richardson,[10] a "Down-Easter" out of Stockton, Maine, young, but a steady married man of experience on the seas, went out as mate of the *Celeste,* and Andrew Gilling was second mate. She had a crew of five; the steward and cook was Edward William Head of

New York; the four seamen, all apparently of German or Scandinavian origin, were Volkerk Lorenzen, Boas Lorenzen, Arian Harbens, and Gottlieb Goodshaad.[11] The crew, despite later calumnies, appear to have been stolid, dependable seamen, and all that is known about them, as Horatio L. Sprague, U.S. Consul at Gibraltar later pointed out, "inspired confidence rather than otherwise."

The *Celeste's* cargo was 1,700 barrels of alcohol, valued at $36,-943, belonging to Meissner, Ackerman and Co., of 48 Beaver Street, New York City, to whom she was under charter, and consigned to an Italian firm in Genoa. The "cargo was insured abroad but the freight interest was covered by the Atlantic Mutual Insurance Company [to the extent of $3,400] and other local companies."

Details of the *Celeste's* last days in New York are incomplete,[12] although at least one lurid book has been written which purports to describe at length the circumstances before and at her sailing.

It is known that one of the *Celeste's* two boats, which was carried on top of the forward house, was smashed when a sling slipped while cargo was being loaded at Pier 44, East River, and she had no time to replace it before sailing.

And it is also known that the brigantine *Dei Gratia* of Nova Scotian registry, Captain David Reed Morehouse commanding, was in New York loading cargo while the *Celeste* prepared for her voyage into history.

Skipper Briggs and Skipper Morehouse were old friends; they had encountered each other in many of the ports of the seven seas; Morehouse, like Briggs, was part owner and master of his ship, and sometimes took his wife along on his cruises. Mrs. Briggs and Mrs. Morehouse, like their husbands, were also old friends and had met at ports-of-call in various parts of the world. And so it was natural that the two masters should see something of each other while their ships were loading—the *Celeste* with her barrels of alcohol, the *Dei Gratia* with a mixed cargo[13] (apparently) for Mediterranean ports. Some say that Briggs and Morehouse even had dinner together at the old Astor House the night before the *Celeste* sailed, but there is no evidence of this and no certainty that the two skippers did meet.

But this—and even her date of sailing—are still matters for dispute. Most writers—and the records of the Atlantic Mutual Insurance

Company—put the *Celeste's* sailing at November 7 or 8, but in the New York Custom House, an entry in a musty ledger, entitled "Index of Foreign Clearances" for the year 1872, plainly lists, under date of November 4, as having cleared the port, the brig (sic) *Mary Celeste,* bound for Genoa, Italy. And on November 11, another sailing vessel, dropped down channel with the tide, procured her clearance papers and got ready to take her departure from the Hook and lay a long course for Gibraltar. She flew the British flag, and she was the brigantine *Dei Gratia,* Captain David Reed Morehouse, commanding.[14]

The *Dei Gratia* had been at sea about twenty days that December fourth, when she sighted the strange brigantine and hauled up to speak to her. In those days of long ocean crossings any sail was a welcome sight and Morehouse, as he closed the stranger and came to recognize her as the *Celeste,* ship of his friend Briggs, was particularly pleased. But his pleasure soon changed to bewilderment.

There was no man at the *Celeste's* wheel; he could see that clearly now as the two ships approached. That explained her erratic sailing; there was none on deck to check her and keep her fair upon her course. Perhaps they were lying ill below—his old friend Briggs among them—with plague.

He signaled—no answer; again, and finally "he gave her an urgent hoist." Close aboard now, Morehouse broke out his speaking trumpet and hailed her:

"*Celeste* ahoy!"

The great bellow surged full above the wave tops and echoed away in rumbling syllables across the sea—but there was no answer. Again Morehouse tried, and again. There was but silence.

He ordered a boat away, and Oliver Deveau, his Nova Scotian mate, and two men manned it. The oar blades plumped into the sea as Morehouse leaned on the *Dei Gratia's* rail and squinted with some alarm and amazement at the *Mary Celeste* swagging along aimlessly there, yawing to each puff of wind. He saw again that the *Celeste* was on the starboard tack (heading westward) but that her jib was set to port. Only the jib and the foretop-staysail were set; the lower foretopsail was hanging by the four corners, and all the rest of the sails were furled. He speculated, as he watched the boat row under *Celeste's* stern and come alongside—it wasn't like Captain Briggs to leave the wheel untended and the ship footing it free with no one on deck. What was the explanation?

Morehouse soon had the answer. There was no one aboard; *Celeste* was a derelict.

Deveau and his men had rowed under the brigantine's stern—the stern with the name painted fair (*"Mary Celeste*—New York"). They had ranged up alongside forward and had gotten aboard by climbing up the chain plates. The mate and a man had handed it up to the deck; one man had stayed in the boat towing alongside by her bow painter.

On deck there was "nothing and no one." There was little more below. Deveau proceeded to inspect the ship.

The "first thing" he did was "to sound the pumps which were in good order" and showed a depth of 3½ feet of water in the hold.[15] "The pump gear was good, but one of the pumps was drawn to let the sounding rod down. . . ." The "fore hatch and the lazarette hatch were both off (the cargo hatch lying on deck upside down[16] near the entrance to the hold it had covered) and the binnacle was displaced with its compass broken. There was a great deal of water between decks; the forward house [was] full of water up to the coaming." The yawl—the only boat aboard when the *Celeste* left New York—was gone from its place of stowage on the main hatch and a section of rail on the port side abreast the hatch, which apparently had been removed to launch the boat, was still lying on deck.

The masts were good, the spars all right, the rigging in bad order; some of the running rigging carried away. The upper fore-tops'l and foresail gone apparently blown away from the yards, lower fore-tops'l hanging by the four corners. The main staysail hauled down and lying on the forward house loose as if it had been let run down. Jib and foretop stay-sail set. All the rest of the sails being furled.

There was one other slightly unusual circumstance; there were six windows in the after-house—"two in the captain's [cabin], one in the mate's, one in the W.C., one in the pantry and one facing the bow of the ship," and they "were all battened up with canvas and boards." Deveau knocked the battens off one window in the mate's room and started exploring the after house (or cabin, which was raised about two feet above the upper deck).

Everything was in order, though wet, and it was evident there had been "a great deal of water" in the house. "The clock was spoilt by the water." The sky light of the cabin was open and raised. Charts, books, clothes, furniture were in order; the captain's bed was made but wet and soggy; in the mattress there was an impress "as if a child had lain there." Two or three "loose charts" lay over the master's bed. The log book was in "the mate's cabin on his desk," the log slate on the cabin table.

There was "an entry in the log book up to the 24th November, and an entry on the log slate, date 25th November." These entries showed that at noon on November 24, ten days earlier, the *Mary Celeste's* position by observation had been Latitude 36-56[17] North, Longitude 27-20 West, "about 110 miles due west of the island of Santa Maria in the Azores." The slate entry, entered as of 8 A.M. on November 25, recorded a bearing of the eastern point of Santa Maria, SSW, distance six miles. That was the "last record of any kind."

Deveau looked further. The things in the cabin "were all wet," but the rosewood melodeon was dry and unharmed. The dish rack was on the table, but there were no edibles, though the mate found "preserved meats in the pantry" and plenty of provisions aboard. Deveau found clothes, a small amount of money, jewelry, including a gold locket. Under the bunk in the captain's cabin he found an old sword, with a blade that seemed to be covered with rust when he took it from its scabbard, and with a "cross of Savoy" on the hilt. There was one other thing—a few words on the log slate[18] on the cabin table, apparently in the handwriting of Albert G. Richardson, Captain Briggs' mate:

"Francis [sic] my own dear wife, Francis N.R.——"[19]

There were no ship's papers—except the log and the mate's notebook. The captain's sextant, the chronometer, and navigation books were gone. There was no log line, either trailing astern or ready for use.

Forward in the forecastle (or forward house) were the same signs of sudden and inexplicable abandonment. The seamen's chests and baggage[20] were standing in a few inches of water, but were all there, stowed neatly and in order; they had even left behind oilskins and boots, and their pipes (the first thing an old tar thinks about); and the razors on shelves near the bunks were bright and keen, with no flecks of rust. Clothes were hanging on lines to dry as they had been left; there was an English five-pound note in one of the ditty boxes and other articles of value. The galley was deeper in water than the fo'c'sle; the water "slushed out of the door when the ship rolled" and the pots and pans were washing about. There were no cooked provisions in the galley, and nothing to eat in the cabin, but there was a barrel of flour in the galley wet and "one-third gone," and potatoes, meat, and miscellaneous foods of all sorts in the storerooms, enough for about six months' supply. There was plenty of water in the water casks, but the deck chocks in which they were stowed had been moved "as if struck by a heavy sea." The carpenter's tools were in the mate's room, and all the rest of the paraphernalia of the sea was found stowed about the brigantine, most of it in its proper and precise order, though some things were "all in confusion, the hatches off, ropes about."

Deveau's somewhat cursory first inspection satisfied him that not only was there no one aboard the *Mary Celeste,* but there was no ready clue as to why she had been abandoned derelict. After a consultation with Captain Morehouse aboard the *Dei Gratia,* the mate and two men started the job of getting the *Celeste's* rigging in running order and the ship squared away for Gibraltar, to be taken in for salvage. With a wave of the hand Morehouse laid the *Dei Gratia* off on her course again, and the first chapter in the strange case of the *Mary Celeste* was finished.

The *Dei Gratia* arrived in Gibraltar the evening of December 12, and the *Celeste* followed her into port the next morning. When Deveau arrived he was still puzzled; in his days aboard the brigantine he had found no cause for abandonment; she was well-found and sturdy and the men had had no trouble in bringing her in.

Morehouse immediately filed a claim for salvage; the owners and underwriters in New York were notified by Morehouse and by the American Consul, Horatio J. Sprague, and as Captain Winchester in New York prepared to come to Gibraltar, the Vice Admiralty court in Gibraltar commenced hearings on the salvage claim. As the series of hearings started, and surveys and inspections of the *Celeste* were made, there was considerable mystification as to the reason for her abandonment, but at first no great apprehension about the safety of Captain Briggs, his wife, his child, and his crew. It was thought by many that the brigantine had been abandoned hurriedly, for what had been considered by her master some good reason, that her people had embarked in the yawl, and had been picked up by some passing vessel. Some or all of them would surely turn up at some one of the world's ports within the next few weeks.

But the weeks dragged by without news, and the hearings and surveys, conducted with some acrimony, considerable suspicion and much fanfare, developed some amazingly conflicting theories, but little real evidence. The principal investigator was Mr. J. Solly Flood, who bore the imposing title of "Her Majesty's Advocate-General and Proctor for the Queen in her office of Admiralty, and Attorney General for Gibraltar." He was, it appears from the records, an indefatigable legal bloodhound, who early formed a theory of violence and who clung to it through pages of testimony and divers examinations of the brigantine. He tried, however, to leave no stone unturned. On December 18 and 20, and subsequently, Deveau and those of the *Dei Gratia's* people who had boarded the *Celeste* at sea were examined, and on December 23 a thorough survey of the brigantine was made by Solly Flood and experts retained by him. J. Ricardo Portunato, a diver, examined the hull, and John Austin, surveyor of shipping at Gibraltar, made a thorough inspection topsides.

These inspections were later followed by one made by Captain R. W. Shufeldt, USN, of the U.S.S. *Plymouth,* who visited the *Celeste* at the request of American Consul Sprague. Sprague himself boarded the derelict, and in January the indefatigable Mr. Flood inspected the brigantine again with the help of navy officers and a British Army engineer. All of these inspections—formal and informal —official and unofficial, were interspersed with examinations in the proceedings before the Admiralty Court of Mate Deveau and his men,[21] and later of Captain Winchester, who arrived from New York early in the new year to help have the imposition on his ship lifted. Captain Winchester, apparently a man of frankness, became impatient

at the delays and procrastination of British legal procedure, informed
the court angrily that he was a citizen of the United States of English
descent, "but if I knew where the English blood was I'd open a vein
and let it out," and stamped off home in a huff. The court was delayed
and irritated by the departure of the *Dei Gratia* with the chief witnesses, Deveau and his men. The brigantine went about her business
in the Mediterranean but returned to Gibraltar, whereupon Deveau
testified again and final disposition of the case was made.

All of these inspections and all of this testimony did little to clear
up the mystery, though several minor discoveries were made, and a
number of them apparently were emphasized far beyond their importance. Solly Flood or one of his men found the sword, with the cross
of Savoy on its hilt, somewhere in the captain's cabin of the *Celeste,*
and drawing it from its scabbard, detected signs of what some thought
were rust, but which Mr. Flood was sure was blood.

Suspicious-looking spots of the same dark, brownish-red color were
found on the starboard top-gallant rail, together with "a mark of a
blow, apparently of a sharp axe," and similar spots were found in
various parts of the deck. Solly Flood's dander was up at this discovery.

Apparently he thought that Captain Morehouse, the *Dei Gratia's*
master, had allowed Deveau to "obliterate" some of the stains found
on the sword and on the starboard top-gallant rail, and he therefore
believed it necessary to have an expensive analysis made of the scrapings taken from rail and sword. (Solly Flood thought the blade had
been wiped before it was returned to its scabbard.)[22]

A Dr. J. Patron of Gibraltar made an analysis of the alleged bloodstains, but before it was completed Mr. Solly Flood had addressed a
report to the British Board of Trade in London, pointing with suspicion to the supposed stains and other findings. Alas for theories, for
Dr. J. Patron reported to the court that the stains were not blood,
although even the exact nature of his report was surrounded with unexplained mystery. The analysis was ordered by the Vice Admiralty
Court on March 14, 1873, and the doctor's report was brought in
under seal the same day, although it was later discovered that it was
dated January 30. Despite Consul Sprague's attempts to obtain a copy
of the analysis for the U.S. State Department, he was unable to do so

until *1887, fourteen years later.* Then, during a revival of interest in the *Mary Celeste* mystery, Consul Sprague addressed a letter to Edward W. Baumgartner, Registrar of the Court, requesting a copy of the analysis. In complying with the request Mr. Baumgartner discovered that the seal on the original copy of the analysis had remained unbroken for fourteen years "until I opened it for the purpose of giving you the copy." Presumably Dr. Patron had made a verbal report to the court and the court had not opened, or permitted the opening, of the written analysis.

That written analysis, since derided by some writers as inadequate for a proper analysis of the stains, and as even laughable in the light of present-day knowledge,[23] described Dr. Patron's methods and procedure. A copy of that report sent by Mr. Sprague to the State Department in 1887, declares that Dr. Patron inspected the *Mary Celeste* to determine whether "any marks or stains of blood could be discovered on or in her hulk."

After a careful and minute inspection of the deck of the said vessel [the report continues] *some red-brown spots about a milimetre [sic] thick and half an inch in diameter with dull aspect were found on deck in the forepart of the vessel; these spots were separated with a chisel and carefully wrapped in paper No. 1. Some other similar spots were also gathered in different parts of the deck and wrapped in papers numbered 2, 3 and 4. Paper No. 5 contained a powder grated from a suspicious mark seen on the top-gallant rail part of which was obtained on board and part from a piece of timber belonging to the said vessel in Her Majesty's Attorney General's Chambers.*

I carefully examined the cabin both with natural and with artificial light; the floor, the sides of the berths, mattresses, etc. were minutely searched and nothing worth calling attention was seen that could have any relation with the object of my inquiries.

The good doctor took the sword and his carefully labeled papers, and commenced his analysis. He simply placed the scrapings from the sword, decks and rails in filtered water, and later heated the water with a spirit lamp, after letting it stand.

. . . as no precipitate or cloudy aspect appeared I considered the experiment over and of a negative character.

*From the preceding negative experiments I feel myself authorized
to conclude that according to our present scientifical [sic] knowledge,
there is no blood either in the stains observed on the deck of the* Mary
Celeste *or on those found on the blade of the sword I have examined.*

So much for the "blood" discovered in the various inspections of
the American brigantine. Those inspections developed one or two
other circumstances (as well as a host of details) which puzzled the
investigators then and have continued to puzzle posterity in the three-
quarters of a century since then.

One of those circumstances concerned a peculiar and unexplained
"injury" to the bows. "On either side of the bows of the ship, some
two or three feet above the water-line, a narrow strip had been cut
away," Lockhart reports, "from the edge of one of the outer planks,
to a depth of about three-eighths of an inch, a width of about an inch
and a quarter, and a length of about between six and seven feet. The
injury was recent. . . ."

This "injury" (it was more of a superficial scratch than a serious
"injury") "had been sustained very recently," John Austin, Gibraltar
Surveyor of Shipping thought, "and could not have been effected by
weather, and was apparently done by a sharp cutting instrument continuously through the whole length of the injury." Solly Flood himself, and his board of naval officers and an army engineer, agreed
"that the injury to the bows had been effected intentionally by a sharp
instrument." Captain Shufeldt, the American skipper of the *Plymouth,*
did not, however, concur in this opinion, but considered that the
gouges, marks, or "spauls" (as they were variously described)
amounted "merely to splinters in the bending of the planks, which were
afterward forced off by the action of the sea," and not in any way
betokening any intention of "wilfully damaging the vessel."

One other find on the brigantine—the log of the *Mary Celeste*—
interested the investigators greatly. Both the working chart and the
ship's log were "complete up to noon of the 24th. November . . .
the deck or slate log is continued . . . up to 8 A.M. on the following
day, at which hour the eastern point of St. Mary's [Azores] bore
SSW, distant six miles."

The *Celeste's* position by observation on November 24, according to the log, had been 36-56 North, 27-20 West. The next morning, according to the log slate, she was off the island of St. Mary's to the northward. Ten days later she was sighted by the *Dei Gratia,* unmanned, some 500 to 750[24] miles to east and northwards from her last recorded position. Solly Flood thought "that she must actually have held her course for ten days after November 25th, the wheel being loose all the time." Lockhart, with the blessing of Dr. Cobb,[25] then the young nephew of the mysteriously missing Captain Briggs— concurs in this.

Other investigators, however, believed it impossible, or at least highly improbable, that a ship could sail such a distance unmanned, and even Lockhart admits that if his assumption is correct, that it "was pretty good going for an unmanned ship."

Evidence as to the weather the *Celeste* experienced is mixed; some other ships during that period reported heavy gales, but the *Dei Gratia,* following practically the same course, encountered heavy weather and high seas but no stress of wind or wave severe enough to cause alarm, much less abandonment. And the *Celeste's* surveys showed no evidence of storm damage; when Deveau boarded her the paltry amount of water in deckhouses and hold, and the confused state of her rigging and gear were the only evidences (and negligible ones at that) of "damage."

For the rest, there was little enough. The repeated explorations and searches of the derelict brigantine revealed few tangible clues. One barrel of alcohol in the opened hold looked as if it had been tampered with, or started. There was, however, no evidence that the *Celeste* "had sustained any injury whatever, the hull, the copper with which it was covered, the stern, sternpost and rudder being all in good order and condition."

As regards the interior of the ship a very minute survey showed most clearly that not only had the vessel not sustained any accident but that she could not have encountered any seriously heavy weather. The whole of the hull, masts and yards were in good condition, and the pitch in the water ways had not started, which must have been the case had any bad weather been experienced. The house, made of thin planking and six feet in height above the deck, was perfect, there not being a crack in the planking, nor even in the paint. The seamen's chests and clothing found on board were perfectly dry, some razors even being quite free from rust. Moreover a small phial containing oil for use with a sewing machine, was found in a perpendicular position, which together with a thimble and a reel of cotton[26] discovered near it, had not been subject to any stress of weather. Spare panes of glass were also found stowed and unbroken.

. . . almost the whole personal effects of the Master, and . . . of his wife and child, and of the crew have been found in good order and condition. They are of considerable value. In the Captain's cabin were a harmonium in a rosewood case, books of music, and others mostly of a religious tendency; gold lockets and other trinkets, jewelry, and female attire of a superior description were in the lady's boxes.

Captain Shufeldt found the vessel upon his inspection "staunch and seaworthy"—with "no evidence of violence about the decks or in the cabins."

John Austin, the Surveyor, also found the *Celeste* "thoroughly sound, staunch and strong and not making water to any appreciable extent . . . the whole appearance of the vessel showed that she had never encountered any such violence as would have accounted for her abandonment . . . did not discover the slightest trace of there having been any explosion or of a fire."

J. Ricardo Portunato, the diver, also found nothing in his examination of the underwater hull. There was "no trace of damage or injury, or any other appearance that the vessel had been in collision or had struck upon any rock or shoal or had met with any other accident or casualty. The hull, keel, sternpost and rudder were in thoroughly good order and condition."

Mr. Solly Flood summarized the general mystification in his report to the Board of Trade when he stated that the *Celeste* had been found to be "thoroughly sound, staunch, strong and in every way seaworthy and well found; that she was well provisioned and that she had encountered no seriously heavy weather; and that no appearance of fire or of explosion, or of alarm of fire or explosion, or any other assignable cause for abandonment was discoverable."

Neither he nor other investigators attempted to explain the water in the cabin, deckhouse, and galley which Deveau, the mate, reported, nor did they regard the battened-up cabin windows as suspicious.[27]

But Solly Flood still clung to his theory of bloody violence, and concluded his report (made apparently before Dr. Patron's analysis of the alleged bloodstains) with the following passage:

My own theory or guess is that the crew got at the alcohol, and in the fury of drunkenness murdered the Master, whose name was Briggs, his wife and child and the chief mate; that they then damaged the bows of the vessel with the view of giving it the appearance of having struck on the rocks, or suffered a collision, so as to induce the Master of any vessel which might pick them up, if they saw her at some distance, to think her not worth attempting to save; and that they did, some time between the 25th November and the 5th December, escape on board some vessel bound for some North or South American port or the West Indies.

This was a popular theory with officialdom of that day, though Captain Shufeldt did not endorse it. He reported that "I reject the idea of a mutiny from the fact that there is no evidence of violence about the decks or in the cabins. . . . I am of the opinion that she was abandoned by the Master and crew in a moment of panic and for no sufficient reason. She may have strained in the *gale through which she was passing* [Captain Shufeldt offers no further explanation of this "gale"] and for the time leaked so much . . ." as to induce her people to abandon her. "Someday," Captain Shufeldt's report continued, "I hope and expect to hear from her crew. If surviving the Master will regret his hasty action. But if we should never hear of them again, I shall nevertheless think they were lost in the boat in which both Master and men abandoned the *Mary Celeste* and shall remember with interest this sad and silent mystery of the sea. . . ."

The United States Treasury Department, from the reports forwarded by Consul Sprague and others, decided that the mutiny and murder theory was at least tenable, and issued instructions to its Customs Officers that "the circumstances of the case tend to arouse grave suspicions that the Master, his wife and child, and perhaps the chief mate, were murdered in the fury of drunkenness by the crew, who had evidently obtained access to the alcohol." The Customs Officers were ordered to be on the lookout for any of the crew of the *Celeste*.

Captain Winchester, the principal owner of the brigantine, who had been exasperated by British legal procedure and who had sailed back home in a huff, always believed (his descendants, the relatives of Captain Briggs, and the descendants of Captain Morehouse still believe so today) that the hatch to the cargo hold and the cargo itself were the clues to the mystery. He thought it probable, or at least more probable than the other theories, that the alcohol in the hold had heated up and generated fumes, that a small explosion had occurred, which blew off the hatch, and that Captain Briggs and his people had hurriedly embarked in the yawl, intending either to make for the island of St. Mary's, or to rejoin the *Celeste* later if a feared larger explosion did not eventuate. The overloaded yawl was lost . . . and Briggs and the others passed out of the world beyond the ken of man. . . .

Deveau, the salvage mate, expressed his opinion in his testimony before the court:

"My idea is," he declared, "that the crew got alarmed and by the sounding rod being found lying alongside the pumps, that they had sounded the pumps and found perhaps a quantity of water in the pumps at the moment, and thinking she would go down, abandoned her."

Such were the theories then—theories which were to propagate and multiply mightily (some of them into weird perversions) in after years. But the Gibraltar Vice-Admiralty Court was not concerned with theories, and on March 14, 1873, it "gave judgment" in the *Mary Celeste* salvage case and awarded the sum of £1,700 to the master and crew of the *Dei Gratia* "for the salvage services rendered by them, the costs of the suit to be paid out of the property salvaged." The *Mary Celeste,* a Gibraltar Chronicle report of the award notes, was valued at $5,700[28] and her cargo at $36,943, so that the "award may be set down as one-fifth of the total value."

The official proceedings were ended; the *Celeste,* under a new captain and with a new crew, had cleared for Genoa where she delivered her cargo, and a large part of officialdom settled back to wait until some wind-jamming tramp should put into a foreign port, with the crew—and perhaps the master—of the *Celeste* aboard. The personal effects found aboard her were turned over by the Admiralty Court to

Consul Sprague to be returned to relatives. The inventory ("two lady's hats . . . night shirt . . . mosquito net . . . a doll . . . an envelope containing two free mason's documents . . . a fan . . . two lady's breast pins . . . a crinoline . . .") listing the items makes pathetic reading even at this late date. The consul did not succeed in forwarding these belongings for some months. They were shipped home in the fall of 1873 by the American barkentine *John J. Marsh,* and eventually reached the Briggs family in Massachusetts, Mrs. Albert Richardson, wife of the missing mate, in Brooklyn, and the Collector of Customs at New York, who held the belongings of the missing crew. The "rosewood harmonium" or melodeon, as it has been variously called, was in the possession of Captain Briggs' son until his death a few years ago; the "crinoline," the doll, the hats have probably long since faded into the dust.

There was just one other occurrence relating to the *Mary Celeste* in that year 1873 which Consul Sprague duly and meticulously reported. Under date of 4 April, he notes the receipt of a letter from Nettersum, Isle of Föhr, Prussia, signed by a T. A. Nickelsen (who said he was writing in behalf of the mother and wives of two of the missing sailors) inquiring for information about two sailors—brothers and natives of his village—who, the writer declared, had been members of the crew of the *Celeste*. Curiously enough, as Consul Sprague reported, the letter from Prussia did not give the names of the men about whom information was asked. But nevertheless Sprague comments in his report that "it is somewhat gratifying to learn that three out of five men composing the crew of the *Mary Celeste* were known to the writer of that communication as being peaceable and first-class sailors, as it further diminishes the probability that any violence was committed on board of this vessel by her crew." The consul further reports under the same date that he has been confidentially informed that the Judge of the Vice-Admiralty Court has refused to permit the copy of the analysis made of the supposed bloodstains "to be opened for the present, even for the purpose of furnishing a copy to the Governor of this fortress."

That was all. The days, the months, the years, went by and those who waited lived their lives and died. Their theories died before them, and the sea held its mystery.

In 1887, under date of 26 July, more than fourteen long years after a derelict brigantine had been sighted footing it alone across the blue, Consul Sprague sent a copy of the analysis of the supposed bloodstains to Worthington C. Ford in the State Department at Washington, and remarked in a letter:

This case of the Mary Celeste *as you justly remark is startling, since it appears to be one of those mysteries which no human ingenuity can penetrate sufficiently to account for the abandonment of this vessel, and the disappearance of her Master, family, and crew, about whom nothing has ever transpired.*

The case of the *Mary Celeste,* puzzling enough to those investigators of 1873 (but then still open to reasonable explanation) quickly became so tarnished with the verdigris of fiction that to the investigators of the twentieth century, it has become extremely difficult to distinguish fact from fancy.

A young Englishman, who was to create two of fiction's most famous characters—Sherlock Holmes and Dr. Watson—was chiefly responsible for this, though indirectly and probably unintentionally so. Arthur Conan Doyle, after the appearance of various newspaper accounts describing the finding of the derelict, wrote a story, titled "J. Habakuk Jephson's Statement," which purports to tell of the finding of the *Marie*[29] (sic) *Celeste,* and to describe with many and horrible details what happened to the captain and crew (whose names the author fictionized). "J. Habakuk Jephson's Statement" (supposed to be the statement of a survivor) was first published anonymously in the *Cornhill Magazine* in England in January, 1884, with no indication as to whether it was intended as fact or fiction. Much of the public, including many subsequent writers who were more facile at making phrases than zealous in research, took the story to its collective bosom, and knowing little of the *Mary Celeste* case anyway, accepted the "Statement" as fact. Sir Arthur Conan Doyle, however, undoubtedly never intended it as such, and today "J. Habakuk Jephson's Statement" is accepted fiction.

There followed a great host of *Mary Celeste* "solutions," "revelations" and "explanations," with at least one whole book, called *The Great Mary Celeste Hoax* woven around a series of fantastic and entirely unprovable happenings. Dying sailors all over the world made "death-bed confessions" or left behind them in ditty boxes or sea bags "true stories" of the *Mary Celeste* case. "Survivors" and "members of the crew" by the score turned up in Bangkok, Liverpool, or Key West, and fed newspapers and magazines (particularly the British journals which were avid for news of the case) with weird tales of mutiny, insanity, murder, swimming races in mid-ocean, "baby's quarterdecks" built out like a platform over the bow of the *Celeste* (to explain the gouges in the bow); and other impossible things. Messages in cipher purporting to explain the mystery when deciphered, and the interpretation of the mystery in astrological terminology were recorded. Three novelists, as Lockhart points out—Barry Pain, H. A. Vachell, and Arthur Morrison—added their highly imaginative "solutions" to the rest of the fictional treatments that accumulated on top of "J. Habakuk Jephson's Statement."

The *Mary Celeste* case—a plain, straightforward, though unexplained mystery of the sea—became a gargantuan monstrosity of a story, its true basis so hidden in the obscurity of fiction that even the name of the ship has been distorted by most writers to *"Marie Celeste."*[29] The *Celeste* became a veritable flying phantom of the seven seas; her captain a bully or religious fanatic by turn, her crew murderers and cutthroats or freaks and lunatics, and in some accounts even Captain Briggs' baby, little two-year-old Sophia, has been identified as a baby piano, and the name of Morehouse, master of the *Dei Gratia,* has been perverted to Boyce! Few of those who have written about the case, strangely enough, have taken the trouble to investigate the source material available in the files of the Admiralty Court in Gibraltar, so that even such recorded facts as the number of boats aboard, etc., have been twisted and garbled. Out of some of these fictional accounts grew the fable that the remains of a meal—still hot to the touch—were on the cabin table when the *Dei Gratia's* mate boarded the *Celeste;* this is one of the most persistent errors in the whole scope of *Mary Celestiana* and landsmen from Toledo to Mobile will swear to you that the *Celeste's* two boats were still both aboard and that there was hot food cooking on the galley range!

With such distortion of facts distortions of theories were sure to follow, and they came thick and fast, most of them based on alleged "survivors' " tales. Some authors doubted that Captain Briggs was dead; others impugned the motives of Captain Morehouse, and others spoke of pirates. A number of writers—even those few who have taken the trouble to dig a little deeper into the mass of intermingled fact and fiction—have expressed a belief that Deveau and other witnesses before the Admiralty Court might well have held back pertinent facts, and that the *Dei Gratia's* mate and captain knew more than they told. The inference—and some of these writers express it—is obvious; either that Morehouse and his men murdered Briggs and his people for the salvage value of the *Celeste* and her cargo, or that Morehouse and Briggs conspired to the same end. In view of the known friendship of Morehouse and Briggs, their past reputations, and the miserable reward that such a dangerous enterprise would promise, these "solutions" also seem untenable, to put it mildly.

There is no evident reason, judging from his recorded testimony, to suspect Deveau of evasion or lying, despite Mr. Solly Flood's suspicions, or the later ones of Mr. Harold T. Wilkins, expressed in the *Quarterly Review* in 1931. After reviewing the circumstances of the mystery and some of the testimony given, Mr. Wilkins concludes:

> . . . *it must seem strange that the authorities at Gibraltar in 1872– 73 did not set in motion legal machinery in London which would have led to the arrest of the Captain, mate and crew of the British brig* [sic] Dei Gratia. *It is evident that, in the hands of a skilful cross-examiner at the Old Bailey, acting for the Public Prosecutor or his Crown contemporary in the 1870's, Deveau, mate of the* Dei Gratia, *might have been forced to tell truth, and thereby have put the police on the track of the criminals who made away with the captain, his wife and family, and the officers and crew of the* Mary Celeste.

Mr. Wilkins' conclusion is interesting—and based more firmly on fact than many others, but it is, after all, but another theory, and one arrived at second-hand, sixty-three years afterwards.

And so too is the latest "solution"—that Briggs and his men were captured by Riff pirates—which was advanced in 1933 by J. L. Hornibrook in *Chambers' Journal*.

This investigator does not intend to make the mistake of theorizing;

at this range of time it is worse than futile; the verified *Celeste* facts speak for themselves; each reader may draw his own conclusion.

But that conclusion, until the sea gives up its dead, must forever remain in the realm of conjecture. For when the *Celeste* died, there died with her her secrets. She was much of a "hoodoo" ship the rest of her days after that time when she was taken in derelict to Gibraltar, but she sailed the seas under different masters and with different crews. In January, 1885, she piled up on Roshelle Reef off Haiti, a total wreck. Even in death she was accursed, for her captain, G. C. Parker of Winthrop, sent her to her doom, heading her with "all canvas set and with a fair wind . . . fair and square on the reef." Parker was arrested for barratry, but he died before he came to trial, and the *Celeste's* ribs lay broken and bleaching on a tropic reef.

No one of the people who sailed in her that November day of 1872 was ever heard from after. Deveau, the salvage mate, has been dead these many years, and Captain Morehouse, he who was the friend of the missing Captain Briggs, he who had commanded the *Dei Gratia* in that year 1872, died in 1905. He believed to the last, as his son, Harry Morehouse, and as Dr. Cobb (Briggs' nephew) did after him, that the *Celeste* was abandoned in a moment of near panic (probably because of the fear of explosions from the alcohol in the hold) and that her people were lost in the yawl.[30]

But not until that day when dead men rise and speak and the sea disgorges the bones of wrecked ships can man know with certainty the fate of those ten people of the brigantine *Mary Celeste*.

NOTES The detailed explanation—here given—of Dr. Cobb's theory of the abandonment of the *Mary Celeste* will be of interest to those readers who have followed this celebrated mystery of the sea through its maze of facts and theories. Dr. Cobb writes:

I, for many years, was inclined to blame the captain for failing to provide a line to act as a tow-rope and keep the boat in connection with the vessel. It now seems strange to me that with the evidence plainly before them, no one seems to have realized that the peak halliards were used for that purpose. The evidence given that there was no sign of a tow-rope on the bitts or the rail indicates that this angle of the case was considered and dismissed, but when Mr. Deveau wanted to set the main sail he found no peak halliard. One of the sailors said "the peak halliards were gone." Another said, "were broken and gone." If broken, there must have been a piece left. It is passing strange that Mr. Deveau, Captain Morehouse or one of the sailors did not realize that the peak halliard was the tow-rope. My theory is that Captain Briggs in the afternoon of November 24, 1872, fearing an explosion of the cargo of alcohol, put his wife and child in the boat with Mr. Richardson and one sailor to care for them. Another sailor would hold the boat clear of the vessel. Mr. Gilling (the 2nd. mate) with a sailor unrove the main-peak-halliard to be used as a tow-rope. The fourth sailor would be at the wheel. The captain went below and got the chronometer, sextant and ship's papers. The cook was getting supplies to take in the boat. The cook evidently gathered up what cooked food was available as no cooked food was found on board the Mary Celeste. *Probably at this time came a minor explosion which landed the hatch upside down on deck. They made haste to get away. The man who was at the wheel tried to get the compass from the binnacle. Probably the Captain was shouting to him to bring the compass. The binnacle was displaced and the compass broken.*

During this time the vessel was hove to on the starboard tack with a southerly wind. The topsails and course would be aback and the vessel standing nearly still. Probably there was little wind. The main sail was down. The halliards were available for a tow-rope and were probably bent on to the boat's painter. The boat was pushed hastily away from the brigantine. Just at this time I think a breeze came from the north, and filling the square sails, took the vessel away on an easterly course. When the tow-rope came taut with the loaded boat standing still at the end, the tow-rope leading from its place of attachment to the gaff out through the gangway (where a section of the rail had been taken out to facilitate the launching of the boat) the rope would be brought at an acute angle across the corner, and likely parted at the rail leaving the boat adrift and about 400 feet away.

With even a moderate breeze the vessel would sail faster than the yawl-boat could be rowed. Captain Morehouse used to say "they must

*have rowed like mad in that boat." If Mr. J. Solly Flood had asked
the sailor who said that the peak halliards were "broken and gone"
where he thought they had gone and how long a piece was left, he
would have elicited some very useful information which would have
cancelled all the suspicion engendered by the examination of the sword.*

*It is strange that in all these years nobody has even mentioned this
very obvious use of the peak halliard.*

*I do not hold that my theory absolutely solves the mystery, but I
do hold that every step of my theory is supported by the evidence.
A piece of rope, maybe fifteen feet long, might have been the key to
this whole matter.*

A detailed explanation of Dr. Cobb's theory together with a homely
and delightful account of the life of the Briggs family is to be found
in his little book *Rose Cottage,* published in 1940 by the Easthampton
(Mass.) News Company. In this booklet is reprinted Dr. Cobb's account of the *Mary Celeste,* first published in the magazine *Yachting.*

The extensive notes below which refer to various points in this
chapter indicate the "who-done-it" nature of the *Celeste* case. The
literary verdigris that has tarnished the facts of seventy-five years ago
has been removed as much as possible by diligent research—but even
so many of the "facts" in the *Celeste* case are still in dispute:

1. December 5, reckoned by the "sea time" kept aboard the *Dei
Gratia,* according to later testimony.

2. The *Dei Gratia's* mate figured his longitude as 17-25 by dead
reckoning. Fay makes it 17-15 W.

3. Future events cast their shadows before. The *Amazon's* (*Mary
Celeste*) first master died while taking his new ship from Spencer's
Island to Windsor, N. S., where she loaded her first cargo.

4. Actually a hermaphrodite brig, known in America as the one
half-brig rig—or just brig; in England described as a brigantine.

5. Still doing business in the Whitehall Building, New York, and
still meeting requests for information, at the rate of one or more a year,
about the *Mary Celeste.*

6. Sylvester Goodwin, 2/24; Daniel T. Sampson, 2/24; Simpson
Hart, mortgagee of 1/3.

7. Briggs had taken command "ten or twelve days" before the *Celeste* sailed. Richardson, his mate, had been in command previously and had brought the *Celeste* with a cargo of coal from Cow Bay to New York. Part of her cargo was already loaded when Briggs took over.

8. He made it a "daily practice," Lockhart says, "when at sea to read a chapter of the bible."

9. Arthur S. Briggs died some years ago. He had at his New Bedford home the melodeon which his parents took aboard the *Celeste*. Captain Briggs had a brother, Oliver, also a master mariner, who lost his life about the time the *Celeste* arrived at Gibraltar, when his ship, the brig *Julia A. Hallock* foundered.

10. ". . . an experienced and courageous officer in whom I had great confidence," Captain Winchester later testified. Richardson was married to Francis (sic) Spates, niece of Mrs. Winchester.

11. As Lockhart points out, in nearly every account of the *Celeste* these names vary; in some accounts (generally the fictional, or less reliable ones) totally different names are substituted for them; in others the spelling varies from that given above; sometimes other names are added. I am satisfied that there were only five men in the crew of the *Celeste* (in addition to the mates and Captain) and that the spellings given are substantially correct.

12. Letters written by Captain and Mrs. Briggs give some of the details and adequately refute stories of unusual circumstances.

13. This, according to Harry Morehouse, New York hotel manager, and son of Captain Morehouse. Morehouse testified his cargo was petroleum.

14. A ship usually leaves port on the same day soon after she procures her clearance papers. The November, 1872, files of the New York *Herald* record under date of Nov. 6 (in the same paper announcing "The Battle Won"—Grant's re-election) the *Celeste's* clearance on the fifth, and under date of November 12, the *Dei Gratia's* clearance on the eleventh: "Brig (sic) *Dei Gratia* (Br.) Morehouse—Gib. for orders—Heney & Parker." Morehouse later testified the *Dei Gratia* sailed on the fifteenth. Mrs. Briggs' letter to her mother rather clearly fixes the sailing date of the *Celeste* as November 7 or 8.

15. In an empty hold this would probably indicate a serious leak but in a hold closely stowed with barrels it was not so significant.

16. There is confusion on this point; there is no conclusive evidence that the cargo hatch was "upside down," although all accounts agree it was off.

17. Captain Winchester thought this might have been 36-36.

18. These words were found on the last line on the left-hand side "engraved and scratched on the slate," and according to Captain Winchester, the handwriting—that of Richardson—differed from that of any of the entries on the slate.

19. Dr. Cobb's version is that this note was on a sheet of paper lying on the open log book and read:

"Fannie, My Dear Wife . . ."

20. There is conflicting evidence, but apparently the clothing in the chests was not wet. Seamen's chests were usually waterproof.

21. Morehouse did not testify until March 3, 1873, an unusual, but not a suspicious, fact.

22. Solly Flood somewhat cryptically reported that "the sword has been cleaned with lemon, which has covered it with citrate of iron, which has destroyed the marks of the supposed blood, which, therefore, is not blood at all as at first supposed; but another substance put there to disguise the original marks of the blood which were once there." There is no explanation in the record of this puzzling statement; indeed, the records of the court are obscure on many points as Wilkins emphasizes. Sir James Cochrane, Judge of the Vice-Admiralty Court, apparently censured Deveau, the mate, for "doing away with the vessel which had rendered necessary the analysis of the supposed blood stains." There is no explanation of what the "vessel" was and only Deveau's offhand excuse: "It did not occur to me that there had been any act of violence. There was nothing whatever to induce one to believe or to show that there had been any violence." In his final decree the judge directed that the cost of the "blood" analysis be borne by the salvors, i. e. Morehouse, Deveau, etc.

23. Wilkins says: "In fact, so impossible were his methods of analysis that any bungling agent of an American or European police

force who treated exhibits as Patron did would be instantly dismissed."

24. The obscurity of the years and the paucity of accurate facts as well as the conflicting and hazy testimony given at the hearing have made precise determination of distances and positions in the *Celeste* case almost impossible.

25. Dr. Cobb writes: "750 miles in the 240 hours would be but little over three miles per hour. With topsails and fore course drawing the vessel would do that easily. I think she continued on easterly course for ten days. I think she encountered a squall, backed her square sails, shipped a sea, lost the upper topsail and foresail, and filled away on the starboard tack but a short time before meeting the *Dei Gratia.*"

26. No mention of the oil can or spool of thread is made in the testimony given before the Vice-Admiralty Court, but the quotations are taken verbatim from a summarized newspaper account of the testimony before the Court published in the *Gibraltar Chronicle* of January 31, 1873, and forwarded by Consul Sprague to the State Department, where it is now a part of the official records. Because the testimony was not taken down in question and answer form and since the official record displays discrepancies and evident omissions it may well be that this pertinent evidence, as well as numerous other facts, were not included in the official transcript, although they may have been adduced in the hearings before the court.

27. Dr. Cobb explains these two circumstances as follows: "One moderate sea which probably came on board as the vessel headed into the sea and turned around would account for all the water found, the galley door being open and the fore hatch off, and the forward companionway of the cabin being open." (This does not seem likely to the author; a sea which could unship a battened-down hatch would be likely to do more damage than was done.) Dr. Cobb continues: "I think it quite probable that there was a bit of window dressing [literally; he refers to the battened-up cabin windows]. There is a difference in the testimony regarding these windows. One man said that only the windows on one side were covered." To the author it seems that more importance than they warrant is attached to the battened-up cabin windows. During an Atlantic crossing in winter

during heavy weather, it would be both logical and far from unusual to batten-up windows which otherwise might be broken by boarding seas.

28. Dr. Cobb says $8,700.

29. The name of the *Mary Celeste* has been perverted to *Marie Celeste* even in the redoubtable card catalogue of the New York Public Library.

30. See Dr. Cobb's detailed explanation of his theory under Notes.

ACKNOWLEDGMENTS   The *Mary Celeste* case presents to investigators one of the most tangled skeins in nautical research. For the facts here presented the author is primarily indebted to source materials, particularly to the transcript of the testimony and hearings and reports given and made before the Vice-Admiralty Court in Gibraltar, a copy of which was expressly purchased by me for this story. This document is quoted extensively in this chapter.

The reports of Consul Sprague and other documents in the U. S. State Department files, including contemporary Gibraltar newspaper clippings, data in the possession of the Navy Department, Custom House (N.Y.) records for the year 1872, and the old records of the Atlantic Mutual Insurance Company were all kindly made available to me. Curiously enough, one of the most important documents in the *Mary Celeste* case, the brigantine's log book, is as mysteriously missing as is her crew. The log book apparently was forwarded to the American Consul at Genoa after the investigation at Gibraltar had been completed, but all trace of it has been lost.

In addition to primary documentary material I consulted by letter or in person a number of persons with intimate knowledge of the *Celeste* case who were extremely helpful with both facts and theories. Dr. Oliver Cobb of Easthampton, Mass., nephew of Captain Briggs and a great authority of *Mary Celestiana,* supplied me with several pertinent details and read and checked this story of the *Mary Celeste.* Mr. Harry Morehouse, manager of the Hotel Elysée, New York City, son of Captain Morehouse, also furnished details, which would have been even more complete had not Mr. Morehouse unfortunately lost a large collection of papers about the *Celeste* in a fire some years ago. Mr. Winchester Noyes, of J. H. Winchester and Co., grandson of Cap-

tain Winchester, was also patient and helpful, although his firm is
queried frequently by those hoping to find a "solution" of the *Mary
Celeste* mystery.

In addition to these primary sources the author has consulted contemporary newspaper files of the period and all available literature,
both in book form and in magazines, on the *Mary Celeste*. Books or
articles consulted—some of which are mentioned, and a few which
are briefly quoted in my story—include: *A Great Sea Mystery, The
True Story of the* Mary Celeste, by J. G. Lockhart (who, with Wilkins,
is one of the sounder and more thorough writers on this subject); *The
Great* Mary Celeste *Hoax* by Laurence J. Keating (an unsubstantial
and factually highly inaccurate and extravagant account); an article
in the *Nautical Magazine* for 1914; J. L. Hornibrook's article in
Chambers Journal, 1933; "Light on the Mystery of the *Mary Celeste*"
by Harold T. Wilkins in the *Quarterly Review,* 1931; *Literary Digest,*
condensed account by John Lafitte, from Boston *Sunday Post; Ninety
Years of Marine Insurance,* Atlantic Mutual Insurance Company;
"Mystery of the *Mary Celeste,*" *Overland Magazine,* H. H. Dutton,
1906; an account written for *Sea Sequel to the Weekend Book,* and
others of less importance. By far the most accurate and best accounts
of the mystery are two most recently published. *Mystery Ship* by
George S. Bryan is excellent, but Charles Fay's Mary Celeste—*The
Odyssey of an Abandoned Ship* published by the Peabody Museum,
is undoubtedly the definitive work on the subject. In all instances
where accounts differed (and there are many) I have preferred the
primary sources, and thus the record of the Vice-Admiralty Court
(though in itself somewhat incomplete and inconclusive) has resolved
many of my difficulties.

1916

Admiral Death—

THE BATTLE OF JUTLAND

IRON DUKE, 24TH JUNE, 1916

SIR—BE PLEASED TO INFORM THE LORDS COMMISSIONERS OF THE ADMIRALTY THAT THE GERMAN HIGH SEA FLEET WAS BROUGHT TO ACTION ON 31ST MAY 1916 TO THE WESTWARD OF THE JUTLAND BANK OFF THE COAST OF DENMARK.

Dispatch of Admiral Sir John Jellicoe
Commander-in-Chief, Grand Fleet

It was two o'clock in the afternoon watch, May 31, 1916. A rusty tramp—the *N. J. Fjord*—with the flag of Denmark painted large upon her sides and splotches of red lead showing on her weather-beaten plates, steamed slowly across the North Sea. On the far horizon the top hamper of a ship rapidly took shape: the light cruiser *Elbing* of the Imperial German Navy. There came the peremptory orders of the sea, "Heave to!" The *N. J. Fjord* stopped. "Her steam blowing off shot skyward in a cotton-white jet which mixed with her funnel smoke to spread into a listless cloud visible for miles against the leaden atmosphere." German destroyers nosed alongside—boarding and search, the routine procedure of wartime.

Aboard H.M.S. *Galatea,* flying the broad pennant of Commodore

Alexander-Sinclair, the white steam of the *Fjord* was sighted. The light cruiser, far on the wing of Beatty's Battle Cruiser Fleet then turning away to the northward, stood on to investigate. At 2:18 she signaled to the fleet: "Enemy in sight!"

The rusty *N. J. Fjord* had lifted the curtain on "the greatest drama of modern naval warfare." *Der Tag* had come.

It had been slow in coming. Sir Roger Casement was treading the road to death after the abortive Sinn Fein rebellion in Ireland, and muddy dying Frenchmen were still blocking the Crown Prince's road to Paris when Reinhard Scheer, with the German High Sea Fleet, groped into battle with the much stronger British Grand Fleet under Admiral Sir John Jellicoe. The operation of May 31, 1916—a sortie resulting from the more aggressive German naval policy of 1916— had been planned originally as a raid on Sunderland on the British coast. But because of unfavorable weather Scheer's Zeppelins were unable to scout ahead of the High Sea Fleet and protect the Germans from surprise. Scheer therefore had abandoned the dangerous Sunderland operation and substituted for it a sweep to the north toward the Skagerrak, in hopes of luring the British Grand Fleet into submarine-infested waters, and of inflicting injuries upon detached and isolated portions of that fleet.

From the efficient British Intelligence Service Jellicoe knew that the Germans were planning some considerable movement, and the Grand Fleet actually had put to sea before the Germans left the Jade. Vice-Admiral Sir David Beatty, with the Battle Cruiser Fleet from Rosyth, had been ordered to scout to the east toward the Skagerrak before turning northward to join the main body of the Grand Fleet. At the same time Scheer, cruising northward off Denmark, had sent Hipper well ahead of his main body.

The opposing fleets, groping toward each other through the mists of the North Sea, were disproportionate in physical strength but not in courage, seamanship, or professional skill.

The Great Britain of 1916, with the Empire—Upon-Which-The-Sun-Never-Set—had passed its golden age; Jellicoe who commanded the greatest battle fleet that ever put to sea epitomized Quintus Fabius, the cautious Roman, rather than the dash and daring of Drake and

Hawkins and Nelson. He understood his position of towering responsibility as the "only man who could lose the war in an afternoon"; but
he had an almost unreasoning respect for enemy mines and the torpedoes of German U-boats and destroyers. Unlike his famous predecessors, he felt, in his own words, that he could not leave *anything
to chance in a fleet action, because our Fleet was the one and only
factor that was vital to the existence of the Empire."*

The gods of war never smile upon those who do not pay obeisance
at the shrine of fortune, but the Admiralty—and, indeed, the British
Government—endorsed the "to have and to hold" caution of Jellicoe.

Scheer was an admiral of different stripe, bearing different responsibilities and representing a Germany nurtured on nationalism, weaned
on Bismarck's "blood and iron," eager to acquire. Scheer knew his
fleet was far inferior to Jellicoe's; he was pursuing a policy of attrition;
he hoped by his sorties—and by luck—to entice elements of the Grand
Fleet to destruction.

And so the fleets—by far the mightiest of their era—stood forth to
battle, neither anticipating the clash of arms that shook the world.

From Scapa Flow in the Orkneys and from Invergordon and Rosyth
in Scotland, the British Grand Fleet that sortied to sea numbered
twenty-eight battleships and nine battle-cruisers, mounting twelve-
inch, thirteen-and-one-half-inch, fourteen-inch and fifteen-inch guns.
Jellicoe also commanded eight armored cruisers, twenty-six light
cruisers, and seventy-eight destroyers and destroyer flotilla leaders.
Scheer's High Sea Fleet that stood out from the Jade counted twenty-
two battleships (some obsolescent) and five battle-cruisers, armed with
eleven- and twelve-inch guns, eleven light cruisers, and sixty-one destroyers and flotilla leaders. The British advantage in weight of broadside was large, in numbers of ships less so, in armor there was little
difference, save that the British battle-cruisers had defects in design
which cost them heavily during the battle. Frost estimates that the
British had a material superiority in strength of about 8 to 5.

The battle that ensued, fought entirely in the sullen, heaving cockpit
of the North Sea, was naturally divided by circumstance and tactics
into four principal phases. Beatty, who commanded the British scouting force, built around the battle-cruisers, and Hipper, who commanded the German screen, had been sent ahead of the main fleets,

each feeling for the enemy. The first phase of the battle ensued when Beatty and Hipper made contact and dueled with their battle-cruisers as Hipper led Beatty southward toward the bulk of the German High Sea Fleet, hidden in the mists. When the German main body was encountered Beatty turned north and steamed toward his own main fleet, with the Germans coming hard after him and the great guns echoing over the waters. The third phase was the brief encounter of the main bodies, when Scheer with the High Sea Fleet steaming in column met the Grand Fleet "crossing them" or steaming at a right angle across Scheer's course. The final phase, after the Germans turned away back toward port was a sprawling, inchoate night action, chiefly between the light forces.

But it was units from the scouting forces of both fleets, both investigating the smoke of the *N. J. Fjord,* that made the first contact of the battle of Jutland. Beatty and Hipper opened the ball.

H.M.S. *Galatea,* steaming at twenty-eight knots, fired the first gun of the battle; its unexpected concussion almost blew a surprised officer who had been basking in the sun down a fo'c'sle ladder. The Germans drew first blood: an enemy shell struck the *Galatea* below the bridge but did not explode; a cockney seaman came upon it and tried to pick it up; he jumped back, wringing his scorched fingers: "Crikey, the blighter's hot!"

As *Galatea* felt out the enemy, a strange-looking, awkward vessel, H.M.S. *Engadine*—just over the horizon from the Germans—stopped dead in the water, swung out a boom, launched a seaplane. The *Engadine's* seaplane made a fifty-two-minute flight (interrupted by one landing on the sea due to a broken petrol pipe—repaired with a rubber tube); sighted the German battle cruisers, reported their course, position and numbers by W/T (radio), and became immortal in the annals of naval history, even though her report never reached Beatty. It was the first plane to participate in a naval battle; a quarter century later in the Pacific the history of the world was to be decided by *Engadine's* descendants.

By 3:48 the battle was fairly begun, and within five minutes the *Tiger* was struck, and Beatty's flagship *Lion.* Shells made geysers alongside the speeding ships; dead fish floated belly up, killed by

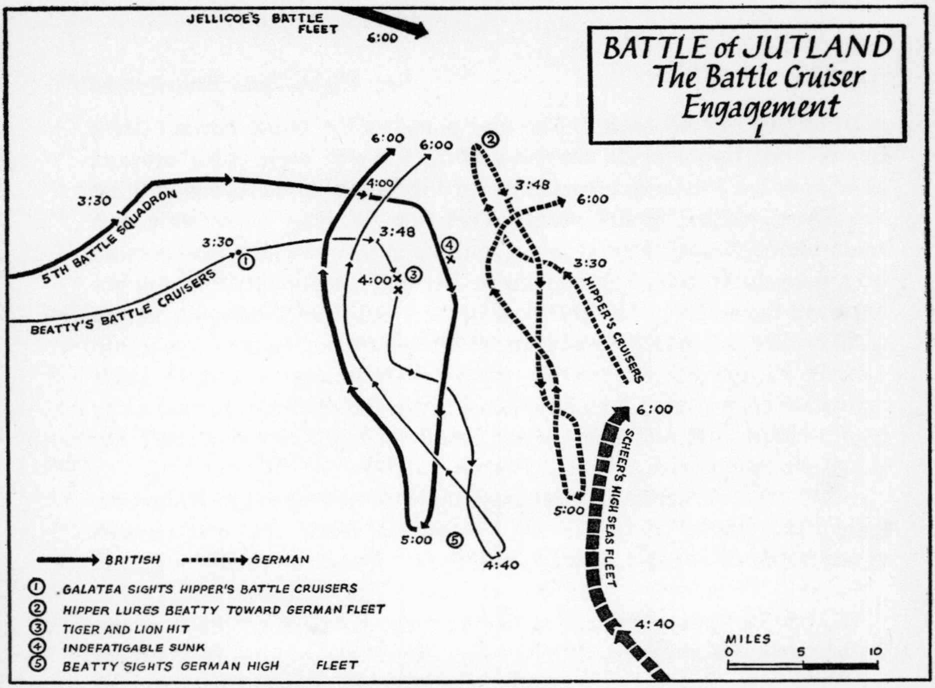

BATTLE of JUTLAND
The Battle Cruiser Engagement
I

JELLICOE'S BATTLE FLEET
6:00

3:30
5TH BATTLE SQUADRON
6:00 6:00
4:00
3:30 ① 3:48 ④ ×③ 3:48
BEATTY'S BATTLE CRUISERS 4:00 ×
②
6:00
3:48
3:30
HIPPER'S CRUISERS
6:00
5:00 ⑤ SCHEER'S HIGH SEAS FLEET
4:40 5:00
4:40

→ BRITISH ┅┅► GERMAN

① GALATEA SIGHTS HIPPER'S BATTLE CRUISERS
② HIPPER LURES BEATTY TOWARD GERMAN FLEET
③ TIGER AND LION HIT
④ INDEFATIGABLE SUNK
⑤ BEATTY SIGHTS GERMAN HIGH FLEET

MILES
0   5   10

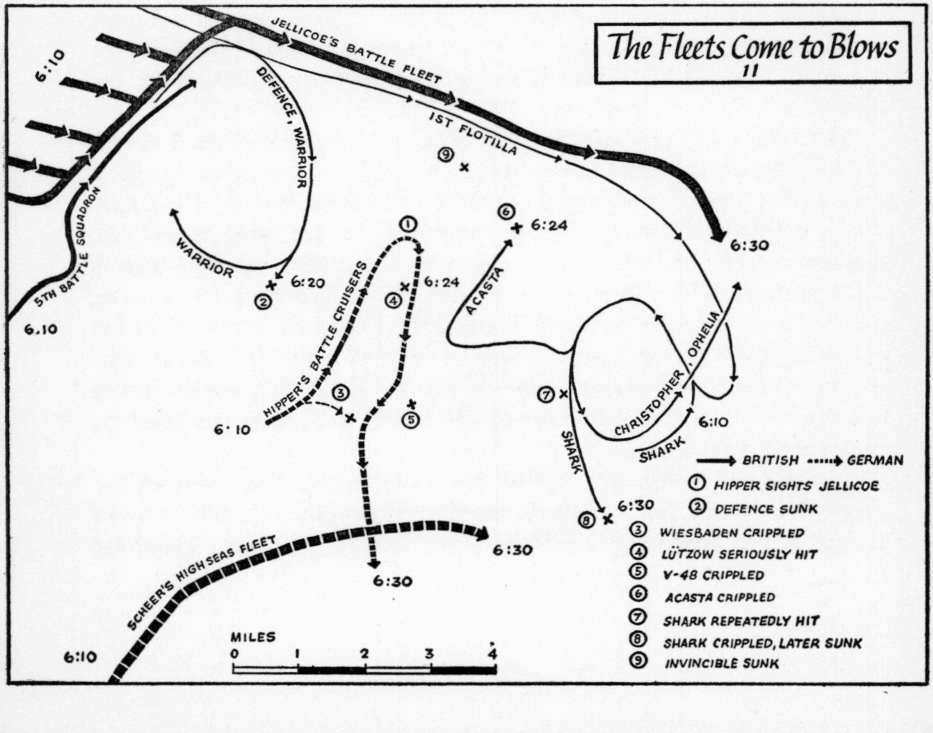

The Fleets Come to Blows
II

6:10
JELLICOE'S BATTLE FLEET
DEFENCE, WARRIOR 1ST FLOTILLA
⑨ ×
6:30
WARRIOR ① ⑥ × 6:24
6:10 5TH BATTLE SQUADRON × 6:20 × 6:24 ACASTA
② ④
6.10 HIPPER'S BATTLE CRUISERS CHRISTOPHER OPHELIA
③ ⑦ × 6:10
6:10 × ⑤ SHARK SHARK
SCHEER'S HIGH SEAS FLEET × 6:30
⑧
6:30
6:10 6:30

→ BRITISH ┅┅► GERMAN
① HIPPER SIGHTS JELLICOE
② DEFENCE SUNK
③ WIESBADEN CRIPPLED
④ LÜTZOW SERIOUSLY HIT
⑤ V-48 CRIPPLED
⑥ ACASTA CRIPPLED
⑦ SHARK REPEATEDLY HIT
⑧ SHARK CRIPPLED, LATER SUNK
⑨ INVINCIBLE SUNK

MILES
0   1   2   3   4

the detonations. The sun—shining through a gray haze—dazzled the eyes of the German gunners, but the wind rolled the battle smoke toward the British line. From the turret ports, or through the slits in the armored conning towers, men saw the red-black bursts of shells on steel.

At four sharp, the *Lion* took its fourth hit from the *Lützow;* and Major Harvey of the Royal Marines won his posthumous V.C. in the shambles of Q turret. The shell had penetrated the turret amidships and exploded with horrible effect, killing the turret crew, jolting open the breech plug of a loaded gun, and igniting the powder bags. Harvey, in the officers' booth at the rear, had both legs severed from his body by the explosion; but he sent his wounded sergeant to Flag Captain Chatfield to report Q turret out of action, and dragging himself to a voice tube ordered his handling-room crew to flood the magazines; the flash of flame met a rising tide of water, and the *Lion* was saved.

At 4:03, after two rapid salvos from the *Von der Tann,* the *Indefatigable* was finished. She disappeared in a great sheet of flame and smoke; boats, debris, armor plate, and bodies mushroomed two hundred feet into the sky—and she was gone, with a thousand British seamen.

Flames rose from the decks of stricken ships; below decks, mattresses and shores plugged shell holes against the water; surgeons with bloody scalpels bent above the wounded; the acrid odor of cordite smoke seeped into every casemate, and burned men screamed in agony.

Only the *New Zealand* escaped the raging hail of steel plunging now all along the British line—and she was a lucky ship. Her Old Man, Captain Green, with Admiral Pakenham beside him, wore a Maori war mat through all the heat and flame and fury of Jutland. It was called a *piu-piu* and resembled a kilt of black and white. It had been given to the ship with the admonition that the captain wear it when the *New Zealand* cleared for action. Below-decks thought it lucky, and it was; the *New Zealand* was hit only once that day, and lost no men.

To port—from the British line—the scene of battle looked "red, lurid, and beastly." Shell splashes cascaded foaming water across the splintered decks. Fair between the lines, with screeching death from turret guns arching high above her, lay a full-rigged merchant ship in ghostly beauty, like the *Flying Dutchman,* a portent of death and destruction. At 4:06 Evan-Thomas coming hard from the northwest with his four splendid battleships (which were operating with Beatty's battle-cruisers), opened fire at nineteen thousand yards. A fifteen-inch shell from the *Barham* sliced through the *Von der Tann's* armor, and six hundred tons of water sluiced into the German ship. The tempo of battle speeded up; Hipper stood southward at twenty-three knots, leading the British battle-cruisers and Evan's battleships into the jaws of the German fleet.

The *Lion* was a moving pillar of smoke and flame; the German gunnery was good and Beatty took heavy losses. At 4:26 came the *Queen Mary's* end. She was struck near Q turret, again and again and again. Terrific yellow flame spurted from the broken decks; then smoke hid her from the speeding ships. When it had been blown clear, the *Queen Mary* was on her beam-ends; great fluttering clouds of paper were blowing from her after hatch; black specks that were men were clambering about the slimy bilge keel, and at her stern, lifted clear of the cold North Sea water, her propellers were still turning futilely as if to speed her to her grave. A second explosion shook the torn hulk. Long later, when the battle had passed, a little midship-man and eight others were rescued from the sea: only survivors of the crew of 1,275 men.

Beatty, his cap cocked at a rakish angle, his hands thrust into the pockets of his "non-reg" uniform coat, stood on the *Lion's* exposed bridge—a bridge shredded by flying steel splinters, shaken by concussion and explosion, and coolly charted the course of battle. He had seen his two ships go, and to port through the wreathing smoke watched the German battle-cruisers pounding the British line. *Lion* was on fire; *Tiger* was badly hit; only *New Zealand* had escaped. A German salvo struck the *Princess Royal;* a signalman on the *Lion's* bridge, seeing the burst of impact and the licking flame, mistakenly reported: *"Princess Royal* blown up, sir."

Beatty turned his keen blue eyes and jutting jaw toward his flag captain: "Chatfield, there seems to be something wrong with our bloody ships today. Turn two points to port" (toward the enemy).

H.M.S. *Nestor*—Commander the Hon. E. B. S. Bingham, V.C.—
was waiting for her end. Of what was in store for her there was now
no doubt. The *Nestor,* the *Nomad* and others of the 13th Destroyer
Flotilla had made a mad dash toward the German battle-cruisers, as
Beatty and Hipper dueled. They had launched torpedoes; but the
Nomad had taken a shell in the engine room and the *Nestor* was soon
disabled and unable to steam. Drifting, wrecked, they lay in the oily
swells full in the path of the German High Sea Fleet steaming up from
the south.

The German battleships of Scheer's High Sea Fleet were first sighted
at 4:33 from light cruiser *Southampton,* well in the van of the British
battle-cruisers. The destroyer recall signal was hoisted from *Lion* in
ten minutes, and by 4:50 Beatty had his battle-cruisers—reduced now
to four—turned away to the north and pounding hard to lead Scheer
and Hipper into the guns of Jellicoe.

But *Nestor* and *Nomad* were done; as the British disappeared to
the northward the disabled destroyers lay square between the lines of
the mighty German battleships.

The *Nomad* took it first. Commander Bingham saw her smothered
in clouds of smoke and columns of spray, as scores of German guns
riddled her. She died game; she fired her final torpedo at two thousand
yards and sank at last under the fire of the oncoming German battleships.

The *Nestor* was next. While her crew was waiting Commander
Bingham threw overboard the lead-backed signal books, saw the
boats filled with biscuits and water, and hoisted out the Carley floats.
Then, to keep the men busy and their minds from the British fleet
vanishing to the north and the German columns approaching from the
south, he had the cables ranged on deck.

The van of the German column—twenty-two battleships, surrounded by a swarm of destroyers and cruisers—looked larger and
larger. The Germans opened fire at five miles, far beyond the range
of the *Nestor's* popguns; but Bingham fired his last torpedo before
it was too late. By that time shells had made sieves of the light steel
decks; spray from the splashes alongside were pattering on stacks
and masts. The crew was decimated; the ship had filled and was starting to sink.

"Abandon ship!" Men climbed into the motor boat and the Carley floats. Commander Bingham looked at his wrecked command and turned to Lieutenant M. J. Bethell.

"Now where shall we go?"

"To heaven I trust, sir." Bethell, "that gallant spirit," turned aside "to attend to a mortally wounded signalman, and was seen no more." The *Nestor* sank, her crew singing "God save the King." 5:30 P.M.

At the Admiralty in London deft-fingered men work in guarded rooms with coding boards and signal books. Radio direction finders are trained on the German High Sea Fleet. Messages from Scheer to Hipper are intercepted, the ciphers are broken, the code is translated from a code book captured earlier in the war, and Jellicoe—steaming hard to Beatty's assistance with the whole British Grand Fleet—is informed at 5:45 of the exact position of the German main body as of 4:30. The British Intelligence Service is "amazingly efficient"; not so the Admiralty's judgment: Tyrwhitt, champing at the bit, is kept useless in harbor with the powerful Harwich force, until *Der Tag* is almost done.

At the Admiralty in Berlin German naval officers bend stiffly above charts—tense and waiting. In imagination they can hear the thunder of the guns above the North Sea; shell bursts obscure the rumble of traffic in the Wilhelmstrasse . . . Germany's challenge for sea power is come to fruition at last; the doctrines of Mahan are translated into the voices of the guns. But they know less of the course of battle than the British; the deciphering unit at Neumünster has but little luck. And the German public knows nothing of the North Sea action; they face the Western Front, where for months the Crown Prince had been battering at Verdun, gateway to Paris.

The sun was low and the mists were gathering before the main fleets met at last, about 6:15 on that day of battle.

From about 5 to 6 P.M. the British battle-cruisers, screened by their light craft, drove to the north towards Jellicoe's battleships steaming southwestward to join them. Evan-Thomas' four 25-knot battleships —*Barham, Valiant, Malaya, Warspite*—attached to Beatty's command brought up the rear in the "Run to the North," and were blanketed with heavy straddling salvos from the guns of five German battle-cruisers and seven dreadnoughts in the German column. The four British battleships got "the full hate of the German Fleet, which was far from pleasant." The British ships were hit repeatedly—particularly *Malaya*, the rear ship—but they gave better than they received, and the tender-skinned German battle-cruisers—already badly damaged by fire from the *Lion, Tiger, Princess Royal* and *New Zealand*— were struck many times. All of *Von der Tann's* guns were out of action; she stayed in line and surged on to the north—a floating target, her deck a shambles.

By 6 P.M. *Lützow, Derfflinger,* and *Seydlitz* were seriously damaged; *Seydlitz* was afire; *Derfflinger's* flooded bow was dropping low in the water; the German stokers—stripped to the waist, sweating and exhausted—scooped coal furiously into the boilers, to keep up the steam. Hipper—now well ahead of Scheer's main body—had pursued Beatty and Evan-Thomas almost into the jaws of the Grand Fleet, and the dying afternoon put him at a serious disadvantage. The British ships— except for gun flashes on the horizon—were hidden in the mists; "the low slanting rays of the setting sun made impossible any effective German reply" (Frost). Hipper turned away, and about the same time —in *Iron Duke*—Jellicoe hoisted the signal for deployment. The two fleets came together—torpedo craft, cruisers, battle-cruisers, battleships—as the darkness crawled above the sea. It was "Windy Corner" —a melee of stabbing gun flashes, of white froth upon the sea, of speeding ships and dying men—the confused chaos of battle.

The destroyer *Shark,* Commander Loftus Jones, R.N., with three others of the 4th Flotilla, *Acasta, Ophelia, Christopher,* tiny pawns in a titanic struggle, were assigned to Hood's Third Battle Cruiser Squadron. The great guns of the battle-cruisers roared above the destroyers' mast tips; *Invincible, Inflexible, Indomitable* were firing at the German light cruisers, *Wiesbaden, Pillau, Frankfurt.* Bödicker, the German, turned away from Hood's smothering salvos, fired his torpedoes at the giant British ships, ordered his destroyers to the attack. The white wake of the "tin fish" streaking underwater towards the battle-cruisers warned Hood; he too turned away and sent Loftus

Jones and his four destroyers dashing madly in the foam-flecked sea to parry the German thrust.

Yellow cordite smoke bellied and eddied between the fighting lines; ripples of fire burst in shining flashes from the mist-hidden ships on the dark horizon. Their propellors lashing a frothy wake, the *Shark,* the *Acasta,* the *Ophelia,* and the *Christopher* raced towards the enemy.

It was a brief Armageddon. "Right ahead and close aboard" of the racing British destroyers were the *Regensburg* and two columns of "nine or ten" German destroyers on either hand. Farther off—half-hidden in the smoke and mist—were Bödicker's cruisers, their guns still flashing, but this time at Loftus Jones and his four ships. The British attacked at close range with torpedoes and guns, firing to port and starboard at the destroyers, launching their torpedoes at the cruisers, their screws working at top speed before annihilation.

The spitting flashes of crimson stained the horizon to west and southwards; the little *Shark* and her sisters, tearing along at 30 knots, careened and shivered as shell splashes geysered high alongside and roaring waters cascaded down upon their decks. It was only a question of time. . . .

The *Shark* lived for perhaps ten minutes in this, her last mad dash. Loftus Jones on the bridge kept her headed west and slightly southwards, where streamers of smoke bannered across the misty sky. Far on the horizon dim shapes began to form out of the haze and gun smoke; the *Shark* was speeding towards the whole German fleet. But Jones had more modest aims; the *Regensburg* was his target; he brought the *Shark* into firing position, launched a torpedo—and turned to go. But the enemy had found his range and salvos were straddling the straining ship. A shell struck her amidships; roaring steam wreathed above her in a pall of white; "the pipes to her oil suction were damaged"; a greasy slick oozed from the tortured steel and spread across the swells. The *Shark* slowed down. A shell struck the forward four-inch; the entire crew was killed; the gun dismounted. Flying splinters of steel shredded the bridge structure; Jones was wounded; another shell tore away the steering wheel, smashed the bridge. The *Shark* stopped . . . so slowly, her lifeblood spilling quietly on the waters, her panting breath steaming above her for all the fleet to see.

Loftus Jones, his blood staining the gold braid of his rank, staggered painfully aft across the broken and littered deck past the bodies of his men, mangled and torn. . . . The after and midship guns were still firing; the flag was still there.

Brief respite. The *Canterbury,* light cruiser, headed out of the battle smoke into the no-man's land between the fleets and drew the punishing fire of the *Regensburg,* the *Frankfurt,* other enemy light cruisers and the German destroyers. Quietly, the *Shark* waited for the coup de grâce. *Acasta,* Lt.-Comdr. John O. Barron, who had been with Loftus Jones in previous actions, pulled up alongside, wanted to tow. But Jones waved her away; he told Barron "not to get sunk for him."

"Soon afterwards" a number of enemy destroyers, probably of the 9th and 6th Flotillas, came up and "opened a heavy fire." The after gun was hit squarely, and its entire crew wiped out; Jones, who had been directing its fire, lost a leg at the knee. "But he continued to encourage his men," and lying there upon the deck among his dead and wounded, the blood swimming out upon the shattered deck plates, he noticed the White Ensign, the gaff shot away, drooping down the mast.

He asked "what was wrong with the flag and appeared greatly upset as he lay on the deck wounded. Twice he spoke of it." Seaman Hope, one of the only two men left unwounded, climbed the mast, unbent the ensign, and passed it down to Midshipman Smith, who hoisted it on the yardarm. "Commander Jones seemed then to be less worried when he saw the flag was hoisted again."

The enemy destroyers were closing down to the kill. The midship gun, manned by a crew of blood-stained, staggering spectres, was firing slowly as the *Shark* settled.

The British destroyer was on fire and dying fast; the flaming flashes of the enemy almost ringed her round. But still the lone gun spoke; its crew of wounded aimed it well; British shells crashed into the German *V-48.*

There came the end. Close by, a speeding enemy launched two torpedoes; one ran true and struck the battered *Shark* amidships near the funnel. The loud roar of the last explosion; the little destroyer lurching heavily. "She took a heavy list and sank," the White Ensign flying from the mast, the midship gun still firing. "So, maintaining to the last the finest traditions of the service, she came to her end, and it was in the heart of the battle she found it."

Vice-Admiral Reinhard Scheer in the *Friedrich der Grosse* had had little warning of the presence of the Grand Fleet; intent on pursuing Beatty, he had led his ships full into Jellicoe's overwhelming force. But he was a German General Grant, "direct and simple and cool as ice." He stood on into the jaws of death.

The Germans had had the best of the fight until now—even until 6:20 when German gunfire sank the *Defense:*

> . . . *in one sullen roar*
> *Of flame the furious incandescence tore*
> *Her symphony of steel to molten heat,*
> *And wrapped 900 men in one red sheet.* . . .

—the tide of battle had flowed their way.

But Jellicoe now crossed the German's T: before the path of Scheer lay England's mightiest ships—*King George V, Ajax, Iron Duke, St. Vincent, Temeraire, Marlborough, Agincourt, Collingwood,* and a host of others bearing proud and ancient names and flying the cross of St. George.

The range, in the gathering dark, had closed to 11,000 to 16,000 yards; at long last the battle lines slugged toe to toe. The Germans could see little of their enemy except stabbing flashes ringing the horizon to the northward: the van of the German line was under concentrated fire. At 6:24 Von der Decker in the *Derfflinger* recorded, "*Lützow* heavily hit forward. Ship on fire. Much smoke." At 6:36 came the command *Gefechtskehrtwendung nach Steuerbord,* the famous simultaneous battle turn to starboard, to the reverse course. The Germans swung away from the destructive fire, the *König* flaming and smoking like a volcano and the *Lützow's* forecastle nearly under water —so badly damaged that Hipper ordered her home to Wilhelmshaven and transferred his flag. *Markgraf* and other ships were hit. The *Von der Tann's* heavy guns had not spoken for an hour; she was a shambles, turrets jammed, steel sides ripped, dead and wounded littering her decks. But again, just before the turn-away, Scheer drew blood, and

the *Invincible,* with Hood her admiral—well beloved and efficient—
went to join the *Indefatigable, Queen Mary,* and *Defense.*

The *Wiesbaden* was slowly sinking now. She had found her death
wound in the thick of the fight, fair between the lines. Helpless, she
had lain the target for ship after ship, replying with her puny guns as
best she could; man after man killed, gun after gun dismounted. Lower
she sank. The grimy stokers long since had drawn their fires; the grate
bars, where the glowing coals had been, were under water. Her few
survivors had seen the end of *Defense* and *Invincible;* had seen the
Gefechtskehrtwendung nach Steuerbord; had watched in the gathering
dusk while Scheer returned again to the fight, and the hell of battle
screamed round them. Then, at last, while the cold North Sea lapped
upward toward the slanted decks, Scheer had turned away. The battle
flowed past them and the long hours under fire were over.

Out of the battered hulk, from behind the shattered plates the seamen crawled—what was left of them. They got the wounded up from
below and waited, dead and dying and those soon to die, for the end.
It was slow in coming, so a few of them sang while they waited, songs
of the Fatherland. The *Wiesbaden* went with the long North Sea day.
There was none there to see her passing when she slipped at last,
slowly, slowly, into the darkness. The cold water took her crew one by
one. Her only survivor, Chief Stoker Zenne, was rescued by a small
steamer after thirty-eight hours in the rough and icy sea.

The first brief contact of the main fleets was quickly broken off as
Scheer turned away. But at 6:55 the German admiral returned to the
attack, partly to try to save the foundering *Wiesbaden* and the damaged *Lützow.* At 7:04 the battle fleets slugged again; again Jellicoe
had the advantage of light and position; the broadsides of many of his
ships bore upon the van of the German line, whereas only Scheer's
leading ships could bear upon the British.

"The Germans were headed directly into the center of the Grand
Fleet . . . in a regular death trap . . ." (says Frost). "They were
in the most unfavorable and dangerous situation imaginable. Jellicoe
enjoyed the overwhelming advantages of position, visibility, and numbers, each in a very great degree." Scheer's attempt at surprise by

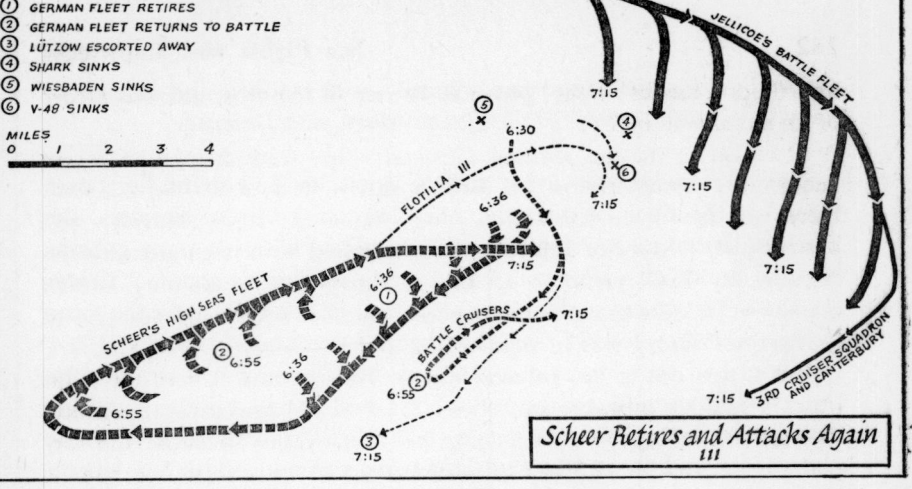

BRITISH ━━━▶ GERMAN ┅┅┅▶

① GERMAN FLEET RETIRES
② GERMAN FLEET RETURNS TO BATTLE
③ LÜTZOW ESCORTED AWAY
④ SHARK SINKS
⑤ WIESBADEN SINKS
⑥ V-48 SINKS

MILES
0   1   2   3   4

JELLICOE'S BATTLE FLEET

7:15

⑤ ✕
6:30

FLOTILLA III

6:36

④ ✕
7:15

⑥
7:15

7:15

SCHEER'S HIGH SEAS FLEET

6:36

①
7:15

6:36

②
6:55

6:36

BATTLE CRUISERS

7:15

6:55

②
6:55

7:15

3RD CRUISER SQUADRON
AND CANTERBURY

7:15

③
7:15

Scheer Retires and Attacks Again
III

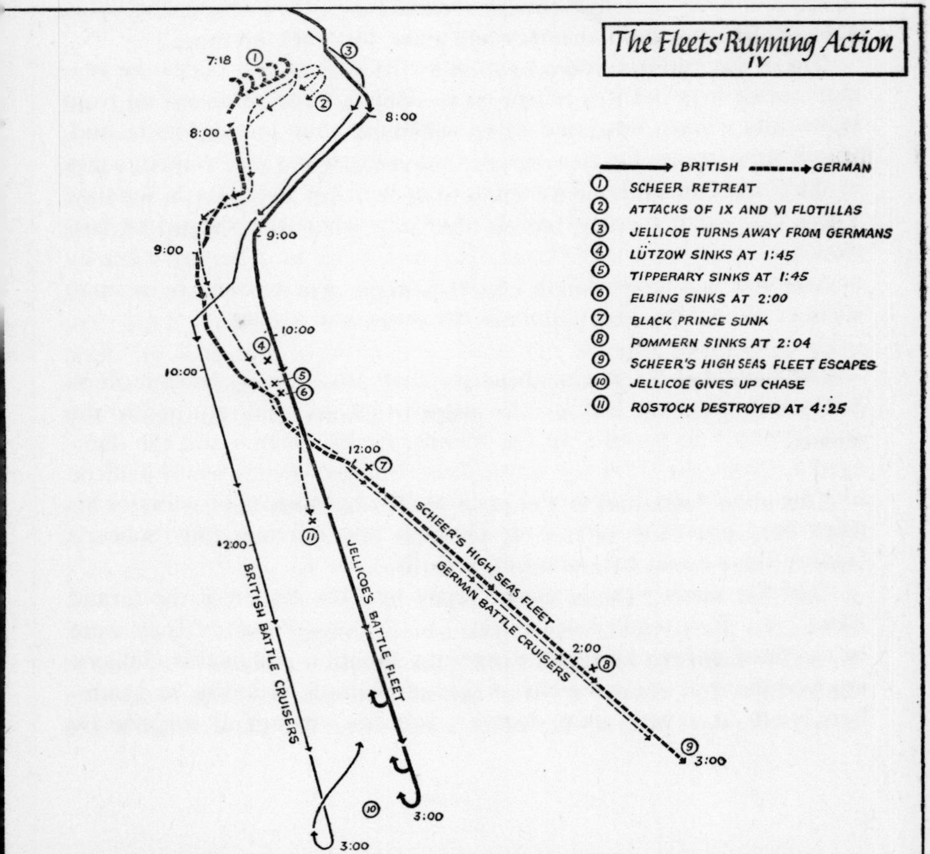

The Fleets' Running Action
IV

7:18 ①

③

②

8:00

8:00

9:00

9:00

10:00

④ ✕

10:00

⑤ ✕

⑥ ✕

12:00 ┗ ⑦

BRITISH ━━━▶ GERMAN ┅┅┅▶

① SCHEER RETREAT
② ATTACKS OF IX AND VI FLOTILLAS
③ JELLICOE TURNS AWAY FROM GERMANS
④ LÜTZOW SINKS AT 1:45
⑤ TIPPERARY SINKS AT 1:45
⑥ ELBING SINKS AT 2:00
⑦ BLACK PRINCE SUNK
⑧ POMMERN SINKS AT 2:04
⑨ SCHEER'S HIGH SEAS FLEET ESCAPES
⑩ JELLICOE GIVES UP CHASE
⑪ ROSTOCK DESTROYED AT 4:25

2:00

2:00

⑪

SCHEER'S HIGH SEAS FLEET

GERMAN BATTLE CRUISERS

BRITISH BATTLE CRUISERS

JELLICOE'S BATTLE FLEET

2:00 ⑧

⑨
3:00

⑩
3:00

3:00

unorthodox tactics might "prove to be one of the most colossal errors of all naval history."

From 7:12 on the leading German ships were blanketed in an "enormous concentration" of British salvos. It looked like the end. Here was a chance for annihilation; the God of Opportunity had knocked at the door of Jellicoe—he who might have been greater than Nelson. By 7:17 virtually all of the thirty-three remaining British capital ships were firing at the enemy—the first such concentration of the battle. Victory was in sight—God and St. George!

But it was not to be. Jellicoe was no Nelson; and Scheer the Bold quickly saw his mistake, and about 7:18 turned his battle line away, covered by a torpedo attack from his destroyers. To avoid the torpedoes, the British Grand Fleet—that fleet of the resounding names, blood and bone of British history—turned *away* from the enemy—not *towards* him—and opportunity had gone, to knock no more.

There was more scattered action in the waning day, and just after the sun set at 8:19 Beatty caught the oldest German battleships and the battered enemy battle-cruisers silhouetted against the after-glow, and in a few brief minutes registered seven hits and received only two. It was—though none could know it then—the last contact between heavy ships of the battle; indeed, the last capital ship action of World War I.

The rest was a sprawling chaos of night action between the light forces—as the German High Sea Fleet retired toward the Jade. The coup de grâce to cripples, the numbing surprise in contact in the dark, the crimson flare of guns and the stabbing beams of searchlights—the last act dragged on with all the props of drama. But the climax had passed.

The main fleets had lost contact in the darkness but all that night until well after dawn of June 1, when the German High Sea Fleet was safe at bases beyond Horn Reefs, a fierce melee between the light craft waxed and waned. Death struck many in the sudden flare of searchlights and the roar of guns at point-blank range. The *Elbing,* which helped to open the battle, did not quite live to see it end; she died in the night action, though most of her crew were saved. The *Frauenlob* sank in the dark with all her officers and men. The crew of her No. 4

gun, standing in water up to their waists, continued to fire to the last
and just before she capsized those on board cheered for their Kaiser
and the German Empire.

The *Tipperary's* crew, crowded on a tiny raft in the freezing water,
sang "It's a Long Long Way to Tipperary," and died one by one.

Friend and enemy collided in the dark; friend crashed into friend.
A British destroyer rammed a German cruiser and backed away with
a crumpled bow and sixty feet of German plating. Her own masts and
stacks and superstructure were swept clean by the blast of the German
guns which could not be depressed sufficiently to hit. The *Lützow*
sank; the *Seydlitz* was beached at the mouth of the Jade. The British
drew last blood: the old battleship *Pommern* was sunk "with a tremendous roar of flame and sound" in a dawn torpedo attack, and at
5:20 A.M., June 1, the *Ostfriesland,* inward bound to the Jade, struck
a mine and was seriously damaged.

The first of June drew on to an unpleasant day, with a cold raw
wind and the sea making up. The battered British ships, working their
way back to harbors, struggled with the sea, with fires and wreckage,
and with the wounded. All over the North Sea, that day, the English
were burying their dead:

> *We have fed our sea for a thousand years,*
> *And she calls us, still unfed—*

Creeping back to port the burned and blackened ships, with gaping
decks and guns awry, were greeted with cheers by the dockyard
workers at Invergordon and Rosyth. But the *Warrior* gave up the
battle half-way home, and in the *Malaya,* the "smell of burnt human
flesh remained for weeks."

Along Unter den Linden Skagerrak was hailed as a glorious victory. The German Navy had come of age. The Kaiser with the withered
arm—last of the Hohenzollerns—bestowed the Order *Pour Le Mérite*
on Scheer and Hipper and promoted them. Congratulatory telegrams
from all over Central Europe sped to the German naval bases. But
beneath the North Sea waters, or in plain coffins in the dock-yards,
ranged row on row, lay 160 German officers and 2,385 German men
—the price of "victory."

NOTES   The German code book which aided the British Intelligence was recovered from the German ship *Magdeburg* which had struck a mine near the island of Odensholm, off the Esthonian coast, earlier in the war. She drifted on to a sand bank and was shelled by Russian cruisers; her crew surrendered. According to a story by an "Old Naval Officer," published in *Pravda,* one officer jumped overboard and sank immediately. To quote the story: "Marking the spot where this occurred, we sent down divers as soon as possible and they brought up the body of the officer. Secured to the body were a number of secret German naval signal codes in the usual weighted covers." Though the author has not been able to check the accuracy of this account published in a Russian paper, it is, nevertheless, accepted history that the German code books were first secured from the wreck of the *Magdeburg,* and that the Germans continued to use the same code for a long period.

Though the Germans celebrated the "victory" of Jutland, Jellicoe still controlled the sea. More than six thousand British seamen died in Jutland's brief holocaust of flame and smoke, but *Der Tag* had for the Germans a hollow meaning. The strangling power of the British blockade was unbroken, and some thirty months later, with the red flag flying over Kiel, Von Hipper, hero of Jutland, sent the pride of the German Fleet to Great Britain for internment.

Soon after the echo of the guns above the North Sea had died, there followed an aftermath of bickering and recrimination. The British Navy was a house divided against itself. "Jellicoe men" and "Beatty men" quarreled about the tactics of Jutland; the British public gradually came to realize that Nelson had long since died. The Germans— who called the battle Skagerrak—celebrated it as a moral victory as well as a victory so far as material and personnel losses were concerned. Undoubtedly Britain lost considerable of her naval prestige in those bitter hours in the North Sea; but Germany, two and a half years later, lost the war.

The real victor at Jutland was "Admiral Death," but the dispute as to which nation won the great sea fight still endures. Frost's summing up in his book, *The Battle of Jutland,* probably the most impartial and thorough account of the battle, calls attention to the British loss of face: ". . . it is strongly believed that a 'Trafalgar' on May 31, 1916, would have re-established British naval supremacy for a long time to come. Such ascendency depends as much upon moral as upon material factors and . . . the British lost that imponderable and invaluable moral ascendency at Jutland. Jellicoe forgot what Napoleon had said: 'The moral is to the physical as three to one.' Calculations of cold tonnage are by no means all that count in naval warfare. Never again would American or Japanese sailors be overawed by the powerful, even overwhelming, force of British naval tradition." And Winston Churchill, in his *World Crisis*, states: "The ponderous, poignant responsibilities borne successfully, if not triumphantly, by Sir John Jellicoe during two years of faithful command, constitute unanswerable claims to the lasting respect of the nation. But the Royal Navy must find in other personalities and other episodes the golden links which carried forward through the Great War the audacious and conquering traditions of the past; and it is to Beatty and the battle-cruisers, to Keyes at Zeebrugge, to Tyrwhitt and his Harwich striking force, to the destroyer and submarine flotillas out in all weathers and against all foes, to the wild adventures of the Q-ships, to the steadfast resolution of the British Merchant Service, that the eyes of rising generations will turn."

On the other hand, extravagant German claims can be dismissed; the German ships and seamen—like the British—spoke for themselves. The battle, in retrospect, is somewhat reminiscent of Southey's "The Battle of Blenheim":

> *"But what good came of it at last?"*
> *Quoth little Peterkin.*
> *"Why, that I cannot tell," said he;*
> *"But 'twas a famous victory."*

ACKNOWLEDGMENTS   This article in abbreviated form was first printed in the *New York Times Magazine,* and thanks are due to Mr. Lester Markel, Sunday editor, for permission to reprint it. Additions and changes have been made in the first published version.

In writing *Admiral Death—The Battle of Jutland,* I have drawn upon all the standard sources and histories of the period. I am particularly indebted to *The Fighting at Jutland,* compiled by H. W. Fawcett and G. W. W. Hooper; to Commander H. H. Frost's *The Battle of Jutland;* to Harper's and Gibson's *The Riddle of Jutland;* to Winston S. Churchill's *The World Crisis, 1916–1918;* to Scheer's *Germany's High Sea Fleet in the World War;* to *Kiel and Jutland,* by Commander George Oskar I. von Hase; to Corbett's account of the battle in the *British Official History of the World War, Naval Operations, Vol. III;* and to the *Encyclopaedia Britannica* (1954 edition). The quotations used and incidents recounted in this article are drawn from one or the other of these books.

1893

Death of an Admiral

The lamps of London gleamed brightly above the muddy Thames. Gladstone hurled thundering paragraphs across the halls of Parliament. Sir Arthur Pinero's new play, *The Second Mrs. Tanqueray,* minced—beneath flickering gas jets—across musty theater boards. And at home in Eaton Place, Lady Tryon, wife of Vice-Admiral Sir George Tryon, K.C.B., Commander-in-Chief of the Mediterranean Squadron, received her guests.

It was a warm London evening: June 22, 1893; the drawing-room curtains were looped back, and the French windows stood ajar. Bare shoulders gleamed above low-cut bodices; bustled dresses flared in rustling rivulets of silk; ladies curtsied; men bowed deeply, with all the gallantry of Victoria's England.

Lady Tryon moved sedately among her guests, chatting with this one, tapping that one lightly with her fan. Somewhat breathless, an elderly woman tripped up to her:

"Is Sir George here?"

"Sir George *here!* Now Constance, what an idea! You know very well that Sir George is in the Mediterranean. What?——"

"Yes, I knew that, but James swore he saw him in the drawing room."

Later, when the news was known, there were others who had "seen" Sir George that night in the crowded drawing room of his Eaton Place home.

On June 22, 1893, Sir George Tryon's flag flew from the battleship *Victoria,* anchored with the twelve other ships of the Mediterranean Squadron in the harbor of Beirut, Syria. A brilliant sun burned down on the date palms and the sand dunes and the sea. Sir George, one of the most experienced and skillful tacticians in the Royal Navy, paced his cabin, wiped the moisture from his brow, and sank somewhat wearily onto a transom. Just recovered from a bout of illness, he would not be sorry to leave this place, even though the nearby Syrian town of Tripoli, with its swarms of sore-infested beggars, was to be the next port.

At 10 A.M. the squadron got under way and steamed northward along the coast toward Tripoli. The ships were formed in line abreast —eight battleships and five cruisers—with the flag of Rear Admiral Markham, in command of the second division, flying from the *Camper-down.* It was a lazy and uneventful cruise past the sands of Lebanon, with the distant purple hills shimmering like a mirage in the heat waves. Sir George kept his cabin after lunch, and at four bells in the afternoon watch called his staff about him to give instructions about entering port. Captain Maurice Bourke, his flag captain, Staff Commander Hawkins-Smith, and Lord Gillford, flag lieutenant, listened as the admiral told them he intended to form the squadron in two columns, with the *Victoria* leading one column of six ships and *Camperdown* leading the other column of seven ships, steaming on parallel courses some six cables (or twelve hundred yards) apart. After passing a coastal landmark near Tripoli, known as the Tower of the Lions, the two columns were to reverse their courses upon signal, turning inward toward each other. Each ship in succession, headed by the *Victoria* and the *Camperdown* leading their columns, was to put its rudder hard over, swing about in a wide semicircle, and head back in the direction from which the squadron had come. Then, when abreast of the Tripoli anchorage, the squadron was to make another turn toward port and anchor.

The instructions were clear in all respects, except for the specified distance between the columns. That distance—six cables or twelve hundred yards—made the maneuver impossible, since the leading ships, *Camperdown* and *Victoria,* each required six to eight hundred yards leeway in which to make a 180-degree turn. Both Captain

Bourke and Hawkins-Smith suggested that the distance between the columns be increased, and Sir George agreed:

"Yes, it should be eight."

The younger officers left the cabin and went on deck, and Lord Gillford began to carry out the admiral's orders. Flag hoists whipped in the hot breeze; the Mediterranean sparkled in the sun glare. At quarter past two Lord Gillford was recalled to the cabin and ordered to make the signal: "Columns to be six cables apart." There was no mistake about it; Sir George gave him careful verbal instructions and handed him a slip of paper with the figure six written upon it. The flag lieutenant made the signal; Hawkins-Smith hurried aft and told him there must have been some misunderstanding; the admiral had agreed to a distance of eight cables or sixteen hundred yards. The fatal flags still fluttered from the yardarm as Gillford went below again to Sir George's cabin. Captain Bourke, still chatting with his chief, supported the younger officer:

"You certainly said it was to be more than six cables."

"Leave it six cables," Tryon repeated to Gillford.

The young officer went back to the bridge. The signal had been answered; across the calm wind-rippled sea the Mediterranean Squadron was steaming in two parallel columns—six cables or twelve hundred yards apart.

Down in the cabin Captain Bourke again remonstrated, pointing out that the *Victoria's* turning circle was eight hundred yards.

Tryon was brusque: "That is all right; leave it at six cables."

Five bells were struck. The admiral's flag fluttered from the truck. The hot breath of the desert beat upon the steel sides of the ships; the slow thump of the propellers throbbed monotonously. The bow waves and the frothy wakes were white as Her Majesty's men-of-war, steaming slowly at 8.8 knots, headed up on the brief passage from Beirut to Tripoli.

At 3:15 Sir George left his cabin and went to the forward charthouse. To starboard lay the coast of Syria, with the Tower of the Lions almost on bearing. To port was the quiet Mediterranean, the inland sea, bordering shores where civilization had begun; the Mediterranean, scene of triumphs and disasters. Beneath and about him was his command; in two columns as he had ordered, six cables distant—his practiced eye saw that. One column, the first division, stretched out astern: *Victoria, Nile, Dreadnought, Inflexible, Collingwood, Phaeton;* brave names in England's history. The second division, to port twelve hundred yards away, was headed by the *Camperdown,* with her stout stem and heavy underwater ram. The *Camperdown,* the *Edinburgh,* the *Sans Pareil, Edgar, Amphion, Fearless,* and *Barham*—all his command.

The admiral turned to Lord Gillford. Stout British arms jerked the flags from their flag bags, and from the masthead of the *Victoria* fluttered the 2 flag, 2 pendant, the compass pendant, 1 flag, 6 flag; from the yardarm the 2 flag, 1 pendant, 1 flag, 6 flag, and compass pendant. The meaning was unmistakable:

Second division alter course in succession sixteen points to starboard, preserving the order of the fleet; first division alter course in succession sixteen points to port, preserving the order of the fleet.

Rear Admiral Markham on the bridge of the *Camperdown* saw the signal, thought the columns too close to execute it, exclaimed:

"It is impossible; it is an impracticable maneuver!"

He kept the signal at the dip and ordered his flag lieutenant to send a message by semaphore to Tryon:

"Am I to understand that it is your wish for the columns to turn as indicated by the signals now flying?"

But the message was never sent; the Tower of the Lions was on the bearing, and Admiral Tryon, impatient, stepped to the after part of the *Victoria's* chart house to see if any of the ships in the second division had failed to read the hoist correctly. All the hoists were two-blocked except the *Camperdown's.*

"What are you waiting for?" snapped out the waving flags across the six cable lengths of water between the *Victoria* and the *Camperdown.* Admiral Markham hesitated no longer; the flag hoist was two-blocked, and at 3:31 down came the flags from the *Victoria's* masthead and yardarm; rudders went hard over and the two ships, leading their divisions, started to turn inwards toward each other.

Almost immediately, as the great steel bows were swinging, Captain Bourke spoke again to Sir George:

"We had better do something; we shall be too close to that ship."

He got no response, and turning to Midshipman Lanyon:
"Take the distance to the *Camperdown,* Mr. Lanyon."

As the gap of shining water between the two ships decreased the
tension in the chart house heightened. Only Sir George Tryon seemed
lost in a strange lassitude.

"The distance, Mr. Lanyon, the distance," Captain Bourke barked.
"What is the delay? Give me the distance to the *Camperdown.*"

"Yes, sir. Just . . . 3½ cables, sir."

Captain Bourke to the admiral: "May I go astern full speed on the
port screw?"

The admiral stood looking out at his command—the *Victoria* and
the *Camperdown,* the *Fearless* and the *Sans Pareil,* the *Dreadnought*
and the *Nile*—England's steel bulwarks. . . . He gave no answer.

"May I go astern full speed, port?" And again: "Admiral, may I go
astern full speed on the port screw?"

At last an answer: "Yes."

The brass handle on the port engine-room telegraph flashed round
the dial; the pointer stopped at FULL ASTERN. A bell jangled far
below decks; the propeller lashed the sea into froth; the ship shivered.
Almost immediately and without further orders Captain Bourke reversed the starboard engine. The sea's sunlit green foamed into white
surging water; the great propellers, thrashing mightily, tried to halt
the steady advance of the trembling ship. On the *Camperdown,* too,
first the starboard engine and then the port had been reversed—but it
was too late. The *Victoria* and the *Camperdown* surged struggling onward toward each other.

A gong sounded on the flagship; boatswain's pipes signaled: "Close
all watertight doors."

Men on the upper decks who could see disaster advancing stood
braced and tense, waiting for the shock. Those below, who knew nothing, thought: "Another of old Tryon's maneuvers."

At 3:34 the *Dreadnought* and the *Nile,* the *Amphion* and the *Barham* and the rest of the Mediterranean Squadron saw and heard it
happen. The *Camperdown's* ram buried itself deep in the starboard
bow of the flagship. There came the awful scrape of wounded metal;
the bow of the *Victoria* was flung bodily to port sixty or seventy feet
by the ten thousand steel tons of her sister. Startled cries arose in the

first moment of disaster, then, sudden silence. Only the steady thump of screws still backing in a troubled sea.

And on the chart house the figure of Vice-Admiral Sir George Tryon, K.C.B., Commander-in-Chief of the Mediterranean Squadron, could be plainly seen.

A startled petty officer in a messroom, far below-decks, saw the ram of the *Camperdown* burst in a cloud of black dust through coal bunkers and bulkheads. Commander John Jellicoe, tossing feverishly in his bunk, struggled into a life belt, made his way topside in his pajamas, helped at the signal halyards, was washed into the sea, and lived to command England's greatest fleet in England's greatest battle.

The sick were brought on deck; the prisoners in the brig were released; bugles called to quarters; men struggled to close the watertight doors and hatches. The *Victoria* and the *Camperdown,* grinding and groaning, remained locked together with the *Camperdown's* twisted ram buried deep in the shattered steel of the flagship, about twenty feet forward of her turret and some sixty-five feet from the bow. Then, with engines backing, the *Camperdown* pulled clear: a jagged hole in her port bow, her stem broken, some forward compartments flooded, but in no danger.

On the *Victoria's* chart house Captain Bourke spoke: "I think I had better go below and see about the doors."

Admiral Tryon: "You go below to look after the doors: I will attend to the engines."

The *Victoria* was mortally stricken. Into the great breach below the water line—one hundred square feet, lined by broken metal, open to the sea—rushed the Mediterranean, gurgling green water filling and flooding at three thousand tons per minute. Almost as soon as the *Camperdown* tore out her ram the *Victoria* had taken on a list to starboard, with her bow drooping. Men on the settling forecastle struggled with the thrummed collision mats in vain efforts to stopper the gaping hole. The bow sank deeper; the list increased; within four minutes water was washing through the hawse pipes.

The admiral spoke: "It is entirely my fault!"

The Mediterranean Squadron—in confusion—lay scattered about the dying *Victoria*. The *Dreadnought* lowered her boats. And Sir George made another mistake, signaled: "Annul sending boats," and ordered the *Victoria's* engines half ahead in an effort to beach the wounded ship.

Slowly she crawled about, her screws flopping, slowly she straightened for the white sands not so far away.

But she settled quickly, listing more and more, drooping to meet the calm waters. The engines speeded up; far below-decks steel bars sliced into fiery coals as sweating men kept up the steam. They were forcing her full speed now; it was man against the sea—but the men below-decks didn't know that, though it was queer (they thought) the anchor chain rattling out when the ship was under way. They sent an artificer topside to find out. He found out, but could never tell them; the *Camperdown's* ram had ruptured the chain locker, and the chain was rasping out through the ship's bottom into deep water.

Six minutes after the crash the men handling the collision mats on the forecastle were working in water up to their waists; they were ordered away from the hopeless task. The bow was deep now; water was washing toward the open turret ports; almost half the length of the *Victoria* was submerged. The men had fallen in on the upper decks —those not on watch or working—in long ranks, their backs to the sea. They stood there waiting with British stoicism and discipline, the water lapping about their ankles, then their knees. With them stood Chaplain Morris, arms folded across his chest, lips moving in prayer.

"Steady, men, steady," he said, as the list deepened.

Ten minutes after the collision, with the port screw thrashing wildly in the sunlight and the ship still slowly heading for the beach, the admiral turned to Staff Commander Hawkins-Smith:

"I think she's going."

"Yes, sir, I think she is."

Bunting once again fluttered to the canted yardarm of the stricken *Victoria:* "Send boats immediately."

Activity at last. The Mediterranean Squadron leaped into life. Boats were lowered; with long sure strokes men pulled toward the flagship. But again it was too late. The *Victoria* was going swiftly. The men ranged on the canted decks, with their backs to the sea, turned on order to face their death. On the top of the chart house Vice-Admiral Sir George Tryon noticed that a young midshipman was still standing by his side:

"Don't stop, there, youngster—go to a boat."

The boy did not move.

Captain Bourke, who had been below trying to stem the inrush of
the sea, came above decks, climbed up the after-bridge ladder, and
started forward along the fore-and-aft bridge to report to the admiral.
He never got there.

The heavy list turned into a lurching heave to starboard; an officer
shouted to the ranks of men to jump; some leaped into the sea; some
scrambled up the tilting decks onto the ship's port side. A great wave
met Captain Bourke and lifted him into the Mediterranean. On the
bridge Vice-Admiral Sir George Tryon, K.C.B., refused a life jacket
offered him by his staff commander.

Boats rocked from their skids as the ship turned over; weights fell
with sickening thuds and hammered out the lives of swimmers close
alongside. Screaming men were crushed against the bulwarks. Below-
decks, where the bare-armed stokers shoveled to the last, the careening lurch meant death to all on watch. A rush of water, flaming coals,
and steam . . . and that was all.

The *Victoria* turned over, stern high, bow deep. The untended engines still raced as if to push her shorewards; the great bronze blades
of her propellers flailed, half out of water, lopping arms, legs, and
heads of helpless swimmers. The red weed-grown keel and bottom
strakes of the *Victoria* were black with men; the sea was pocked with
froth and wreckage—struggling men and gouts of blood. Boats were
coming from all sides; but the *Victoria* did not wait. She floated, bottom up, rolling; then, with a loud explosion, she plunged downward,
dragging swimmers with her. The sea boiled; two muffled explosions,
two geysers of water and wreckage and bodies, and the Mediterranean
gathered seething above the grave of Vice-Admiral Sir George Tryon,
K.C.B. . . .

And in far-off London Lady Tryon, at her home in Eaton Place,
gave the butler directions for her evening's reception.

The *Victoria* carried down with her the Commander-in-Chief, 22
officers, and 337 men; the boats rescued almost three hundred others.
The *Camperdown* limped to port without loss.

After an investigation a court-martial was ordered of Captain

Bourke and other surviving officers of the flagship. It resulted in acquittal. The conclusion was that the Commander-in-Chief of the Mediterranean Squadron, "as the result of a temporary aberration, made a most inexplicable and fatal mistake, for which he paid with his life." The court also expressed its regret that Rear Admiral Markham "had not protested more strongly against the fatal maneuver, but considered that it was not in the best interests of the Service to censure him for obeying the orders of his superior officers. . . ."

Unending speculation followed the court-martial findings, but no more tenable conclusion was ever reached. But the reaction to disaster helped to lead to a more intelligent interpretation of the past's rigid and inflexible adherence to orders—the "blind obedience"—which has always been at one and the same time the cornerstone of discipline and the refuge of the weak.

NOTES The *Victoria* disaster did lead to considerable research in ship design and construction and was indirectly, if not directly, responsible for marked improvements in the watertight integrity of men-of-war.

The *Victoria* case raised again that age-old problem of the military —the limits of proper obedience. Some months before the disaster, Admiral Tryon had issued an order to the Mediterranean Squadron pointing out that maneuver orders did not relieve any subordinate of responsibility for the safety of his ship; if collision threatened as a result of superior orders, "paramount orders direct that the danger is to be avoided, while the object of the [maneuver] order should be attained if possible." But the Commander-in-Chief had also introduced the unexpected in his maneuvering orders; he was known to his subordinates as a practical student of "fleet evolutions," and whether his orders were understood or not, his subordinates had come to have faith in them and obeyed them readily. Admiral Markham pointed to this faith in his superior's capabilities at the court-martial and added that he thought when he acknowledged Tryon's signal that the *Victoria* was going to circle outside of the *Camperdown*. He felt that if he failed to obey the signal he might—not knowing what was in his commander's mind—cause a collision. Markham was justified. As *The Review of Reviews* in its August, 1893, issue pointed out (quoted by Lt. Bassler):

"You cannot maneuver a fleet on the principle of limited liability or qualified obedience."

ACKNOWLEDGMENTS Republished from *Esquire* with permission of the editor.

I have drawn upon various British Admiralty papers, as well as upon J. G. Lockhart's *Mysteries of the Sea*. I have also quoted from an article, "Tryon and the *Victoria*," by Lieutenant R. E. Bassler, USN, in the September, 1934, *United States Naval Institute Proceedings*.

1945

The Greatest
Sea-Air Battle in History

This is the story of "the Last Battle" of World War II, the gigantic struggle at Okinawa, in the East China Sea. between the "fleet that came to stay" and the Japanese "Kamikazes"—a battle which Winston Churchill correctly described as one of "the most intense and famous of military history."

Easter Sunday, April 1, 1945, a time of prayer and hope in a world at war, is a shining day in the East China Sea. The ocean is calm, the weather cool, the visibility good, the sun strong; the escarpments of Okinawa, dim and distant island soon to become forever warp and woof of American traditions, are shadowy on the horizon.

The greatest naval armada in history—more than forty carriers, eighteen battleships, two hundred destroyers, hundreds of transports, cruisers, supply ships, net layers, submarines, minesweepers, gunboats, landing craft, patrol vessels, salvage ships and repair vessels, some 1,321 ships transporting 183,000 assault troops—is steaming deep into Japanese waters. The objective is "Operation Iceberg"—the seizure of Okinawa.

After the months of intensive preparation and weeks of hair-trigger tension that always precede battle, the start of the operation seems anticlimactic.

Well offshore cruises famed Task Force 58 under "Pete" Mitscher, the admiral with a gnomelike face framed in a peaked baseball cap.

Southward, where the swells of the East China Sea break against the rocky pediments of Sakishma Gunto and Formosa, a British carrier task force, first to operate in the Pacific, rakes Japanese airfields. Off Blue Beach and Purple Beach, the transports and landing ships and cargo vessels are disembarking their Marine and Army assault units with almost incredible ease. The bright waters are laced with the wakes of small boats and landing craft. In the distance the guns of battleships flame and thunder—but they are American guns. In the skies the planes dip and wheel and bomb—but they are American planes.

The enemy is strangely silent. An infantryman of the Seventh Division, the tightness gone from his chest, wipes his brow after climbing one of Okinawa's knoblike hills and says:

"I've already lived longer than I thought I would."

Okinawa, largest of the Ryukyu island chain stretching southward from Japanese Kyushu, is a lizard-shaped land mass fringed with coral reefs, about sixty miles long and from two to eighteen miles wide. Its two-mile waist divides the northern two-thirds of the island—rugged, mountainous and heavily forested—from the rolling, hilly land of the south. It is in the southern sector, seamed by escarpments and ravines, dotted with ancient Okinawan tombs and limestone caves, and with every foot of arable ground planted in sugar cane, sweet potatoes, rice, and soybeans, that the Japanese have erected their main defense lines.

The assault upon Okinawa is a logical development of the Pacific strategy of the United States. The island is within medium-bomber range of Japan, and it is estimated that 780 bombers can be based there to intensify the assault being conducted by the B-29's from the Marianas. From Okinawa and its satellite isles planes and ships could sever virtually all Japanese shipping routes. Okinawa also is wanted as a supporting position for "Operation Olympic"—the invasion of the Japanese island of Kyushu, 350 miles away, which is scheduled for the ensuing November 1.

In retrospect it may be argued that the assault upon Okinawa was not essential to final victory; less than two months after its capture the enemy was ready for peace. But at the time the predominant military opinion was that Japan would fight on for at least another year to eighteen months. The Japanese defeat at Okinawa was, moreover, a major contributory cause to the enemy's quick surrender. The final

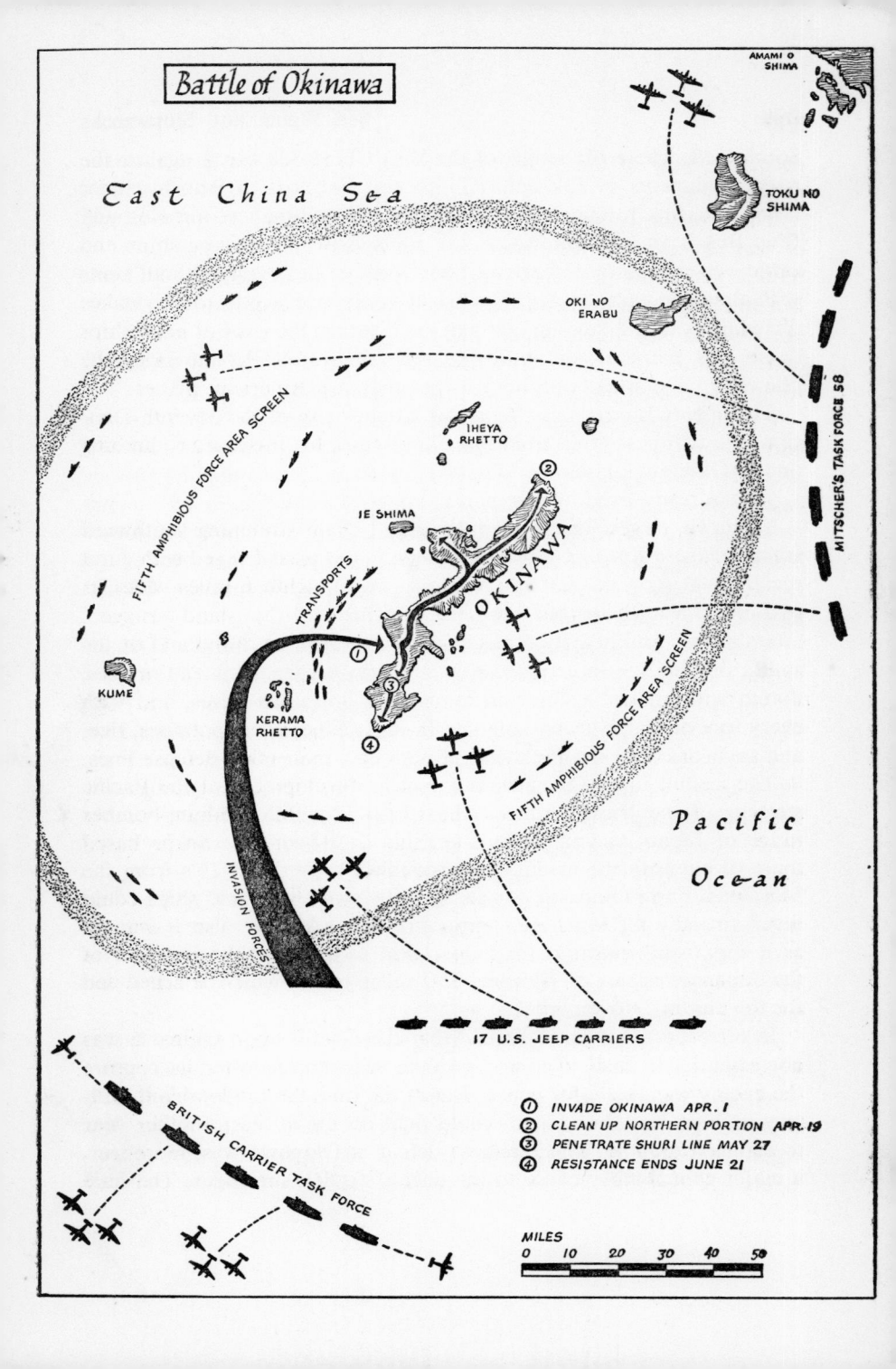

Battle of Okinawa

East China Sea

AMAMI O SHIMA

TOKU NO SHIMA

OKI NO ERABU

MITSCHER'S TASK FORCE 58

IHEYA RHETTO

IE SHIMA

OKINAWA

FIFTH AMPHIBIOUS FORCE AREA SCREEN

TRANSPORTS

①

KUME

KERAMA RHETTO

③

④

FIFTH AMPHIBIOUS FORCE AREA SCREEN

INVASION FORCES

Pacific

Ocean

17 U.S. JEEP CARRIERS

BRITISH CARRIER TASK FORCE

① INVADE OKINAWA APR. 1
② CLEAN UP NORTHERN PORTION APR. 19
③ PENETRATE SHURI LINE MAY 27
④ RESISTANCE ENDS JUNE 21

MILES
0   10   20   30   40   50

desperate hope of the militarists—to force a negotiated peace—died at Okinawa.

The invasion is envisioned as a "quick" operation, lasting a month or less. Intelligence estimates that the enemy has about 55,000 to 65,000 troops on the island and 198 artillery pieces of major calibers. But Intelligence is to be rudely surprised and hopes of a quick victory are soon to bog down. More than 110,000 of the enemy are to die and 7,400 to surrender; more than 26,000 Americans will be killed, wounded, or missing before the "Last Battle" ends.

For the Japanese high command is determined to hold Okinawa and to employ the major portion of the Empire's remaining air and sea strength to destroy the American armada that is making the invasion possible. The destruction of our fleet is the major enemy objective. To accomplish this, the enemy is counting chiefly on bomb-laden planes guided to their targets by suicide pilots, members of the Japanese Navy's Special Attack Corps, better known as the suicidal Kamikaze (Divine Wind) Corps.

A shadow of the terror impending at Okinawa has touched the invasion fleet even before the first landings. *Indianapolis,* the flagship of the armada under Admiral R. A. Spruance, commanding the Fifth Fleet, has been hit on the port quarter by a bomb-carrying Kamikaze suicide plane on March 31; the *Adams* also has taken a suicide hit; the *Murray* has been disabled by a torpedo; the *Skylark*—strange, lilting name for a plodding sweeper—has been blown up by a mine. By April 3 the sheltered anchorages at Kerama Rhetto already are beginning to clot with limping and crippled ships.

April 6, 1945, is clear, with wind riffling the East China Sea. Ashore, around a hill called "The Pinnacle," where Matthew Perry had raised the American flag almost a century before, a desperate battle rages—the first in a bruising, terrible struggle to break the enemy's fortified Shuri Line.

Afloat, the great armada is spread wide around the island. To the southeast are seventeen United States "jeep" carriers, their planes furnishing air support for the ground troops ashore and flying C.A.P. (combat air patrol) for the surface ships. Cruisers and battleships steam back and forth within easy range of Okinawa's high escarpments, shelling the Japanese positions. Huddled off the beaches are the landing ships, transports and cargo vessels which keep the stream of men and supplies moving over the coral reefs and through the surf to the fighting men ashore. And ringing the whole island and the amphibious force, in a great circle some fifty miles out from the beaches, are the "tin cans," the "spitkids," the "small boys," officially designated the "Fifth Amphibious Force Area Screen" but universally called the radar picket line.

The "small boys," clustered in fifteen main picket stations, detect the enemy first; the Kamikazes show up as points of light on the radar screens long before the diapason of their engines can be heard.

The mid-watch notes enemy snoopers on April 6, and, before daylight, "heavy air attacks." Nine enemy planes are "splashed" in the transport area by AA fire. The day clouds up; by afternoon the sky is heavily overcast, and from all directions the "bandits" roar in. The radio-telephone T.B.S. (talk between ships) circuits chatter as the Japanese attack, and the C.I.C. (Combat Information Centers) aboard the destroyers are a babel of radioed reports: "Pedantic, this is Riverside; I see bogey one eight zero. Do you concur? Over?"

"This is Pedantic. Affirmative. That makes three raids . . . out."

Between 1 and 6 P.M. of this gray and somber day 182 enemy planes in some twenty-two different attacks reach the Okinawa area. Many drop bombs or torpedoes, but more than a score crash into American ships in suicide dives. The victims are mostly the lowly sweepers, destroyers, escorts, and landing craft in the far-flung radar picket line.

One of the victims is U.S.S. *Rodman,* which has her rendezvous with destiny at about seven bells in the afternoon watch. The sea is smooth and *Rodman's* white wake scarcely roils the surface as she loafs along at eight knots, screening—with her sister destroyer-sweeper, the *Emmons*—a group of sweepers. The crew is at general quarters, but there are no pips on the radar screen. Suddenly three planes break out of the thick cloud rack close aboard and commence a coordinated attack. One crashes into the port side of the main deck and a great sheet of flame burgeons over the superstructure, to be followed seconds later by a blinding spray of water from a near-miss close aboard to starboard.

The whole bow of *Rodman* is opened to sea and sky. The struggle for life commences; steering control is lost as *Rodman* backs into the wind to keep the fire forward, the bridge clear of flame and smoke. The ship settles deep; the main deck is awash. Overboard go the top-side weights; jettison the anchor, pump clear the ballast. Working near the licking flames, seamen manhandle the ammunition out of the fire's path and dump it overboard. Lighten the ship, lighten the ship! Fight fires! Plug leaks!

By eight bells the fire is under control, but the Japanese come again. They come from all directions—the young men of Japan who would die for their Emperor—and their wishes are fulfilled as their blazing planes flame, like meteors, across the skies. Many of the Japanese, shot down by the C.A.P., crash close aboard the *Rodman*. One Kami-kaze nearly cuts her in two with a bull's-eye on the port side water line; the rupture extends almost to the keel. Four five-inch powder charges detonate; most of the others in the forward magazine are tumbled and torn, but—miraculously—the magazine does not "blow." Another suicider smacks into the captain's cabin; the flames gut the superstructure and force "conn" to shift from the bridge aft.

Some of the crew are blown overboard, some jump. Fifty-eight remain aboard as salvage crew; the rest—those that still live—shift to rescue vessels. As dusk begins to settle down, the fires are out, the rudder is cleared, the ship has worked up to a speed of six knots, and at 0325 the next morning, April 7, the torn ship limps into Kerama Rhetto, the bodies of her dead, singed and battered, still aboard. *Rodman* has survived; she is of the "fleet that came to stay."

But *Emmons* is not so lucky; she is among those who got "theirs" that day. The score card is ominous; besides foundered *Emmons* two destroyers are sunk; an LST is burned "end to end"; the *Logan Victory*, an ammunition ship, dies in an awesome pyrotechnical display after being crashed by two suicide "Zekes"; another ammunition ship is sunk and nine escort types are heavily damaged, one by depth charges attached to floating planks pushed by swimmers.

But the blanks in the radar picket line are filled in; the unloading continues, and the Japanese losses are huge—almost four hundred planes on April 6 and the early morning of the seventh. Of these, three hundred are stopped at the picket line at the cost of only two United States planes. And on this day—the seventh—there dies in sudden

convulsive shudder and pyramid of spiraling smoke the largest battleship in the world, the last pride of the Japanese Navy—the eighteen-
inch-gunned *Yamato*. Planes of Task Force 58 get her far to the north,
as she steams toward Okinawa, accompanied by one cruiser and eight
destroyers, in a gallant but desperate effort to drive the brash invaders
far from the Emperor's realm.

Ashore, the Marines clean up the northern part of the island against
limited resistance, but the doughboys, driving south, meet the enemy's
"iron defense."

The "Sons of Heaven" came again in great numbers out of the
clouds on the eleventh and twelfth. The Okinawa area is only harried
on the eleventh; the Japanese concentrate on Task Force 58, one
hundred miles to the east. *Enterprise*—"the Big E"—one of the
"fighting-est" carriers of the Pacific war—takes "considerable damage"
from two suicide near-misses; *Essex* is damaged; destroyers and DE's
get theirs.

The twelfth—the day of Roosevelt's death—is a day of great attack.
At home, a nation mourns; at Okinawa, the news spreads suddenly
from foxhole to flight deck to gun turret, but there is no time to mourn,
scarce time to pray. That day many another American dies with his
President. In the clear bright afternoon perhaps 175 enemy planes in
seventeen different raids reach the Okinawa area. They are met by
a strong C.A.P. and the guns of the most powerful fleet in history, but
they exact a grim toll. The picket line takes the brunt of it.

At 1:58 P.M. *Cassin Young* splashes four "Vals," but takes a
suicider in the forward engine room. One killed, fifty-four wounded.
At 2 P.M. *Jeffers,* in Picket Station No. 12, is lashed by fire from a
near-miss. At 2 P.M. the new destroyer *M. L. Abele* has her back
broken and sinks. Six killed, thirty-four wounded, seventy-four missing. The battleship *Tennessee* is hit; blisters on the *Idaho* are flooded;
the *New Mexico* is holed by a shell from a shore battery.

Meanwhile, in the foxholes in front of the still-unbreached Shuri
Line, the Japanese propaganda leaflets already are proclaiming:

*We must express our deep regret over the death of President Roose-
velt. The "American Tragedy" is now raised here at Okinawa with his
death. You must have seen 70 per cent of your CV's* [Carriers] *and*

73 per cent of your B's [BB's—battleships] *sink or be damaged causing 150,000 casualties. . . . A grand "U.S. Sea Bottom Fleet" num-
bering 500 has been brought into existence around this little island.*

*Once you have seen a "lizard" twitching about with its tail cut off,
we suppose this state of lizard is likened to you. Even a drop of blood
can be never expected from its own heart. . . .*

April 17 is another bad day. The carrier *Intrepid* is hit, a destroyer
sunk, many of the "small boys" damaged. The "hot corners" of the
radar picket line—Stations 1, 2, 3 and 14—are given a standing C.A.P.
of two planes each and each station is "doubled-banked with two
destroyers to provide greater anti-aircraft fire power." But Spruance
reports to CINCPAC (Nimitz): "The skill and effectiveness of enemy
suicide air attacks and the rate of loss and damage to ships are such
that all available means should be employed to prevent further attacks.
Recommend all available attacks with all available planes, including
Twentieth Air Force, on Kyushu and Formosa fields."

The attacks are made; the Japanese fields are raked and pounded
relentlessly by bombs and rockets, but the Emperor's Special Attack
Corps is well dispersed and carefully camouflaged; the suicide raids
continue. The damaged ships clog the anchorage at Kerama Rhetto;
there is a trail of limping cripples all the way across the Pacific; the
fire-gutted *Franklin,* hurt in Task Force 58's preliminary strike against
Japan, even transits the Panama Canal for repairs at New York.

But the fleet has come to stay, the traffic across the Pacific is two-
way. The cripples steam home; replacements of flesh and steel move
steadily westward; destroyer divisions from the Central Pacific, the
North Pacific, the Atlantic are ordered to Okinawa to take up their
stations in the battered picket line.

Gone now—afloat and ashore—are the hopes of a quick victory.
The Shuri Line is still intact. The "bong, bong, bong" of General
Quarters sounds by day and by night. The fleet settles down for a long
trial by blood and fire. By the end of the month twenty United States
ships have been sunk—fourteen by suiciders—and 157 damaged,
ninety by Kamikazes.

With the end of April the Kikusui (Special Attack) operations do
not falter; the terrible battle is to drag on for almost two more months.

But never again are the ship losses and damages to be so threatening. During May and June Okinawa becomes less and less a struggle of bombs against steel and more and more a sheer test of human will and endurance.

There are alerts unending. For more than forty consecutive days—until foul weather brings a brief but blessed break—there are air raids every night and every day. Sleep becomes a thing yearned for, dreamed about. Heads droop over gunsights; nerves frazzle, tempers snap; skippers are red-eyed and haggard. "Magic"—the Navy's system of breaking the enemy's codes and divining his intentions—has enabled the fleet to forecast the days of big attacks. Loudspeakers sometimes warn the crews the night before to be prepared. But this practice has to be stopped. The strain of waiting, the anticipated terror, made vivid from past experience, sends many men into hysteria, insanity, breakdown. Only that saving American trait—a sense of humor—keeps some from the brink of horror. On one picket station a tiny gunboat, its crew, fed up with close brushes with death, rigs up a huge sign with a pointing arrow: "To Jap Pilot—This Way to Task Force 58."

Ashore, the bloody, slogging progress inches into the Shuri Line, but the Japanese defenses are still intact, and on May 22 the commanding general of the Third Amphibious Corps reports that the marines are encountering the most effective artillery fire yet met in the Pacific. The "plum rains" deluge Okinawa in late May: fields become swamps, tanks are mired. Mud is king and ammunition and fuel are moved to the front in amphibious vehicles.

Back in the rear areas, the gyrenes, huddled in the dripping tents, raise their cans of beer and let forth with the famous MacArthur parodies:

> "Now the greatest of generals is Douglas, the proud,
>   Writer of fine flowing prose.
> He paces the floor as his orders ring out
>   Down through his aquiline nose. . . ."

Afloat, as ashore, the "no-quarter" fight goes on. Enemy submarines, midget submarines, and suicide boats join the Kamikaze planes in harassment of the fleet. Many submarine contacts are reported, but some of them are false; the sonar gear detects a school of fish or a "knuckle" in the current; the sailors dub the contact the "underwater ghost of the Ryukyus." In one suicide boat attack the Japanese use everything "from a thirty-foot raised-deck cruiser to an open dugout canoe with paddlers."

Then they try a new twist. They bomb the American airstrips ashore at Yontan and Kadena, and follow up with an air-borne landing. Five bombers try to make it; four are shot down in the air; the fifth makes a wheels-up belly landing on a Yontan runway, and ten or eleven Japanese jump out and begin to shoot up the neighborhood. Before their riddled bodies line the airstrip they have destroyed seven American planes, damaged twenty-six others, ignited 70,000 gallons of gasoline and in general raised "pluperfect hell."

The suiciders come again in swarms and coveys on the twenty-seventh, and 115 enemy planes are "splashed" that day. The destroyer *Drexler* joins the company of her peers fathoms deep, and a long list of ships with lyrical names—*Gayety, Anthony* and *Braine, Sandoval* and *Forrest, Gilligan* and *Loy,* the *Mary Livermore* and the *Brown Victory*—are hurt.

At midnight of the twenty-seventh, Admirals Spruance and Mitscher, who have commanded the greatest land, sea, and air battle Americans have ever fought, turn over command to "Wild Bull" Halsey, he of the rakish air, and Sidney John McCain, the tobacco-chewing Admiral.

By the end of May, the flower of the Thirty-second Japanese Army, 50,000 men, lies dead in the rubble and shell-pocked debris of their fortifications, and Lieut. Gen. Mitsuru Ushijima withdraws his remaining troops for a last "back-to-the-sea" stand in the south.

The flag now flies above the site of Shuri Castle, the strongpoint of the Japanese line. Built by an ancient, long-forgotten king, the castle has walls twenty feet thick. They are now reduced to rubble out of which the marines dig two antique bells, scarred and dented by shell fire, and inscribed in Chinese:

". . . And how will the bell sound? It will echo far and wide like a peal of thunder, but with utmost purity. And evil men, hearing the bell, will be saved."

Round about in the craters where men have lived hangs the unforgettable stench of rotting human flesh.

But the end is not yet. The war diary of the Third Fleet soon is noting "alarming losses of ships on the radar picket stations."

On Okinawa, the weary, destitute survivors of the Thirty-second Imperial Army stand along a rocky line of hills and bluffs from Itoman to Hanagusuku. On June 3 the Kamikazes come again in eighteen raids by seventy-five planes and on June 4 nature joins the malevolent forces of the enemy. A typhoon, with gigantic waves, tosses the invasion fleet like chips upon rapids; shears off the bow of the cruiser *Pittsburgh* and damages the carrier *Hornet* and many other ships. On June 5 the *Mississippi* and *Louisville* are struck by suiciders; on June 6 there are heavy raids from the north. The enemy is dying hard.

Still victory is in sight. But there are many now who never will savor the triumph. Ashore the principal commanders on both sides are among the dead. Simon Bolivar Buckner, Lieutenant General, United States Army—he of the rolling name, the rugged frame and distinguished heritage, who commands the Tenth American Army—dies on June 18 when a Japanese shell bursts above a Marine observation post, and a fragment of coral, broken off by the explosion, strikes him in the chest.

On June 21 General Ushijima, commander of His Imperial Majesty's Thirty-second Army, and his chief of staff, Lieut. Gen. Isamu Cho, die the ceremonial death of hara-kiri in a cave Americans hereafter will know as Hill 89. A captured Japanese diary later describes the event:

Their [the generals'] *cook prepared an especially large meal to be served shortly before midnight. When the meal was finished, the two generals and their staff drank numerous farewell toasts with the remaining bottles of Scotch whiskey which had been carried from Shuri. . . .*

Alas! The Stars of the Generals have fallen with the setting of the waning moon over Mabuni. . . .

That same night the world is told that organized resistance has ceased on Okinawa. The next morning, as the band plays "The Star-Spangled Banner," the color guard raises the American flag over the blood-drenched island. "A sudden breeze swept the flag out full against a blue and quiet sky."

In retrospect, the battle for Okinawa can be described only in the grim superlatives of war. In size, scope, and ferocity it dwarfed the Battle of Britain. Never before had there been, probably never again will there be, such a vicious, sprawling struggle of planes against planes, of ships against planes. Never before, in so short a space, had the Navy lost so many; never before in land fighting had so much American blood been shed in so short a time in so small an area; probably never before in any three months of the war had the enemy suffered so hugely. There have been larger land battles, more protracted air campaigns, but Okinawa was a combined operation, a no-quarter struggle fought on, under, and over the sea and the land.

The statistics of combat prove "the last battle" expensive. Besides their 110,000 dead, the Japanese lose sixteen combat ships, including the *Yamato;* tens of thousands of tons of commercial shipping sunk by patrol planes operating from Kerama Rhetto; and 287 guns. Of the 12,281 American dead, 5,000 are Navy men—highest toll of all the services.

The Navy ship casualties are 36 lost and 368 damaged (including damage due to storm, collision and grounding) and of this number 26 are sunk and 164 damaged by Kamikazes. Two are sunk and 61 damaged by conventional air attack.

But 7,830 Jap planes are destroyed in three months, about 3,047 shot down by Navy and Marine planes and 409 others by guns of the fleet. Another 2,655 are lost in operational accidents; hundreds are destroyed on the ground; 558 are credited to the Army's B-29's and hundreds are deliberately wrecked in the suicide crashes.

Our losses, including those of the big Air Force bombers which smashed at Japanese fields, are 768 planes, and only 458 of these are lost to enemy anti-aircraft or in aerial combats. The rest are operational losses. Nothing larger than a destroyer is lost to the enemy; of the larger ships damaged, all except one—an escort carrier—ultimately will be repaired, most of them quickly. The Japanese fail to sink a single American carrier, battleship, cruiser, or transport.

The "fleet that came to stay" and made Okinawa's conquest possible gave far more than it received. The simple accolade applied to the brave men of the little ships, . . . "they stuck it out with demon-

strated valor," is equally applicable to all those of Okinawa, dead and living, who stood, fought and endured in the greatest battle of U.S. arms. But to the "small boys," the "spitkids," the "tincans"—the little ships of the radar picket line—belongs a special glory. They bore the overwhelming share of death and destruction; they were the thin and blood-stained line that stood between the Sons of Heaven and the dominion of the East China Sea.

NOTES   The famous struggle at Okinawa between the "men who wished to live and those who wished to die" ended as all such struggles have since time began—in a victory for life. But not without great sacrifice to death.

According to *The Army Air Forces in World War II* (Craven and Cate), the Japanese flew ten large-scale attacks, totalling 1,465 Kamikaze sorties from Kyushu fields between April 6 and June 22. An additional 185 individual Kamikaze sorties from Kyushu were recorded and 250 from Formosa, plus an unknown number—perhaps double the Kamikaze total—of conventional enemy air sorties. B-29 and other type aircraft were used repeatedly against enemy fields. The Navy insisted, against objections from the Fifth Air Force, that some of the attacks were coming from Formosa. The Navy apparently overestimated Formosa as the base for the Kamikaze suicide missions, but the Air Force underestimated it. Repeated photo-reconnaissance missions had been fooled by the extent of Japanese camouflage and dispersion on Formosa; Japanese planes dismantled and others, well camouflaged, were parked in scattered villages and towns. . . . At a time when "intelligence officers estimated only eighty-nine (enemy) planes (on Formosa), the Japanese had approximately 700. . . ."

Okinawa, the island so dearly won, broke the back of enemy resistance and the long-planned invasion of the Japanese main islands was unnecessary. As an Allied air base, Okinawa was only in the initial stages of development when the Japanese surrendered. Nevertheless, it was an important base in the closing months of the war in tightening the blockade around Japan, and Army Air Force planes, based on Okinawa, flew 6,435 sorties against Kyushu.

ACKNOWLEDGMENTS Personal records, after-action reports, ships' histories, unit and personal diaries, memoirs, and letters provide the grist for much of the drama and human interest material detailed in this chapter. Books and other reference material consulted and/or quoted include: *Okinawa, The Last Battle—U.S. Army in World War II—The War in the Pacific* by Appleman, Burns, Gugeler and Stevens; Historical Division, Department of the Army; Government Printing Office, 1948; *The Campaigns of the Pacific War*—U.S. Strategic Bombing Survey (Pacific)—Naval Analysis Division; Government Printing Office, 1946; *The Army Air Forces in World War II* —Volume V—*The Pacific—Matterhorn to Nagasaki,* edited by W. F. Craven and J. L. Cate, The University of Chicago Press, 1953; "The Marines' War," by Fletcher Pratt; *Parliamentary Debates* (Hansard), Vol. 437, No. 104; Wednesday, 14 May, 1947.

1929
Square-Rigger

Lloyd's agent at Cape Verde Islands telegraph, NOV. 18: SAILING VESSEL *Garthpool's* CAPTAIN AND CREW ARRIVED YESTERDAY. SALVAGE OF SHIP'S GEAR AND MATERIALS VERY DIFFICULT. RECOMMEND SELL VESSEL AS IT LIES. CAPTAIN CONSIDERS VESSEL WILL BREAK UP IF BAD WEATHER CONTINUES.

Casualty Reports, *The Times* of London
November 20, 1929

She had been in the jute trade, working from Calcutta to Dundee; later she had run her easting down and rounded old Cape Stiff, her belly full of Australian grain for English bread. She was old, but stout; only three years before she had nearly hung up a record from Callao to Sydney, and her time of forty-eight days was still one of the best passages for the run.

She came out of the W. B. Thompson yards at Dundee in 1891, and her original name was the *Juteopolis*. She was steel-hulled, 2,842 gross, 310 feet long, 45 foot beam, 25.1 foot draft. She was owned, when her end came, by a lover of tall ships, and she was known as the "oldest, trading, square-rigged, four master under the British flag." Her days of glory were long since ended and she was maintained mainly for sentiment, but she was a good ship still.

She sailed that year from Hull for Australia in ballast.

There was a brief mention in the shipping notes of her departure on October 24, 1929, and *Garthpool* had cleared on her last voyage. The windjammer caught a fine, strong breeze in the Channel and stood southward from Ushant to the Cape Verde Islands in nine days, with her canvas drawing sweetly and her yards squared to the strong pull. She was a braw picture as she stood down Channel and the white cliffs of England faded into the sea behind her for the last time. A braw picture with the sails full bellied, straining at the bolt ropes, and the soft hiss of the ocean swishing along her plates. A braw picture— *Garthpool*—one of the last of a vanishing race. She had a fair wind all the way to Cape Verde and as she stood into the soft brilliance of the tropics, her white wings spread as in the days that were gone, the apprentice boys lazed in the jib netting, watching her dolphin striker jab downwards towards the foam of her passing, watching the golden streaks of phosphorescence in the blue-black sea.

She was logging ten knots and every stitch set, when she sighted Sal in the Cape Verde group on November 11—Armistice Day. Her people were standing with bared heads—remembering the day—about eight bells in the evening when the lookout shouted, "Land ho!" They could see the rugged peaks etched clear in the moonlight, with stars bright and coldly clear high above the deep shadows of the land. They braced the yards 'round and put her on the port tack and ran along thus, with the clean night wind whistling in the rigging for *Garthpool's* last minutes.

She was racing and surging along like a fine thoroughbred when the lookout hailed again:

"Breakers ahead!"

She felt the danger sooner than he called. There was the white spume breaking on the hidden shoals, the foam shining and iridescent in the moonlight, covering the jagged rocks and peaked ledges.

"Hard up your helm!"

Quick she leaped in answer to save herself, though she knew then her time had come. Fast she spun as her people clamored about her decks, and her gear came running free in mad haste. Quick she steadied and headed for a calm passage in the frothing sea, where there rose hard on her port hand a steamer without lights, riding free in that strip of dark, calm water for which she stood. But it was a false passage, and the steamer a ghostly siren that lured her white-winged sister to her death. For the passage led only to a lee shore, and the steamer had been holed and riding high and dry on the rocks of Boavista Isle these past eighteen months. And *Garthpool* was enmeshed, with white creaming breakers roaring close aboard, and the ship still running heavily on to her fate.

They let everything go with a run; the fore-and-afters came down in a crumpled cloud of canvas, and the men were hauling on the main course and crojack, when the lookout sang out again:

"Breakers ahead and on the port bow!"

They put the helm up to try to wear her round; she steadied, resting in the deep water with the skittering breakers all about, and then leaped, as the wind caught her fair, to her death. She crunched aground and the sharp rocks roweled into her hull; the sea roared up, she canted heavily, and the reef tore her flanks. There was the awful screeching scream of steel on stone—and "an epoch died when *Garthpool* took the ground." The sea rolled up, and carried her high, while the white-fanged breakers tore at her stern, her bowsprit angled skywards towards those far cold stars, and her gear went all awry. There was nothing left to do; it was time to leave her; she was high and dry on a tropic reef, with the foam skirling about her bilges, and the green growth of her months in the ocean showing plain in the moonlight. Her yards were cockbilled and her sails half-furled or crumpled downwards in disorderly mountains of canvas, while into her holed hull there roared the hungry sea.

They backed the yards and tried to save her, but it was futile; she grated and groaned on the rocks and opened deeper gashes in her hull. Her masts strained, the yards quivered as she lay canted and aslew, fretting her life out on Boavista reef in the Cape Verde. Each time the surf surged high beneath her counter and ran in spuming freshets along her scuppers she shivered and shook to her beams' ends; each time, from beneath her broken keel there shrilled the jarring scream of steel on stone, the voice of a dying ship. Higher she went and higher on the reef, while the moon shone down on the rugged peaks and cavernous valleys of Cape Verde.

Higher . . . and higher, until she moved no more and steadied, impaled like a stranded leviathan, with the sea licking about her jagged wounds. And her people went about her decks to leave her, and the wind whispered softly in her rigging, caressing with its wandering fingers each shroud, each stay, each cockbilled yard. And the reef points drummed their last tattoo upon the flapping canvas and the buntlines and the braces sagged and swayed as the wind caught them, and all heaped and humped about the fife-rail lay the coiled, snarled lines. And the cringles beat their metallic threnody, while the great blocks swung now and again with dull booming thuds—like the surf beneath her stern—against the masts. The half-furled sails rustled and fluttered—as if still she tried to spread her wings and sweep to sea; the irish pennants and loose ends flicked and flapped in the moonlight, and it was time to leave her. . . .

> *You may make her fast, and pack your gear,*
> *Leave her, Johnny, leave her* . . .

They went about her decks to leave her and they took her log and papers and their instruments and pipes and clothes, and they clewed up the loose gear and swung out the boats. And she lay there in the moonlight, numb and silent.

They left her, rowing through the "maze of reefs and isolated rocks" and frothing waters to St. Vincent in the Cape Verde. And they left her alone, as their oar blades soughed in the sea; they left her alone with the wind wandering across her deserted decks and the surf whispering about her strakes. They left her alone—*Garthpool*—left her alone on a tropic reef, a mouldering monument to an age that is gone.

NOTES   The *Garthpool's* obituary in the New York *Times* of November 14, 1929, described her as "Britain's only surviving four-masted sailing ship . . . the loveliest of them all," skippered by Dave Thompson, a "hardy Scotsman from Anstruther . . . forty years in sail."

In my account of *Garthpool's* end I have purposely omitted the names of any of her crew as I attempted to personify the ship and to describe her last hours in the picturesque prose of the sea.

Garthpool was named in part for her rich owner, Sir William Garthwaite, to whom she was an expensive hobby. She participated in the Australian "grain races" (about which Alan Villiers has written so beautifully) and part of her crew were youngsters who were being given training in sail preparatory to life-long careers beneath the "Red Duster" (in the British merchant marine).

In *Last of the Wind Ships* (Alan J. Villiers; George Rutledge and Sons, London, 1934), the *Garthpool* is credited with a passage of 122 days from Australia to England in 1927; 145 days in 1928, and 130 days in 1929—by no means records, but not too discreditable performances for an old ship with a part apprentice crew. Villiers calls her "the last of the British square-riggers"; Shaw, in *Famous Shipwrecks,* describes *Garthpool* as the "last square-rigged windjammer of deep-sea proportions," and a "memorial of the bygone spacious days of sail."

ACKNOWLEDGMENTS   The end of the *Garthpool,* symbolic of the end of an era, is based primarily upon accounts published in *The Times* of London, the New York *Times,* and upon the eloquent chapter "The Last Windjammer" in Frank H. Shaw's book, *Famous Shipwrecks,* Elkin Mathews and Marrot, London, 1930. The few quoted phrases are from *The Times* of London and from *Famous Shipwrecks.*